Against Innocence

∴

Against Innocence

∴

UNDOING AND REMAKING THE WORLD

Miriam Ticktin

THE UNIVERSITY OF CHICAGO PRESS
CHICAGO AND LONDON

The University of Chicago Press, Chicago 60637
The University of Chicago Press, Ltd., London
© 2025 by The University of Chicago

Published 2025
Printed in the United States of America

34 33 32 31 30 29 28 27 26 25   1 2 3 4 5

ISBN-13: 978-0-226-83873-1 (cloth)
ISBN-13: 978-0-226-83875-5 (paper)
ISBN-13: 978-0-226-83874-8 (ebook)
DOI: https://doi.org/10.7208/chicago/9780226838748.001.0001

Library of Congress Cataloging-in-Publication Data

Names: Ticktin, Miriam Iris, author.
Title: Against innocence : undoing and remaking the world / Miriam Ticktin.
Description: Chicago ; London : The University of Chicago Press, 2025. | Includes
  bibliographical references and index.
Identifiers: LCCN 2025020248 | ISBN 9780226838731 (cloth) | ISBN 9780226838755
  (paperback) | ISBN 9780226838748 (ebook)
Subjects: LCSH: Innocence (Psychology) | Innocence (Psychology)—Social aspects. |
  Innocence (Psychology)—Political aspects. | Social values.
Classification: LCC BF575.I48 T53 2025 | DDC 320.01/9—dc23/eng/20250610
LC record available at https://lccn.loc.gov/2025020248

♾ This paper meets the requirements of ANSI/NISO Z39.48-1992
(Permanence of Paper).

Authorized Representative for EU General Product Safety Regulation (GPSR) queries:
Easy Access System Europe—Mustamäe tee 50, 10621 Tallinn, Estonia,
gpsr.requests@easproject.com
Any other queries: https://press.uchicago.edu/press/contact.html

Contents

Figures

Acknowledgments

I never intended for this book to be written. When Ann Stoler kindly invited me to participate in one of her yearly "Political Concepts" conferences, I was at a loss; but in a conversation soon after, *Funambulist* magazine creator, writer, and editor Léopold Lambert gave me the answer to what I'd write about. He said without hesitation, referring to a podcast he interviewed me for in 2014, "Well of course you will speak about innocence." It seemed both obvious and completely impossible; and I have found the writing of this book to be a combination of those two feelings. While I felt compelled to write it—especially after encountering people at the Political Concepts conference who defended the moral righteousness of the concept, when I found it deeply troubling and even violent—I also struggled and struggled with the genre of the book. I am not trained as an intellectual historian, a philosopher, or a political theorist. My writing has tended toward social theory for many years, but I still felt completely underequipped. The writing was painfully slow—I put it aside for years at a time—as I strained to find my voice. I had no trouble writing other things; in fact, I have never written more! I embarked on a parallel project about border walls and containment, which has now also become about the reverse: political imagination, collective life, and commoning. But I could not write the innocence book. While I am still not sure I have found my voice, this book needs to be in the world; it cannot hide anymore, especially after the second election of Donald Trump, and his fascist MAGA movement, where the discourse of innocence figures prominently, both revealing and solidifying the connections between liberal and illiberal political worlds.

I will never be able to thank all the people that have helped me through this long, protracted process. My writing groups have perhaps been the most instrumental in getting this into the world: the "Snaps"—my dear friends Laura Liu and Rachel Sherman—gave me invaluable help from the beginning. A fellowship at the Russell Sage Foundation in 2019–2020 (interrupted, alas, by the COVID-19 pandemic) provided me with much needed time, but more importantly, it enabled the creation of my precious writing group with Sofya Aptekar and Lisa Sun-Hee Park, with the occasional appearance by Amy Hsin: this book is filled with their wonderful, brilliant insights, their care, and their generosity. I am indebted to the long-enduring, nourishing Oxidate writing group for their unparalleled feedback, although Oxidate was tragically and irreparably altered by the loss of Diane Nelson in 2022. Led by our fabulous Lochlann Jain and Jake Kosek, it includes Joe Dumit, Cori Hayden, Joe Masco, Jonathan Metzl, M. Murphy, Diane Nelson, Jackie Orr, and Liz Roberts.

I could not have written this book without the Multiple Mobilities Research Cluster and the parallel and intersecting fieldwork and writing projects I have been so lucky to engage in with them: Victoria Hattam, Laura Liu, Radhika Subramaniam, and Rafi Youatt. The "mob" is an intellectual lifeline, sustained by laughter!

My colleagues at the New School, where this started, were instrumental in supporting me: those in anthropology—Abou Farman, Larry Hirschfeld, Nick Langlitz, Shannon Mattern, Hugh Raffles, and Ann Stoler—and many beyond. Alex Aleinikoff generously supported the project through the Zolberg Institute. I brought the project with me when I moved to CUNY's Graduate Center in 2021, where I am now very happily ensconced, and I cannot say thank you enough to Jeff Maskovsky for encouraging me throughout, and for organizing a book manuscript workshop for me. I am grateful to Karen Strassler and Gary Wilder for their insightful comments on a portion of this work. All my colleagues at the GC have been wonderful in providing a welcoming and supportive atmosphere for writing.

The book manuscript workshop was a turning point, when I realized the book may actually get finished: I cannot thank Nadia Abu El-Haj, Julie Livingston, Lisa Sun-Hee Park, and Camille Robcis enough for their brilliant, rigorous feedback. While Anne McNevin was not a part of this group, she generously volunteered to read and I have greatly benefited from her equally excellent feedback; and I thank Natasha Iskander for guiding me with such gentleness and grace all the way through.

I am so grateful for all the invitations to speak and to the amazing audiences who asked excellent questions and gave me such helpful comments—the book has been indelibly shaped and improved by these encounters and conversations.

I got some of the best feedback when I presented a chapter in the Center for Place, Culture and Politics's (CPCP) seminar, as a fellow in 2022–2023. This made me all the more thrilled and honored when the larger-than-life Ruthie Gilmore asked me to follow her as director of CPCP. I'm delighted to be working side-by-side with Peter Hitchcock, and to have Ruthie's brilliant guidance.

There are so many others to thank, my dear friends and interlocuters, who have all engaged with this project and supported it (and me!) along the way: Vincanne Adams, Ujju Aggarwal, Bridget Anderson, Rob Blecher, Alexandra Delano, Ilana Feldman, Sarah Gensburger, Pamila Gupta, Rachel Heiman, Rebecca Jordan Young, Nadine Naber, Richard Rechtman, Peter Redfield, Rashmi Sadana, Sahar Sadjadi, Nandita Sharma, Anoo Siddiqui, Sharika Thiranagama, Sylvie Tissot, Ananya Vajpeyi, Richard Wilson, and Zoe Wool. Didier Fassin supported the project by way of a fellowship at the Institute for Advanced Study (IAS), between 2016 and 2017, and I benefited from the wonderful conversations there.

I could not have done this without the immense, generous, and careful help of Julian Gantt, who compiled bibliographies, image permissions, the index, and so much more; I am forever grateful to him for working with my erratic deadlines. Thank you to Clara Beccaro for translating portions of it into French. I give the deepest thanks to Dylan Montanari, my editor at University of Chicago Press, who has been so patient and encouraging; and to Sebastian Budgen, for his enthusiasm and guidance.

My family knows all too well how this book has become almost too heavy to bear. Thank you to my sisters, Leah, Tamara, and Jessica, who, as my best friends, always knew when to ask about the book, and when not to—I have benefited from their wisdom, support, and insight all the way along. Thank you to my brothers-in-law for the many excellent intellectual and political conversations: Norman Belhumeur, Gustavo de la Peña, and Adam Rubin. To my brothers-in-law and sisters-in-law from the other side for always being so generous and welcoming: Patricia Marlier, Gégé Lavarte, and Frank Dodd. To my nieces, all five of them, who have grown up alongside the book and provided accidental insight about innocence: Dahlia, Lola, Kaya, Ylang, and Mabel; and to my nephew, David Marlier, for regular accompaniment in Paris. And to my parents, Marlene and Saul, who have always believed in my ability to do this, and to whom I owe everything, from curiosity to political commitment. They taught me to care. Finally, to Patrick Dodd, who fills my black-and-white world of words and texts with the most vibrant colors; his steadiness, wisdom, and imagination ground this book.

Against Innocence, Beyond Innocence

In June 2022, the landmark ruling *Roe v. Wade* was overturned, undoing the federal right to abortion in the US that had been in place since 1973. While the political road to this result had many twists and turns, the reason given was simple and clear: the embryo/fetus must be protected at all costs, as it is not only innocent, but in the words of Pope John Paul II, "absolutely innocent." It is more innocent than the person carrying the embryo, and hence, its life has more value. Indeed, in the many subsequent anti-abortion laws passed, the language of innocence is central: as Rand Paul, Republican senator for Kentucky, stated in relation to *Roe v. Wade*, "It is unconscionable that government would facilitate the taking of innocent life."[1] There is nothing one can say against a claim to innocence: it stops political conversation.

Innocence also shapes debates about child migrants. In 2018, hundreds of migrant children were forcibly separated from their parents at the US-Mexico border by Trump's policy of "zero tolerance," and held in detention centers. While the ongoing plight of migrants does not generally draw sympathy from either liberals or conservatives, despite the many deaths at the border, there was an unprecedented uproar by the American public as the state was taken to task for engaging in the morally repugnant act of taking innocent children from their parents. Innocence was the key factor, distinguishing children from their parents.

If innocence guides these debates about who should live, and how certain forms of life should be protected, it also guides debates about who should die, and whose lives hold no value. On June 27, 2023, French police shot and killed seventeen-year-old Nahel M., in Nanterre, an urban periphery of (banlieue) of Paris, for a supposed violation of a traffic stop. Subsequent video demonstrated that Nahel was not posing a risk to the police, as they had initially claimed, but that it was more of a public execution. He had no weapon; he had done nothing wrong, except perhaps to be born of Algerian and Moroccan origin, in France. It quickly led to major protests around the country against racism and systemic police violence. But even as the protests raged in all the major cities, media and public discourse turned to the fact that he had been arrested fifteen times; he was not innocent. It did not matter that he was innocent in this instance. Innocence and guilt are fixed to a person, not an act. The implication was that he deserved what happened to him: he was, in essence, a criminal.

When the lack of innocence is attached to a group of people, not simply an individual, it can enable the incarceration—or elimination—of a whole population. In 2018, then Israeli defense minister Avigdor Lieberman declared that "there are no innocent people in the Gaza Strip."[2] This foreshadowed the words of liberal-centrist politician Meirav Ben-Ari in October 2023, after the October 7th attacks,[3] that "the children of Gaza have brought this upon themselves," and those of former prime minister Isaac Herzog that "it is an entire nation out there that is responsible." The impossibility of innocence, repeated by Israeli politicians across the political spectrum, has enabled and justified genocidal violence in Gaza. They are no longer human; Gazans are, as defense minister Yoav Gallant's comments asserted, "*human animals.*"[4]

∴

Innocence clearly mobilizes powerful responses. But what exactly *is* innocence—why are we morally compelled by it? What gives it its power? And why is it so central to contemporary politics? The goal of this book is to see how such moral and ethical terms come to structure what we think of as politics today, and what we can do, think, and feel—how they map political possibilities as well as impossibilities.

Far from being understood as an engagement with the regular stuff of politics, like power or the organization of collective life, innocence is defined as freedom from both the worldly and unworldly. In this sense, innocence provides a conceptual space outside corruption and contamination; it is perhaps as far from politics as we could possibly imagine. Innocence slips between its meanings as lack of agency (helplessness), a lack of knowledge (naïveté), a lack of desire (chastity), and a lack of responsibility (blamelessness). It comes into being in relation to its various binary Others, such as guilt, knowledge, and sexuality. While the concept does different work in relation to these binaries, in each case innocence works to regulate a space of purity. It works as a boundary concept, and in the process it helps produce and regulate humankinds and their constituent outsides—it helps us imagine "humanity," sometimes as its constituent outside, sometimes as its precursor, and often as its hope for the future.

The Latin etymology of *innocence* focuses on harm (*in-* + *nocens*, "not harmful"), which is clearly a central feature of the concept, and yet the etymology of *in-* + *noscere*, "not to know," is perhaps even more significant. What does it mean not simply to be empty of knowledge, but specifically to *not know*? This willful ignorance is what James Baldwin (1998) has called racial (or white) innocence, built on Americans' refusal to deal with deeply entrenched forms of racial injustice. This is something I investigate in depth in the book. Perhaps because innocence is about lack—emptiness—it can be projected into many different contexts. Whatever the case, it has been deployed politically in more or less vigorous ways over time; indeed, this book argues that it has moved into the center of political life today.

Innocence is a flexible concept that intimately shapes why and how we should care, for whom, and whose lives matter. That said, I do not want to suggest that it is one unified or homogeneous concept. Rather, I see it more in terms of what Wittgenstein (1958, 31) described as a concept that works by way of a "family of resemblances." By this, he meant that its identifying features are open-ended. Concepts like innocence "have no one thing in common which makes us use the same word for all, but . . . they are related to one another in many different ways." They may overlap, intersect, or demonstrate similarities at different scales: general or specific. Even as we use the same term, these meanings can be contradictory, just as they can reinforce each other. They can be braided together to create a new, deeper meaning; they can also run parallel to one another. I am interested in how innocence works as a multifaceted concept, meaning many things in many realms. But I am also interested in how it produces underlying and consistent effects: indeed, one of my driving concerns is how innocence regularly enables a deferral of responsibility for perpetuating deep forms of inequality. Even more than that, as I will argue, it works to produce hierarchy and domination.

My focus on innocence began with my previous work on humanitarianism, insofar as the exemplary humanitarian subject is often configured as the innocent victim. But this research made me see that innocence is not a straightforward concept or a way of being; it shape-shifts. Who qualifies as innocent, and when? Are there patterns to this? I started to investigate this in the context of humanitarian claims, but I quickly noticed that "innocence" gets attached to and plays a central role in various kinds of contemporary (il)liberal politics, well beyond humanitarianism. To understand, with some urging,[5] I decided to think about innocence as a political concept, and to trace the work it performs transnationally. While philosophers have started to take concepts like vulnerability seriously and reclaim or repurpose them (i.e., Butler et al. 2016), no one has yet looked at innocence as an important political concept.[6] This has since led me into very disparate areas and challenged me to find areas *not* shaped by innocence.

I trace the work of innocence in its various guises, and through specific political debates: from immigration and sexuality to environmentalism and racial justice. For instance, I demonstrate how claims to innocence are used to protect migrant children, but often at the expense of their parents; and how the claims to the innocence of the fetus work to punish women. I focus on its ethico-moral dimensions in the Euro-American context after the 1960s, which means that I locate the contemporary importance of innocence in a particular transnational, secular, liberal world that is concerned with individual autonomy, freedom, and rationality, as well as with the idea of humanity, of which equality and dignity are key principles. But unexpectedly (to me), this has led to me tracing the way innocence slips into and facilitates a shift to illiberalism.

One of my goals is to denaturalize and expose a commonsense concept that is part of everyday life for many, certainly in the Euro-American context. I am interested in how a concept that consistently appears as a moral good actually ends up creating harm for so many: as I will argue, it gets harnessed as a tool of empire, paving the way to new forms of inequality. I realize that this is counterintuitive to most people; many may not see how a claim to innocence works to divide "good" people from "bad," producing the exclusion, vilification, or imprisonment of those designated unworthy, where the "unworthy" are too often simply the poor. In some ways, then, mine is the quintessential anthropological task: rendering common sense strange, demonstrating how the world that seems given and "natural" actually has a history, and as such, how it could be otherwise.

The Problem of Innocence: From Liberalism to Illiberalism and Back

If innocence is central in political life today, we might ask, why now? Where is the driving force coming from? While this book focuses on the work performed when people call on the concept of innocence, it is nevertheless important to give some context for its political significance. To this end, throughout the book, I trace various histories that have helped shape and create an infrastructure for this desire. I want to emphasize that I do not aspire to a substantive history or genealogy of innocence; that is beyond my capacity here. I simply hint at a few strands or moments. I think of this more in terms of an abridged conjunctural history (Hall et al. 1978), mapping the specificity of the present by way of the separate forces or currents that have merged under the label of "innocence" to shape our current political moment.

Why the search for innocence? I will mention two sources of this desire. First, in this moment of increasing precarity and change, many express a desire for a return to prior, seemingly simpler times—this is in many ways a recurring anti-modernist yearning, a form of nostalgia for a different social order. It is a revolt against rapid change, technology, against the lack of "family values," including a loss of faith, and against new ways of living and being. It is also a symptom of, and perhaps a protest against, the increasing insecurity of life on its many fronts, and the extreme inequality between rich and poor. Anti-modernist discontent is often expressed as a search for a space of purity, a space outside corruption and contamination, a space emptied of the power that can ground both tolerance and action; innocence provides us with such a conceptual space.

But this moment has its specificities too. The Great Replacement, a white nationalist conspiracy theory initiated by French author Renaud Camus in 2011 but now rampant across Europe, the US, and even Tunisia, rages against the usual tropes of modernity, such as industrialization, materialism, and globalization; but it adds a more contemporary twist—it is grounded on resentment about the loss of racial privilege. The theory is that civilization is on the decline, as white, European Christian populations are being replaced by non-white ones (Muslim in particular)—it points to demographic shifts that have resulted in more Muslims in France, for instance, or a growing non-white US population, or Black migrants in Tunisia, "replacing" Arabs. Innocence has persisting Judeo-Christian contours that give it power in worlds shaped by the Religious Right and its anti-modernist adherents: we need only think of the politics of abortion—and its many bans—that have radically altered the US landscape. But as we will see, innocence also helps play into racial politics and racialized resentment, by way of claims to racial innocence; people use it to excuse their complicity in forms of oppression, and to hold on to their privileges.

If anti-modernist sentiment and its illiberal expressions drive one aspect of the search for innocence, the second driving force is the politics of liberalism, and in particular, a search for seemingly apolitical (or morally pure) action. While it may be easier to think that the search for innocence is just a problem of the Religious Right, or a symptom of the turn to authoritarianism or illiberalism, in fact, this story is less focused on the illiberal than it is on a liberal, secular world, that, with the help of the language of innocence, ends up blending into, and supporting, illiberal or authoritarian regimes.

The focus on innocence is part of the spread of what some have called "transnational governmentality" (Ferguson and Gupta 2002) or the complex of NGOs, activists, international organizations, and corporations that now govern in zones the state has ceded or abandoned; these include humanitarian, development, and human rights NGOs, such as those focused on refugees, migrants, and women's rights. This has been happening since the 1980s, accompanying the work of what Gilmore (2009) calls the "anti-state state," or the ways in which people and parties gain state power by denouncing state power, dismantling the redistributive and welfare functions of the state, while growing the state's repressive apparatuses. As I will explain by tracing some of their history, the proliferation of transnational governmentality has centered a suffering humanity as a universal moral category, rather than focusing on political categories or political subjects such as workers, colonial militants, or freedom fighters; here, the central political figure is the innocent, suffering victim. These movements conditioned what counts as "politics," turning it into a constantly expanding search for moral purity, criminalizing people in its wake. That is, as we will see, the language of innocence works in relation to its binary Others: if some are considered innocent, others are produced as guilty (or criminal, corrupt, or desiring) in relation. For instance, today, to be granted asylum, refugees must be seen as innocent (i.e., not involved in the conflicts that they are fleeing); but for them to be distinguished as "real" or genuine, a category of economic migrants has been created as their binary opposite, and framed as guilty, or illegal. While many have written about NGOs and humanitarianism, this book demonstrates that the logic of innocence extends far beyond this, into seemingly unrelated worlds.

In this kind of politics, power is located in the morally pure, the innocent; and thus paradoxically, eschewing power and agency is the route to political recognition—victimhood carries powerful rewards. This is not unlike the Nietzschean idea of *ressentiment*, where moralizing takes the place of political discussion, and where power is critiqued from the position of the injured or the victims, who claim that they themselves are neutral and outside power (Nietzsche [1887] 1998; Brown 1995). In the politics I describe, innocence does not function primarily as an adjective, that is, an innocent claim, an innocent action—but as a noun, or as an essential identity characteristic. It builds on the liberal focus on individuals and essences. It is taken to describe a pure state of being. Throughout the book, I discuss key figures that are enabled or buttressed by the concept of innocence: the refugee/child, the liberal/colonizer/humanitarian, the queer and the criminal, and the nonhuman, including Mother Nature and the fetus. If denaturalizing the concept of innocence is my first goal, my second major goal in the book is to show how, through the lens of innocence, seemingly very different political domains work together to shore up individual identity as a place of innocence; and to encourage a politics based on identity and victimhood, where the more complicated, systemic, and structural relationships of power and responsibility are rendered invisible.

People go in search of innocent subjects to satisfy a desire to protect, purify, and dominate—and to return to a simple moral code. But one of this book's key points is that innocence is unattainable; it is a form of mythical, nostalgic desire for purity and simplicity—one that is constantly out of reach. Insofar as there is no pure state of innocence, a politics based on innocence requires not only the search for but also the production of innocent victims, since the "pure" victim is a placeholder, always just out of reach. We are constantly displacing politics to the limit of innocence in a never-ending quest, and in the process the structural and historical causes of inequality get rendered invisible. In the search for purity, a very particular politics gets produced, and another, disabled.

In this quest, the political and affective dimensions of innocence that are embedded in the NGO logics have traveled across borders and shaped transnational spaces, working hand in hand with capital. For this reason, the stories and dilemmas in this book are not located in a recognized or circumscribed geographic region or nation-state; they cover a set of spaces not bound by nation-states, but by specific histories that involve liberal NGOs and their contemporary imperial and capitalist logics. For instance, Médecins sans Frontières or Doctors Without Borders was founded on the idea that sovereignty and borders do not matter in the face of human suffering. The geographies I cover, then, are often related to colonial or imperial histories and their increasingly illiberal aftermaths. I am particularly attentive to the situations where colonial histories have come home to roost; that is, former metropoles. I move from the US and Canada to France and the UK; from Spain to the Netherlands; but I also explore the current settler colonial regime of Israel and Palestine. I track innocence in relation to migrants from former (or current settler) colonies or those descended from the formerly enslaved.

In this sense, while innocence in its various incarnations does many different things, through this logic of transnational governance, I suggest that innocence functions as a tool of empire, helping in the expansion of power, accompanying (military) intervention, and justifying a world built on inequality. For instance, the French *sans papiers* (or undocumented migrant) movement has long pointed to France's repeated role in regime change in African countries from Libya to Burkina Faso, many of which have produced the wars that the migrants are fleeing. France continues to invest in and extract strategic raw materials from its former colonies, and it maintains a financial stranglehold over large swaths of the African continent: fourteen African nations continue to use a colonial-era French currency that obliges them to deposit at least 60 percent of their foreign reserves in a French bank.[7] That is, the French empire has its vibrant contemporary afterlives. And crucially, these migrants are the ones subject to the rigors of the language of innocence, as they attempt to make asylum claims and squeeze themselves into the figure of innocent victim. In this way, tracing the workings of innocence can help us render visible the contemporary mechanisms of (neocolonial) empire, in intersecting forms: French, US, and other.

If innocence works as a tool of empire, it also reworks the distinctions between liberalism and illiberalism. That is, just as innocence is a crosscutting moral concept, the politics it enables crosses back and forth between the liberal and illiberal, helping remake the distinctions between the two. More specifically, one of the arguments I make is that attention to the concept of innocence can help us expose the connective tissue between liberal and illiberal political visions, and I show how innocence is being used to shift the needle toward illiberalism. By assuming that responsibility can only be individual, the concept of innocence works to maintain forms of domination, and to render invisible relations of power. To be sure, liberalism and illiberalism have never been mutually exclusive, and indeed, some argue that right-wing movements, including authoritarianism, are simply an outgrowth of neoliberal rationality and its focus on the personal at the expense of the collective; an expansion of the personal leaves room only for private interests and family values, allotting a greater place for religion, patriarchalism, and nepotism, key tropes of illiberalism (Maskovsky and Bjork-James 2020; Brown 2018; Toscano 2021). Indeed, both are grounded in the competitive individualism associated with racial capitalism: the key is that the state needs to be strong enough to impose and protect private rights and restrict deliberation (Toscano 2021; Dardot et al. 2021). Both are grounded on white supremacy, built on a chain of racialized moral panics (Hall 1988; Toscano 2021).

Liberalism works to manage and govern difference with the concepts of individual liberty, tolerance, and political equality; it works by cultivating and creating difference that it can exploit, even as it abandons and excludes those who exceed the bounds of acceptable or recognizable difference. These people are criminalized. Illiberalism, on the other hand, works to expunge difference, to repress it, excise it. Current forms of illiberalism protect purity, based on bloodlines and heteronormative families; while its contours are shifting and developing quickly, I think of it here in relation to nativism, authoritarianism, patriarchy, nepotism, hierarchy, and isolationism. The line between liberalism and illiberalism involves constant political work; it is about making cuts, and it is never complete. One of the key distinctions between the two is made by way of the moral limits to violence. Talal Asad (2007, 2015) writes that, when a liberal collectivity is felt to be threatened (i.e., the "we" of the nation-state), violence is seen as morally necessary, however cruel, in order to maintain peace and order. In such a case, the distinction between liberal and illiberal is established by evoking moral conscience, not by the violence itself; that is, to be a liberal, one must feel guilt or regret about the violence committed, even while asserting that it was necessary. The distinction is forged by the ability or inability to respond with horror at cruelty. In this sense, innocence and guilt are critical to the liberal imagination, not violence itself, which infuses both liberalism and illiberalism. With this in mind, my aim is to aid in opening political, moral, and affective grammars beyond innocence, which means going beyond liberalism and illiberalism. I want to clear the way for alternative ontological starting points. What would a world look like without innocence?

Toward an Otherwise: Collectivity and Responsibility

Rather than simply critique the concept and its political deployment, this book makes a political argument about how the world could be otherwise; how a different non-innocent politics is not only possible, but already exists, and in the various chapters I detail, amplify, and imagine with these political possibilities. I want to contribute to a new common sense. After all, politics is a battle over the imagination (Dunne and Raby 2018), where the imagination can help us maintain pre-existing realities, or create alternative visions, denaturalizing the "real." In this pursuit, I draw much inspiration from transnational and women of color feminist theory: feminist theorizing has always been about analyzing the way the world is, while simultaneously reimagining and remaking the world.

I insist on being attentive to what is already out there, making room for people to see differently, to be attuned to the world around them: as French philosopher Jacques Rancière states (2010), the goal of political work is not to engage in the imaginary as opposed to the real. Rather, it involves a reframing of the real: a change in the cartography of the sensible and thinkable. As Rancière states, "The real is always a matter of construction"—a "fiction" that passes itself off as real by creating consensus (2010, p. 148). But I also hope to open the way to think differently, to speculate with the kinds of experiments that are already happening. In this sense, with the objective of creating space for new forms of political imagination, I join a broader move toward speculative thinking in scholarship. I do not mean imagining far or distant romantic futures. Locating itself in current material worlds and working out from there, speculation takes place at the edge of what we can see, at the limit; indeed, it can simply make "real" what is already part of a collective imagination (Dunne and Raby 2018). There are various names for such forms of grounded imaginings, such as concrete, real, or practical utopias.[8] Stated differently, I use empirical research primarily to help imagine an "otherwise" (Povinelli 2011) or an "incipient not-yet" (Zigon 2019). I want to create room in public discourse and practice not just for a counter or oppositional politics—that is, reactions to a dominant form of politics, such as countering closed borders with open borders—but to enable *alter-visions*, or alternative political formations that exist alongside the current political order. By alter—as in the sense of "alter-politics" (Hage 2015) or "alter-life" (Murphy 2018)—I mean a coeval alternative to the current political order, a way of "being other to ourselves" (Hage 2015), which differs from an oppositional politics that tries to resist or defeat it. In this case, what would an alternative world, not grounded on innocence, look like, feel like, be like?

I trace three ways in which alternative political worlds are emerging, helping bring a more just world into being: by way of changed political subject(s), new forms of action, and different affective grammars. First, I question the individual subject. The concept of innocence, when successfully evoked, renders invisible more complicated relationships of power by relying on individual causality or by erasing agency altogether. There is no way to deal with structural racism, for instance. Responsibility is either embodied in and bounded by individuals, or located in institutions and states—which, despite being depicted as moral actors, cannot take responsibility without the individuals and groups that compose them. The language of innocence provides a binary choice with which to grapple with injustice, grounded in direct individual accountability: innocence or guilt. This framing enables people to feel that they have nothing to do with past injustices, or with history at all, since they did not participate in regimes such as slavery or colonialism directly; they are innocent of such crimes. And in this way, the ongoing legacies and afterlives of systems of injustice are denied. A framework structured by innocence enables the denial of collective responsibility.

But what if there were a different understanding of a responsible subject, one that is neither individual nor institutional, but rather, mobile and collective, one that has both historical and contemporary breadth? What if this collective subject could occupy the unrecognized connective tissue that innocence sets up, between the individual and the structural? This is neither a liberal nor an illiberal subject, but a constantly morphing and permeable subject based on understanding the world as inescapably grounded on imbrication, mutuality, and entanglement. And with a shift in political subject from individual to entangled collective, a world of different types of responsibility, relationality, and engagement becomes possible: there are implicated subjects, complicit subjects, beneficiaries, perpetuators, inheritors, and so on. Suddenly, innocence or guilt, victim and perpetrator are not the only subject positions to inhabit in the fabric of responsibility or accountability. What if we centered mobs as collective subjects? Or political subjects who are not innocent victims, but rather, desiring, engaged subjects?

Second, I call attention to the types of actions that are changing the political landscape. With a different set of subjects, different actions can take place—and different actions can prefigure different political subjects. As just one example, abolitionism offers a map that takes us out of the language of innocence. As Ruth Wilson Gilmore (2022) suggests, innocence is neither the problem nor the solution for the prison-industrial complex—we do not need to search to prove the innocence of those (wrongfully) in prison; the problem that organizes carceral geographies is bigger than wrongful accusations or excessive police violence, however horrific those are. Rather, prisons respond to the need to absorb surplus populations; racial capitalism requires that some populations be sacrificed, considered as excess, for others to thrive. Abolitionism is therefore about doing away with this system of power, and the language of innocence and guilt that helps justify and sustain it. While some think of abolitionism just in terms of defunding the police, the prisons, and the detention centers, it is actually a world-building praxis that simultaneously reimagines and rebuilds the world to address forms of organized abandonment; it does so by way of positive life-affirming institutions such as education, healthcare, housing, and so on (Chua 2020; Rodríguez 2019).

Reparations are another related form of action that cannot be addressed with the language of innocence or guilt. And if abolitionism takes a future-oriented temporal perspective focused on world-building, reparations turns to the past, to rectify previous harms; it is perhaps the most important strategy of redistributive justice being put forth today, allowing for complicated combinations of debt, harm, and direct and indirect responsibility and repair that extend over time. Reparations challenge the frame of innocence insofar as they are based on the idea of collective and communal responsibility—this is a form of accountability that touches everyone in society, insofar as the social is about participating in a collective form of life. For instance, the US is so deeply shaped by its history of racial segregation and enslavement that everyone who lives there or has lived there is also in some way implicated in this matrix: the question is not *if* one is implicated, but *how*.

"Commoning" is another related example of political organization and social justice that works against innocence. It has come to mean many things (and is practiced by many different people, from Indigenous and Black communities to ecologists, feminists, and anarchists), and I use it largely as a conceptual placeholder for a set of political practices and imaginations that are grounded on a struggle against enclosures, against the privatization of spaces of freedom, against exclusion, and, perhaps most importantly, against private property. It can also mean the sharing of wealth and resources on the basis of collective decision-making; and the grounding principles of reciprocity, respect, mutuality, and responsibility are usually evoked (Hardt and Negri 2009; Dardot and Laval 2019; Federici 2019). Some might know it under the name of the "commune": a political form based on cooperation and association, practiced from the days of Marx and Kropotkin with the Paris Commune, to today's examples such as Notre-Dame-des-Landes (Ross 2024). Commoning is based on a horizontal model of relationality, unlike the hierarchical and vertical models that claims to innocence institute (like victim and savior). The genealogies I draw on to think about commoning suggest that these practices are based on the principle of non-exclusion, which means it can never be pure, or innocent: it is always contaminated, and people must learn to live with conflict, difference, dislike, and uncertainty. To be clear, to exist, commoning needs—as Chris Harris (2021) has argued—to undo the world as we know it, and its inequalities and forms of domination; but as I will suggest, it is important to acknowledge that commoning already exists all around us, if we look carefully—it grows in the uncaptured excesses of racial capitalism, and prefigures alternative ways of being. It is what Jayna Brown (2021) calls an "alter-frequency." In this book, I trace commoning in the collective practices engaged in by migrants or "people-on-the-move" (a term used by migrants themselves and no-borders activists to get away from legal categories like refugee or economic migrant that are built on hierarchy and exclusion), as they occupy space together, and share resources and knowledge about how to move or stay where they want. Commoning is a way to share and redistribute resources, without temporal limits: it can be a few days, a lifetime, or a way of life over generations.

Third, a world that moves beyond innocence does not rely on sentiments such as compassion, sympathy, or pity, or the more moralized judgments, such as deserving or undeserving. These latter are part of a liberal capitalist landscape of sentiments, which work to connect the autonomous individuals of liberal politics into hierarchical relationships; they serve to justify these inequalities, which are inevitably shaped by racialized, classed, and gendered ideas of who is a worthy subject of compassion or sympathy. As many have acknowledged, compassion, while a notable sentiment, is limited: it chooses a few exceptional individuals and excludes the rest—by its very definition, compassion is unable to generalize. According to Arendt (1990, 85), it can be actualized only in particular situations in which those who do not suffer come face-to-face with those who do.[9] In this sense, it cannot scale up to address structural inequalities or forms of political violence (Arendt 1990; Boltanski 1999; Ticktin 2011a, 2016). Instead, I highlight different affective grammars that subtend horizontal relationships, from respect, comradeship, humility, ambivalence, patience, and indifference to political love. Those who share resources need not have any sentimental affiliation at all; their relations may simply be grounded on the belief that everyone is equally entitled to live. Most importantly, such sentimental grammars are built less on fixed identities than on a constant becoming, part of an embrace of the liveliness of the world.

Histories and Philosophies of Innocence

Innocence means many things: it can be freedom from sin, guilt, or moral wrong in general; freedom from specific guilt; freedom from cunning or artifice.[10] In what follows, I briefly lay out the historical and philosophical groundings of the concept of innocence, and how it functions as a political, not simply a moral, concept. This space of "freedom *from*"—this negative freedom—is so free indeed that it is seemingly free of content; it purports to be a state of *moral and epistemic purity*. Innocence is defined as a state of guilelessness, artlessness, want of knowledge or sense—in the terms of the *OED*, it is a state of ignorance, even a state of "silliness." This emptiness is also innocence's political potential—in other words, its potential to engage with the dominant order and the shape of collective life lies in its ability to define the outer limits of that social order.

Before proceeding, I want to be clear that I will not deal centrally with innocence in its arguably most recognizable guise—that is, as a legal or juridical concept. Of course, early appearances of the concept define innocence as free not only from knowledge but also from specific wrong or guilt. In contemporary legal terms, innocence is about acquittal—a decision to acquit means that the judge or jury had a reasonable doubt as to the defendant's guilt, whether this is because of exculpatory evidence or a lack of evidence to prove guilt. To find someone innocent is not necessarily to make a judgment on who they are, but on whether they committed a particular act. In other words, the legal concept has developed to judge acts, not identities (although, as Janet Halley [1993] has demonstrated, acts and identities may not be as easily distinguished as we might think). The legal concept leaves room for uncertainty. This is not the case of innocence as an ethico-moral concept, which is much less flexible, much less compromising, and which helps constitute identities or kinds in relation to purity. While these different registers certainly work together to determine its meaning, it is the ethico-moral register that has been deployed in more politically salient ways, and so I largely limit my discussion to that. Chapter 3 deals with the blending of legal and ethico-moral concepts of innocence by way of the Innocence Project.

In the context of the dominant Western secular liberal world, innocence comes into view early in relation to its theological interpretations. These locate innocence in the story of Adam and Eve, where innocence means not knowing the difference between good and evil; it means lacking worldly knowledge. Innocence is represented as a state of calm and repose, particularly in the Garden of Eden, before the fall of humanity, when Eve eats from the tree of knowledge. The Fall helps define humanity afterward; the loss of innocence is *how* we become human. In this sense, as philosopher Joanne Faulkner (2008) points out, innocence is inherently unsustainable, overdetermined by its conceptual history within Christian discourse: it is a mythical state, destined to be toppled by humanity. Innocence also implies a lack of responsibility, insofar as innocent life is bound by a divine authority, and the Fall brings to human life a will and responsibility of its own.

This Judeo-Christian history continues to resonate and shape our ideas of innocence, even as it gets deployed to different ends. Recalling the Garden of Eden, Enlightenment thinkers such as Jean-Jacques Rousseau (1987a, 1987b) also imagined a time of innocence that preceded the social contract and the political life of citizens; for Rousseau, innocence is exemplified in the state of nature and conceived of as "oneness with nature." Again, it is understood as a state of unsullied simplicity, where human and animal are not clearly distinguishable. As with the Garden of Eden, the departure from the state of nature is the beginning of our social existence, our start as political animals. These Judeo-Christian ideas continue to echo in the desire for innocence in secular liberalism, even as they are adapted for a different context: both Locke and Rousseau hold on to the desire for a pure state of being but flip it, locating it in humanity's pure and uncorrupt potential—its future, not in its past. As I will describe, we see this evoked in particular in the figure of the child.

Central to this philosophical history is epistemic or experiential purity: the absence of knowledge or experience, or sometimes even the active repelling of it. Such purity structures moral categories, filling out binary notions of deserving and undeserving, the innocent and the guilty, ultimately giving shape to different humankinds. I am interested in how innocence is constantly deployed to *produce* this economy of knowledge, action, and purity—how it regulates what counts as knowledge and what is understood as purity, and for whom. Innocence has worked to produce the idea of a deserving humanity, one that can escape the compromised and often-corrupt nature of political life. In marking off a period of epistemic and moral purity, the concept of innocence has produced worthiness, but only insofar as it is also a space of freedom from desire, will, or agency. While literary theorist James Kincaid (1998, 16) suggests that the empty figure of the innocent allows the admirer to read just about anything into its vacancy, my goal here is to trace what ends up filling this negative state. Sometimes the missing element is attached to desire—it leaves the subject as asexual; sometimes it means lack of will or intention. Almost always, however, the lack leaves one incapable of being a thinking, engaged, active, or informed subject. In valorizing purity, innocence has also produced humanity as a population of unknowing dupes. While it is certainly not my goal to recuperate a normative liberal idea of humanity as composed of rational, autonomous, agentive beings, I do want to mark innocence as the opposite of such a normative humanity, one that leaves no space for other ways of being in the world. That is, innocence acts as the boundary for liberal ideas of personhood, where this constituent outside is simultaneously idealized and denigrated. In this sense, to think beyond innocence also means thinking beyond liberalism—and illiberalism, its purported binary opposite.

Take the archetypal figure of innocence: the child. Capturing innocence in the figure of the child reflects this search for purity in the secular world, this deep yearning for a time before corruption, a space beyond social norms. The child represents a mode of experience that is protected, controlled—it performs the part of tabula rasa, and as such it offers proof that as humans we can be anything, that we are not condemned by our sinful past. Of course, childhood was not always considered the epitome of innocence; this is a modern invention, dating to the eighteenth century (Ariès 1965). Following theories of original sin, which held that all humans carry the guilt of Adam's disobedience, children were understood as inherently sinful; they were small, faulty adults in need of discipline, correction, or worse, since they had no idea how to control their various impulses (Bernstein 2011).

Notions of childhood as soiled by original sin shifted to the now more well-known ideas of Romantic childhood, thanks in part to John Locke (1975), who situated the child as simply a subject without experience and memory. For Locke, the child was an instance of natural humanity, revealing humanity's *capacity* for knowledge and reason, without being tainted by the prejudices of actual knowledge in society. The child was pure and uncorrupt potential. Images of Romantic childhood stress this idea of the child as barely part of the physical world, as belonging to a time out of history. This is achieved by making their bodies seem unreal or as distinct as possible from adults: dimpled and round, with unblemished skin (Higonnet 1998). In this sense, Locke and other Enlightenment thinkers used the child to imagine a secular humanity; as its exemplar, the figure of the child enabled humanity to reimagine itself as also essentially innocent, that is, as having the potential to act and shape its own future (Faulkner 2011). On the one hand, Enlightenment thinkers turned Judeo-Christian notions of innocence on their heads, not simply placing innocence in the past but identifying it as the key to the future; on the other hand, despite its shifting temporal location, innocence—as a space of unsullied simplicity or purity— remains central to how we imagine nature and the limits of humanity.

Innocence demarcates humankinds according to their relationship to knowledge and action. For instance, locating innocence in the figure of the child leaves little space for actual childhood experiences. What happens when these experiences do not fit the parameters of innocence? Innocence carves out a conceptual space and time of unsullied hope, one that is linked to a freedom from knowledge. Yet the borders of this space are profoundly contested; rather than a given, this space is a political battleground. Understanding the work of innocence requires tracing which types of knowledge are named or counted as pure (which experiences slip into a space of epistemic purity, unnoticed) and, by contrast, which ones somehow tip the balance and result in an expulsion from innocence. Child soldiers, for instance, trouble the image of the child as innocent. And as Liisa Malkki (2010) has argued, child soldiers are seen as an abomination, a category mistake that leads to their being labeled "youth" or "teens" as opposed to "children" whenever possible, to set aside and protect a time of innocence, when they are still unworldly and untainted. In the context of Palestine, Nadera Shalhoub-Kevorkian calls this "unchilding" (2020).

This concept of the child as having unmediated access to an imaginary wholeness has also been taken up and critiqued by scholars like Lee Edelman (2004). As he writes, following Rousseau and Locke, the liberal social order is dependent on the universal signifier of the (white) child, and its teleological hope for the future; in some ways, he suggests that the child is the father of man, too, filling a hole in the symbolic. To disrupt the figure of the child is therefore to disrupt the social order. In this sense, innocence is indeed critical to the white liberal social order. However, the way I see it, real, complex children can disrupt the reproduction of the liberal social order, not by positing no future, as Edelman suggests, but a *different* future.

Even as it produces humankinds, innocence marks humanity's limits. Perhaps unsurprisingly, those associated with innocence tend to be at humanity's edges; they mark its border, in the sense that they are not corrupt (as is a normative humanity), yet nor are they fully human in the Enlightenment sense of having reason, will, or autonomy. Women have been figured as innocent, for instance, particularly in the form of mother and child. This may be because white children's innocence was often seen as transferable to surrounding people and things (Bernstein 2011). As we know, sex is a particularly dense site of struggle between knowledge and ignorance; the term *carnal knowledge* illustrates the battle over how to categorize different forms of action and experience.[11] Kincaid describes innocence as simply "virginity coupled with ignorance" (1998, 55). For women, then, sex is considered the primary corrupting form of knowledge. To be innocent is to be chaste. Purity here—to be a "good woman"—is to actively embody performances of passionlessness (Bernstein 2011, 41). This is echoed over and over again in the history of rape cases—women who have been victims of sexual violence are figured immediately as guilty; the burden of proof is reversed, requiring that they prove *their innocence* rather than the guilt of their attackers. Indeed, in this way, innocence has helped produce new gendered and sexual ontologies: the requirement of passionlessness to claim innocence has carried over to homosexuality. As we will see in chapter 3, in the struggle against HIV/AIDS, access to lifesaving treatment required that queer bodies be rendered innocent, which entailed taking homosexuality out of the realm of choice and desire, placing it in the sphere of genetically determined nature or essence.

Building a Desire for Innocence: Humanitarianism and Victims' Rights

I return now to the question of the infrastructures of desire for innocence in the Euro-American political landscape. Earlier I discussed the question of why the contemporary search for innocence and purity; I turn now to lay out a few of the mechanisms and histories that spurred the development of this politics. Once again, this is not a comprehensive genealogy of innocence. I have picked what I see as two significant moments here, but there are multiple histories and starting points to show how innocence has become central to contemporary politics, insofar as it creates a space for seemingly apolitical (or morally pure) action. First, to humanitarianism; and second, to victim's rights movements.

THE NEW HUMANITARIANISM

I turn to France in 1968 and the subsequent formation of Médecins sans Frontières (MSF; Doctors Without Borders), since it was here that a shift in a form of political engagement rendered innocence central to politics. This was not the only moment or place that the shift occurred, but it was certainly a critical one, particularly in the European and, later, global context. This is also the beginning of what Didier Fassin calls "humanitarian government" (2011, 1), or how moral sentiments have become an essential force in contemporary politics, directed from the more powerful to the weaker. The year 1968 marked the largest strike in the history of the French workers' movement—only recently rivaled by the strikes against pension reform under President Macron in 2023—and the largest mass movement in French history (Ross 2002, 3–4). The key players in the formation of MSF were all *soixante-huitards* ('68ers): at the time they were doctors or medical students, and Maoists or members of the Communist Party. These revolutionary doctors, who came together with a group of equally radical journalists, founded MSF in 1971.

While initially guided by the belief in a universal humanity grounded in equality and solidarity, MSF and the "new humanitarianism" soon blossomed into and helped shape an era of moralist antipolitics. After the failure of '68 to transform the social and political order and after the disappointment of anticolonial revolutionary Marxist movements, Bernard Kouchner, one of MSF's founders, and many of his comrades from '68 radically changed their views. They turned away from engagement with what they thought of as politics—engaging with power relations in the struggle for a collective future—and instead embraced the belief that one can ultimately address only individual suffering; in this sense, they attended to what they conceived of as a universal humanity composed of suffering victims (Redfield 2013; Ross 2002; Vallaeys 2004). As former executive director of MSF-USA Nicolas de Torrenté wrote, "Humanitarian action's single-minded purpose [is] alleviating suffering, unconditionally and without any ulterior motive" (2004, 5). That is, politics in terms of the anticapitalist, anti-imperialist revolution dreamed of by the *soixante-huitards* was replaced by a defense of the principles of human rights, and by a view that separated victims from perpetrators, heroes from villains, in order to side with and defend the powerless (Ross 2002). Kouchner and MSF brought a form of action that appealed in its purported ability to *avoid* Machiavellian politics

(Caldwell 2009). It was an ideology grounded in individualism, one that no longer allowed for the possibility of larger political change.[12]

Innocence was central both to the politics of this "antipolitics" and, ultimately, to defining morally legitimate suffering. This "new humanitarianism" was shaped by a frustration with and refusal of politics; consequently, it was driven by the search for an uncorrupted space of action. Innocence offers such a space of imagination, even as it calls forth and protects different versions of epistemic and moral purity. In this sense, the suffering victim driving humanitarian action quickly inhabited the conceptual space opened by the notion of innocence, even if it was not always identical to it—of course, humanitarianism is not *simply* a politics of innocence, and innocence clearly travels beyond its humanitarian deployments. While MSF maintains impartiality as a key principle, meaning that it offers assistance to people irrespective of their race, gender, religion, or political affiliation, in many humanitarian contexts—on the ground—innocence becomes the necessary accompaniment to suffering, required to designate the sufferer as worthy. That is, the suffering victim is best and most easily recognized by humanitarians when considered innocent—pure, outside politics, outside history, indeed, outside time and place altogether (Ticktin 2011a).

On a practical level, humanitarians are guided by the principle of impartiality, but in practice, finite resources limit their action. While the goal is to treat everyone equally, whether they are perpetrators or victims, they themselves admit that they must triage, prioritizing those considered in the most serious and immediate danger. The concept of innocence helps in this process, as a way to grasp and measure vulnerability. Indeed, former MSF president Rony Brauman has criticized how moralist positions have marked humanitarianism, noting that the symbolic status of victim can in effect "only be granted in cases of unjustified or innocent suffering. . . . The point is that he [*sic*] must be 100% victim, a non-participant" (Brauman 1993, 154).

This process of triage is evident in the case of sexual violence. Before the early 2000s, survivors of sexual violence were not included in standard models of humanitarian aid delivery. In the collection of essays by MSF about humanitarian practices in the Congo Republic in the late 1990s, *Civilians under Fire* (Le Pape and Salignon 2003), former MSF-USA executive director Nicolas de Torrenté and former MSF president Jean-Hervé Bradol admit that this is because relief organizations search for the "ideal victims." On the one hand, they acknowledge that this is strategic, insofar as it is a way to get donors interested; de Torrenté writes, "Deeply rooted images put a premium on the innocence of victims, making children, who are by definition blameless, the ideal recipients of care" (Le Pape and Salignon,

2003, x). On the other hand, they suggest that this focus, instrumental or not, pushes other categories of victims into the background. Survivors of sexual violence were not seen as innocent—as Bradol writes, "The raped woman rarely represents the ideal victim" (Bradol 2003, 11). This is because such survivors raised a number of unsettling issues for practitioners around violence and gender roles, which they felt were too political to engage. As a result, de Torrenté states that MSF reproduced forms of prejudice against women in general and survivors of sexual violence in particular. These discussions are haunted by the histories and treatment of women victims of rape, who were (and still are) seen as responsible for and consenting to their own rapes because of how they dressed or behaved, or where they had chosen to be. They are seen as too knowing and too agentive to be innocent.

In many ways, MSF's collection of essays marks the shift, since the early 2000s, in the humanitarian mandate; sexual violence now merits an immediate response from aid workers, and in a complete about-face, we might even see it as the humanitarian issue par excellence. This was not because humanitarianism stopped looking for innocent subjects; rather, there was a shift to seeing these women as innocent enough to be compelling humanitarian subjects. This happened, in large part, through the medicalization of gender-based violence, which is a longer story related to its changing treatment by regimes of human rights and global health (Ticktin 2011b). Attention was transferred to health consequences such as infection with HIV, physical injury and trauma, unwanted pregnancies, reproductive health, and STDs. This medicalization of rape and sexual violence ended up shifting the blame and rendering the victims innocent of the harm they endured. More specifically, a focus on the vulnerable body in biomedical terms brackets off social and political identities and realities. The medicalization was helpful insofar as it allowed women to be abstracted from their political contexts, rendered blameless, and treated; it has been less helpful, however, insofar as it has worked to depoliticize the larger gendered inequalities that lead to such harm.

The conceptual space of innocence has been critically shaped and deployed through the process of medicalization at the heart of medical humanitarianism; biomedicine, in its focus on the physical body, also generally disregards the role of intentionality, desire, or will. The depoliticizing process of medicalization—assessing people primarily through their biologies, not as moral or political persons—enhances people's palatability as blameless, or innocent. They are suffering, and that is all one needs to know. Indeed, the process of medicalization was also important to one of the second movements that helped make innocence central to politics: the victim's rights movement. It helped conflate these two categories and make them into one: "innocent victim."

VICTIMS' RIGHTS

Innocence and victimhood, while conceptually close, have not always been collapsed into one another. The question is how their connection has become almost common sense; and as with humanitarianism, both the process of medicalization and a focus on gender-based violence played crucial roles in this process. The focus on victims has made the language of innocence more politically salient, but perhaps more importantly for me, the connection between the two has made claims to victimhood and injury seem like a legitimate answer to charges of enduring structural racisms. It has suffocated other moral and political responses. As we will see in chapters 1 and 3, discourses of white grievance imply that white people are the primary innocent victims—of crime, for instance; this reframes structural racism and organized abandonment into individual acts, with white people on the side of the morally injured, rather than the reverse.

First, I describe the victims' rights movements of the 1970s and 1980s in both the US and France, because this is what gave victimhood a new public and social presence. Second, I will explain how victimhood and innocence were coupled in such a way to make innocence a prominent part of this politics. This happened by joining three different political concepts: victimhood, innocence, and trauma.

In the US, the victims' rights movement began with the unlikely marriage between feminism and conservatism, each trying to transform the judicial system. On the one hand, it developed as part of a tough-on-crime ideology—a conservative, punitive movement, associated with protecting whiteness; indeed, the idea of "the innocent victim of crime" was forged as part of a white backlash against the civil rights movement of the 1960s (Abu El-Haj 2022). But on the other hand, this was occurring at the same time as liberal, second-wave feminists were fighting for the legal recognition of victims of rape and incest, with the transformative idea that these women and girls were indeed victims, they had not "asked for it." In parallel fashion, in France, the turn to victims' rights began with victims of terrorist acts in the 1980s rather than with other types of crime, but it was also combined with a struggle for the rights of victims of sexual violence. The result was the centering of the "innocent victim" as part of a conservative, moralized politics.

While some say the movement began in 1975 in the US with the publication of a book called *The Victims* by Frank Carrington (sponsored by the Heritage Foundation), others argue that it began in 1966, with movement for effective law enforcement, against the "due-process revolution." The latter worked to protect defendants in very basic forms, including notifying them of their rights and providing court-appointed attorneys. It is actually extremely recent to grant rights to defendants—these are protections against the state and have nothing to do with harms done to victims.

The victims' rights movement was part of a law-and-order rhetoric mobilized against the challenge by civil rights movements to white dominance: political protests against a racist state were recast as a set of criminal acts (Abu El-Haj 2022). "Law and order" Republicans, starting with Nixon but really gaining prominence with Reagan, argued that judges were soft on crime. It is no accident that this followed on the heels of the civil rights movement. The Republicans argued that there was a silent, victimized majority, victims whose voices needed to be heard because of the alarming rise in crime; Reagan suggested this was due to a "hardened criminal class" who had been treated too leniently. After the Warren Court in 1972 ruled the death penalty to be effectively unconstitutional, Carrington coined the term "victims' rights," which called for the restoration of the death penalty and the rights of victims over those accused of crimes (Lepore 2018). Rather than grant rights to victims against unfair government intrusion, this movement changed the procedural balance to lean toward conviction and incarceration—it fought against constitutional protections for defendants. In this sense, from the get-go, victims' rights were for the politically privileged; they were not for subordinated groups. The movement constructed victims as "weak, innocent, and helpless" while the defendants were cast as irredeemable, evil, and powerful, and populated by race and gender stereotypes. They focused on individual responsibility, writing out the very idea of "society." The "criminal" was mostly poor, Black or Latino, angry and violent (Gruber 2007, 775). The victims were passive white women. The context of crime was entirely erased.

What is interesting and relevant here is that the conservative, punitive, lock-them-up law-and-order movement unexpectedly became bedfellows with the liberal feminist movement of the 1970s. Crimes against women had never made it into the law—from marital rape, domestic violence, to sexual harassment—and women's rights activists sought stronger sentences for rape and sexual assault and protections for victims. For instance, these feminists sought to protect rape victims from cross-examination about their sexual history, and to reframe rape as an external event, not something "deserved" by a victim's behavior. To be clear, as Nadia Abu El-Haj recounts, while they insisted on the legal innocence of victim in relation to the particular act of sexual assault, these feminists were not looking just to protect women who were pure, or sexually innocent; it was not, as she suggests, a politics of identity or injury. They acknowledged the rights of women to have sexual pasts and to live alone and be independent.

Despite the acceptance of complexity in the feminist movement, the connection between victims and innocence was solidified by the feminist inclusion of child victims of incest in their struggle (Abu El-Haj 2022). Liberal feminists fought to establish the figure of the innocent girl in relation to father-daughter incest, taking away any blame from the children, while also showing that they suffered harm that could manifest many years later. And this is where trauma comes in. These children (or later, as adults) were diagnosed as suffering from PTSD. The feminist movement argued that the guilt that many felt after sexual abuse—blaming oneself—was entirely misplaced; indeed, they argued that trauma itself brought along an exaggerated sense of control, when in fact, one was helpless. In this sense, then, the diagnostic category of trauma was essential in establishing the innocence of the victim, that is, lack of agency, responsibility, or culpability. To be traumatized was precisely to take on unwarranted guilt.

In these various ways, victims were newly associated with the transformed medical category of trauma (or PTSD), which in turn eliminated the suspicion of them—they were henceforth considered innocent in their claims and deserving of either compensation or treatment (Abu El-Haj 2022; Fassin and Rechtman 2009; Herman 1992). Even as this idea of the helplessness of victims of trauma developed in relation to child sexual abuse, it carried over into the category of trauma more generally, including those traumatized by war (soldiers) or other forms of crime. The idea of a passive, helpless innocent victim played into other existing gendered, classed, and racialized stereotypes: well-off white women fit well into the passive, helpless category, while poor Black men and other men of color matched the category of aggressive criminal. Social or economic issues were now effectively erased as a critical part of this story; the only thing that mattered was criminal justice (Gruber 2007). Indeed, Nicole Brown Smith—the murdered wife of O. J. Simpson—became the poster child for the convergence of the victims' rights and anti–domestic violence agendas, as the ultimate victim: an elite white woman, murdered by a Black man. This turn to the law to deal with gender-based violence, while not initially conservative, subsequently morphed into law-and-order, carceral, or governance feminism (Halley et al. 2019; Bernstein 2018), which has prioritized criminalization over any other form of gender justice.

If we return to France, and the role of medicalization in particular, the role of PTSD in developing the politics of innocence is once again put into relief. As Fassin and Rechtman recount (2009), the victims' rights discourse really came into its own in Paris after the terrorist attacks in the summer of

1995;[13] then-president Chirac called on Dr. Xavier Emmanuelli to respond, who was the secretary of state for humanitarian action and had led the effort to create the social emergency response force called SAMU, which blurred social and medical emergencies. We see the overlaps between humanitarianism and victims' rights, and how they both developed around the subject of innocent victim, drawing on the context of health and medicine to expand its reach to a range of political experiences.

Dr. Emmanuelli went to the site of the attack with a group of psychiatrists to deal with the shock the victims had experienced; he was already involved in a nascent discipline of "psychiatric victimology." French psychiatry has an important tradition of psychoanalysis and long resisted the biomedicalization of trauma, but when it did finally follow that model, it shifted the focus of psychic trauma to all those touched by terrorist attacks: the injured, the survivors, as well as rescue workers, nurses, and TV viewers. Insofar as trauma became a medical category—and increasingly, a biomedical one called PTSD, rather than a psychological or psychoanalytic one—it was applied across the board, regardless of context or relations of power. It was the diagnosis applied to the suffering person, but did not include an analysis of why they were suffering. And as part of this, a new role developed for the doctors, as forensic medical experts, testifying to the rights of victims. The role of experts further solidified their condition as "innocent"—passive, voiceless, and helpless. They now needed doctors and other experts to speak for them. In this sense, the category of trauma allowed for a form of moral collapse (Fassin and Rechtman 2009; Abu El-Haj 2022): it applied the same category to those who suffer from violence, commit it, or witness it, rendering them all "innocent victims."

∵

Humanitarianism and the movement for victims' rights not only put innocence front and center; they did so in part by collapsing or combining different types of innocence. For instance, they conflated sexual innocence and racial innocence. While, as noted earlier, they are clearly part of a "family of resemblances" (Wittgenstein 1958), the meanings of innocence are not identical: sexual innocence is about sexual integrity and chastity, while racial innocence is about ignorance and a will to not know about racial domination. Furthermore, there are different mechanisms by which to reach innocence, and these have real consequences: sometimes innocence is claimed, other times it is assumed, assigned, or imposed. Through these movements, however, the claims to innocence have ended up working intersectionally, and this has given them even more reach and capacious power.

As we can see from both humanitarianism and victims' rights, certain subjects are better positioned to fit into the conceptual framework of innocence. Gender configurations suggest that women are more easily understood as victims and as apolitical, and hence more easily interpellated into the role of moral purity. But a series of combinations of innocence were required to make this so: on the one hand, the focus by victims' rights movements on both sexual violence and criminal justice made white women the ideal innocent victims. Once again, Nicole Brown Smith is a case in point. This played on previous histories and precursors, such as the nineteenth-century panic about white slavery, which focused on innocent white women being kidnapped by foreign men; and to be sure, such tropes have since carried over to the contemporary struggle against human trafficking. As anthropologist Carole Vance (2012) has long argued, the central characters in stories of sex trafficking are teenage girls and young women, putatively devoid of sexuality or knowledge, and sold into brothels. These girls and women are considered innocent victims in the sense of sexual innocence; there is no room for sexual knowledge or experience, and the victims are described as vulnerable, defenseless, lost, and excluded, unable to comprehend their situations. But the victims' rights movements were driven by white men, enabling them, in what we might think of as a counterintuitive move, to *claim* innocence and victimhood too, by identifying themselves in relation to white women—"their" women were being abused, trafficked, murdered. They used this to lean into a form of *racial* innocence, characterizing foreigners or men of color as criminals, preferring not to know about histories such as the organized abandonment of Black communities after the civil rights movement. Here innocence is claimed to assert and retain power.

On the other hand, if white women and men are one kind of victim in this configuration of racial and sexual innocence, the "Third World Woman"—as transnational feminist theorist Chandra Mohanty (1988) has called the stereotypical suffering victim of oppressive patriarchal cultures—is another ideal candidate for the innocent victim, insofar as women from the Third World or Global South are often equated with passivity and apolitical corporeal existence. Yet for them, innocence is not claimed, but *imposed*. They are seen as without agency, docile, and in need of rescue (Abu-Lughod 2013; Mohanty 1988). Indeed, Ratna Kapur has called this "the victim subject" (2002). This plays on a different configuration of sexual and racial innocence; here, the sexual innocence of the Third World Woman is not only about passivity, but pitifulness; and a politics of pity, as Luc Boltanski (1999) suggests, is not about equality or justice. While justice is concerned with fairness and requires recourse to standards or conventions of equivalence, pity sets up two classes of people, the fortunate and the unfortunate, where the unfortunate are often regarded as victims. In this second sense, innocence is part of a conceptual apparatus that demarcates humankinds, purporting to value the most naïve, the most inactive, the most childlike, while simultaneously setting up another class of people on whom these innocents must depend.

Innocence and Its Conceptual Friends

Innocence is part of tangled convergences with concepts that seek to manage and regulate distributions of knowledge and power, deservingness and blame, life and qualified life, potentiality and hopelessness. It is used to name and manage the border between politics and humanity, to set aside a space at the heart of politics that is included by its very exclusion; in doing this, it joins concepts like *homo sacer* (Agamben 1998). It is also part of a cluster of moral concepts, including suffering, victimhood, and vulnerability; these take shape in relation to one another. I conclude by briefly parsing the differences in this latter cluster, to think through the overall structure of the political argument that innocence participates in and, ultimately, to pry open a space to think of a world without or beyond innocence.

Suffering is often thought of in relation to innocence, although to be sure it is not limited to those who are innocent. Rather, today, suffering is associated with the concept of a universal humanity. Nevertheless, innocence helps qualify expressions of suffering, rendering some as more warranted than others; for instance, innocence creates a moral distinction between unnecessary (innocent) and unavoidable (necessary) suffering. This notion of common suffering as the basis of humanity developed in the eighteenth century, with Enlightenment thinkers like Rousseau (Sznaider 2001); one might say it accompanied the democratic project and the shift away from a religious belief in the blessedness of suffering. "Humanity" began to refer to a shared sentiment of sympathy or benevolence—not shared species or biological fact. In this sense, the construction of a humane, secular society required the elimination of suffering; meaningless pain and suffering were eschewed. Humanitarianism in its current form developed to respond to a global humanity, understood as the capacity to suffer. Yet, while the concept of suffering pretends to universality, and while the humanitarian argument is that all suffering should be alleviated, there is a tension at suffering's conceptual core: in the liberal secular project, some kinds of suffering have been seen as gratuitous—as more inhuman—than others. As both Talal Asad (2003) and Samera Esmeir (2012) note, suffering and pain have been used as both tools for and measures of the progress toward a modern, liberal, "civilized" humanity. Asad suggests that some kinds of suffering are justified as helping one become human—those that are seen to be carefully calibrated and used to rational ends, such as modern warfare or prisons; meanwhile, others are considered barbaric, such as torture, which people see as excessive, irrational. Innocence takes shape in and through this tension, qualifying expressions of suffering, justifying some and condemning others. At stake here is what counts as suffering and how we can recognize it. Innocence parses different kinds of suffering, qualifying them; it provides a moral and cultural frame by which to judge them. Differently stated, innocence inserts hierarchy into the concept of suffering. Suffering could be understood in other ways—perhaps as more wide ranging—without innocence.

As we just saw, victimhood is also part of a moral constellation with the concept of innocence; the phrase *innocent victim* occurs so often that it can be difficult to think of *innocent* and *victim* apart. Victims of natural disasters such as earthquakes or tsunamis are the incarnation of this. But innocents need not be victims—children are one such example. And victims need not be innocent. One can be a victim of a crime without being innocent, as we know in the cases of women who kill their abusers. Another example from the 1970s shows some of the complexity within the concept of victimhood: I refer here to debates in the United Nations about whether everyday people (i.e., civilians) who were part of occupying or colonial regimes, and who were killed as part of liberation struggles, should be considered "innocent victims" under the laws of war. This debate took place in the context of struggles for decolonization all over Africa, especially in South Africa under apartheid, and was part of negotiations at the United Nations over the definition of terrorism (Blumenau 2014). Could (violent) acts of liberation be labeled terrorist, and if so, should the victims be considered innocent? Ultimately, it was accepted that victims could be "guilty" but still victims— that is, they were guilty by virtue of being part of an occupying regime (i.e., South African apartheid) and therefore complicit in its violence and oppression. We can extend this logic to Israel as well, as a contemporary example of settler colonialism; Israelis harmed by Palestinian resistance may be victims, but not innocent victims. The coupling and uncoupling of innocence and victimhood can have powerful consequences—we can turn again to Israel-Palestine. Since 2009, the Israeli Defense Forces (IDF) have used the tactic of "roof knocking" to avoid charges of crimes against humanity under humanitarian law; these include telephone calls, leaflets, or warning shots onto the roofs of Palestinian civilians, in buildings suspected to contain fighters or weapons, to tell them to evacuate before Israelis send missiles to destroy them. If Palestinians do not leave, according to the Israelis they are no longer considered "innocent civilians," but as complicit in so-called Palestinian terrorism, and hence killable.[14] Yet civilians are often only given minutes to leave, if that, and there have been many casualties of the "knocks" or warning shots themselves. Does this mean they are guilty? When decoupled from innocence, victimhood becomes a more complicated subject position, which can be tied to an act of harm and not necessarily to a fixed identity as someone pure or undeserving of harm. In other words, victimhood need not be a moral identity; it can also be a medical condition or a legal category, which, as discussed, allows for more flexibility and contestation, and a whole new set of debates, for better or worse.

Finally, innocence is perhaps most often thought of as synonymous with or very similar to vulnerability. Both vulnerable and innocent subjects are seen as needing protection; both cannot fully care for themselves. There is an element of frailty in each; a susceptibility to harm. And in both cases, the subjects verge on being pitiful, even undignified, insofar as a normative, liberal idea of humanity is grounded not simply on ideas of rationality, autonomy, and determination but on physical wholeness (Dean 2015). Feminist theorists like Judith Butler (2016) have attempted to shift understandings of vulnerability, understanding it not in opposition to political agency but precisely as inherent to political action: they mobilize vulnerability as a practice of political resistance to demand the material infrastructures and social conditions necessary for everyone to live. I am not convinced that vulnerability is a fundamental ontological condition, nor am I persuaded by the politics that assumes this to be the case, but these theories nevertheless make clear that vulnerability allows for relationality; one is vulnerable in relation to something or someone. Innocence, however, is a concept that stands on its own, even when contrasted with its binary Others, such as guilt, knowledge, or sexuality; one is innocent or one is not. Because it is about purity, it does not allow for gradations—for being *partly* innocent. Innocence patrols the borders of power and powerlessness, rendering them incommensurable, while vulnerability leaves room for negotiation—it allows room for degrees of powerlessness while allowing some measure of action in the world.

When we parse the moral cluster, it becomes clear that a world beyond innocence would not be a world without morality or care; it would not need to refuse the recognition of vulnerability, suffering, or victimhood. It would also not need to be a world of total guilt or unbridled, unchecked desire. To think beyond innocence is precisely to challenge the binaries that structure our moral vocabularies. It would, however, be a world without purity and absolutism, one that could not be grounded on the idea of a singular place of moral transcendence. The opposite of innocence in this sense is not guilt but *impurity*. A world without innocence, then, would embrace this contaminated reality and let it be the site of new political emergence.

Organization of the Book

Against Innocence: Undoing and Remaking the World is structured as a collection of five chapters, each taking on one aspect of how innocence functions as a method of politics in today's world, helping shape some of our most pressing political debates. Each chapter also focuses on a key figure or figures that are enabled or buttressed by the concept of innocence: the liberal/colonizer/humanitarian; the refugee/child; the queer and the criminal; and the nonhuman, including Mother Nature and the fetus. By thinking across these different figures, I argue against the focus on liberal, individual identity politics that innocence encourages and cultivates, including claims to individual victimhood. I draw on decades of research and political engagement across Euro-American contexts, including the US, France, the UK, Spain, Morocco, and Greece, along with contemporary political examples and historical research, and I combine these with theoretical analysis.

The first two chapters of the book are about those who are considered innocent, with the goal of denaturalizing the category. I start perhaps counterintuitively with those with power, exploring how they assert a form of racial innocence in order to claim and maintain power. Focusing on liberals, colonizers, and humanitarians, I lay out how the concept of innocence not only works to maintain forms of domination, but also helps build bridges between liberal and illiberal political visions. I introduce other concepts of collective responsibility that carry throughout the book—from implicatedness and complicity to the subject positions of beneficiaries and perpetuators. In the second chapter, I consider those who are most often the face of innocence: children, and in particular, refugee children. But rather than take their innocence as given, I explore the historical and aesthetic work involved in producing them as such, and the fallout of this process—the other moral and political hierarchies that result.

If the first two chapters take on the category of those who are seemingly innocent, whether by virtue of claiming it or being assigned it, the third chapter looks at the work of innocence through the lens of those who have been designated as guilty, and work instead to claim innocence. The chapter demonstrates how the category of innocence is invoked and constructed in reverse, primarily through forms of scientific expertise like genetic, DNA, and forensic analysis, and the consequences of this. I focus here on the figure of the queer—in particular, those who were designated responsible for getting and propagating HIV/AIDS, and their subsequent claim to being "born this way" as an assertion of innocence and lack of responsibility. I also look at "Black guilt" and the figure of the criminal, and the Innocence Project's goals in using science to absolve the exceptional few. I conclude with a look at both queer theories and abolitionism as alternative, non-innocent politics.

The fourth chapter continues to look at the dynamism of the category of innocence, arguing that it works through a logic of expansion not unlike that of capitalism, insofar as a politics based on innocence requires not only the search for but also the production of innocent victims. As a key part of racial capitalism, innocence works to help differentiate, racially and otherwise. I focus on the animal, and the fetus—the latest frontiers of innocence—and finally, on Mother Earth. I end the chapter thinking about ontologies of interconnection, contamination, and co-imbrication as the necessary place for non-innocent politics to take root, insisting that these collective ways of being and sharing are the only way to survive.

The final chapter is a speculative engagement with non-innocent political worlds. I am interested in different ways of living and being together that are not grounded on innocence. From visual experiments that counter or undo the affective structures and grounding logics of innocence to "no-borders" movements that are already pushing beyond many of our foundational liberal political terms and concepts, I probe what a non-innocent politics might look like by delving into both the aesthetics and politics of commoning, or a collective regime of living and sharing that refuses a liberal politics of individual identity and victimhood. The goal is to think about a world that takes contamination and complicity as its starting point. I end where I hope others will subsequently begin.

CHAPTER ONE

The Power of Racial Innocence

Liberals, Illiberals, and Humanitarians

In February 2019, a photo of two men was posted online, taken from a 1984 Eastern Virginia Medical School yearbook: one was dressed up in blackface and the other in Ku Klux Klan robes. Virginia Democratic governor Ralph Northam was accused of being one of the people in the photo, as the photo was on his yearbook page. Initially he admitted it, then denied it, and finally admitted to having dressed up in blackface other times, apologizing for his behavior. Despite calls by both Democrats and Republicans for Northam to resign, he refused to step down. To be sure, it was not helped by the fact that his potential successors were embroiled in scandals of their own; the third-ranking official in Virginia, Attorney General Mark Herring, acknowledged that he too had worn blackface as an undergraduate. Instead, several months later, Northam said that he had had to confront truths about Virginia's history of racism, and that "Among those truths was my own incomplete understanding regarding race and equity . . . ."[1] He claimed lack of knowledge about the legacy of racism in Virginia, and by extension, his own. As with his yearbook photo, he located the racism in the past; this included his family's history of slave ownership. The racism of the present was located instead in then President Donald Trump; Northam admitted to his lack of knowledge and asked for forgiveness. In the meantime, he promised to challenge extant racial structures, such as Confederate monuments.

A few months later, in October 2019, photographs emerged of then Canadian prime minister Justin Trudeau in blackface. There were numerous such examples, including him dressed up as Aladdin, complete with blackface makeup and a turban. The latter occurred when he was twenty-nine years old, working as a teacher in a private school. "I apologise profoundly," Trudeau told reporters on his campaign plane. "I didn't think it was racist at the time, but now I see, it was a racist thing to do."[2] While Canada's history of racism has different contours that are arguably more grounded in settler colonialism and the genocide of Indigenous communities, blackface is still one clear symbol of the deeply entrenched racisms;

and Canada, like most nations with histories of settler colonialism and/or slavery, participates in a form of anti-Black racism, even if we understand Blackness to have flexible contours, since it is a political concept, not a biological one. To be clear, blackface has a long and varied transnational history; steeped in centuries of racism, it demeans and dehumanizes those of African descent. It has involved darkening one's face with substances like shoe polish, enlarging lips and exaggerating features. It peaked in the US when demands for civil rights by recently emancipated enslaved people triggered racial hostility, but the practice continues as a way to depict Black people as not fully human, serving to rationalize violence and segregation. It involved people dressing up in blackface for minstrel shows, depicting their characters as lazy, ignorant, superstitious, hypersexual, criminal, or cowardly.

These are just a few examples of racist acts by liberal public officials or those in prominent or privileged political or social positions; there are many more. What is consistent across such examples is that those who enact the racism claim innocence: they ask for forgiveness, explaining that they did not know how hurtful such an act was, and they did not understand how it was racist or demeaning. In this chapter, I am interested in exploring how innocence serves to excuse people for committing such acts—purifying and absolving them—and how this purification enables them to maintain power. Innocence plays an important part in making up the dominant group, and in maintaining hierarchies. That is, by denying culpability or assuming that one is not implicated in oppressive relations toward others, the hierarchies of power are preserved.

The concept of innocence, when successfully evoked, renders invisible the more complicated relationships of power by relying on individual intentionality and causality, or by erasing agency altogether. By discounting the larger scripts that undergird all social interactions—that are not simply individual or structural, but *collective*—infrastructures of power such as white supremacy are allowed to build and grow in ways that are unaccounted for and unrecognized. They underlie collective life and direct action and choice, yet they are rarely made visible.

Further, I will argue that by assuming that responsibility can only be individual, the concept of innocence not only works to maintain forms of domination, but is currently helping shore up the connective tissue between liberal and illiberal political visions. While there is no one clear break between the liberal and illiberal, the work of liberalism is precisely to draw and patrol the line between the two, by deciding what is "acceptable" racism—and it is currently pushing the defining line of liberalism down its political continuum toward illiberalism. This allows all those involved to absolve themselves of responsibility for both contemporary forms of racism and oppression, and their histories.

The refusal to recognize or acknowledge the founding and enduring structural racist inequalities in the US has become a more explicit and acceptable position since Trump became president in 2016 and explicitly supported white supremacist America, and it has been put front and center by banning everything "DEI" (Diversity, Equity, and Inclusion) since he was elected again in 2024. But this supremacist position is a transnational phenomenon and holds true in all the strong-man regimes and increasing extreme-right illiberal and fascist parties that have either taken power, or risk to do so, from Viktor Orbán in Hungary to Narendra Modi in India and Giorgia Meloni in Italy, to Javier Milei in Argentina; this includes the growing power of Marine Le Pen in France, and the new power of the right wing in places like Sweden, Germany, and the Netherlands. But rather than simply locating racisms as an extreme-right problem, I am interested in the way such racially informed discriminations also take shape in liberal spaces and get reproduced and disseminated there, pushing the moving line between the liberal and illiberal into the acceptable zones of the illiberal.

The various meanings of innocence are instructive, and work in counterintuitive ways, against the idea of liberal reason or cognizance, while the Latin etymology of *innocence* focuses on harm (*in-* + *nocens*, "not harmful"), which is clearly a central feature of the concept and perhaps the most familiar to us in definitions like freedom from sin, guilt, or moral wrong, as mentioned in the introduction. I draw attention to a different etymology of *in-* + *noscere*, "not to know," which is particularly significant. What does it mean not simply to be empty of knowledge, but specifically to *not know*? This can be a willful ignorance.

In the context of US history, James Baldwin (1998) thought about this kind of willful ignorance or unknowing in terms of racial innocence; he described this impermissible innocence as Americans' refusal to deal with deeply entrenched forms of racial injustice, by holding on to ideologies of equality that undergird the American dream rather than facing the actual historical evidence (see also Balfour 1999). Baldwin was describing the way Americans want to hold on to the fantasy of a race-blind present and future. Their ignorance allows the posture of innocence. Indeed, racial innocence is a form of deflection (Pierce 2012)—a not-knowing or obliviousness that can be politically useful for those in power and that can prompt and justify further such pursuits of innocence. It allows those who are a part of a white racial formation (by choice or by ascription) to benefit from the system without acknowledging the way the system operates or their central role in its reproduction.

The concept of innocence as such blocks more complicated, nuanced positions that are not only too simple but also rely on a certain ontological stability: one is either innocent, or guilty, but one cannot be both simultaneously, or a bit of one and a bit of the other. Innocence serves as a fixed identity category: it describes a pure state of being. A reliance on innocence to adjudicate relations of power and questions of justice fixes us in what Simona Forti (2014) has called the "Dostoevsky paradigm," which sets "diabolical perpetrators" against "absolutely innocent victims."[3] This binary imaginary focuses on individuals, intentions, and direct moralized culpability, and makes it impossible to think about collective responsibility, structural inequality, or any other kind of relationship to power. By refusing to allow history into the frame—innocence is measured in discrete, individual actions over singular human lifetimes—the afterlives of forms of violence such as slavery or colonialism get erased; and in the process, systems such as racial capitalism remain comfortably in place. There is no room for the "gray zone," as Primo Levi (2015) famously called it; even in the most extreme of situations—such as the world of Nazi concentration camps—Levi notes that there were no easy distinctions between "us" and "them"; all victims were nevertheless marked by shades of complicity. Innocence leaves no room for more complicated relationships of responsibility, such as those who, while not directly involved in the harm, still benefit from earlier injustices; and as such, it will always stand in the way of more radical political transformation.

To be sure, innocence is not equally accessible to all; racial, gendered, class, and religious formations play an important role in how and to whom it becomes available as a source of power, and these positionalities have been honed over time, tamed into naturalized sites of purity. The powerful white men who wore blackface were able to claim innocence by explaining that what they had done earlier, without sufficient knowledge, did not reflect who they were, either then or now. They never intended to inflict harm, and now, they assert, they are capable of change and growth. Others, however—people of color, people from the Global South, or women, for instance—may not be understood as autonomous individuals in the same sense, nor seen as innocent to begin with, as we have seen with Black children (hooks 2013; Bernstein 2011) or Palestinian children. They are also not seen as equally capable of self-transformation. For women, once again, chastity or sexual integrity has been the most important thing about them, not autonomy or rationality; and in this sense, innocence is still inextricably tied to sexual innocence (Miller 2004; Rubin 1993). This means that innocence has worked differently for women; but it also means that women can weaponize a potential violation of their sexual innocence—white woman in particular, as we will see. Innocence is adjudicated in the interstices, despite its purported kinship with purity.

Racial innocence has other variants and counterparts; for instance, scholars have written about "colonial unknowing" in relation to the disavowal of the histories and contemporary relations of colonialism (Vimalassery et al. 2016). There are various concepts that try to make sense of the unknowing of histories of oppression and discrimination, from "white ignorance" (Mills 2007) to "colonial aphasia" (Stoler 2016). Such unknowing is manifest in various places—in former imperial centers, to former slave-owning and settler colonial states. Some call this larger field "agnatology"—the study of the structural production of ignorance, in opposition to epistemology, or the study of knowledge. This can be brought on by neglect, forgetfulness, secrecy, or suppression (Proctor and Schiebinger 2008). In what follows, I discuss these various terms and concepts, in order to then make an argument about how innocence helps us think further about power: in particular, the concept of innocence not only traffics in ignorance, but precludes responsibility by converting the question of harm into purely moral—instead of political—grammars, and then evacuating the possibility of moral accountability. It enables this by denying individual intentionality, knowledge, culpability, or desire, thereby displacing it onto others. In other words, dominance is maintained by way of a collective infrastructure that individuals can tap into without acknowledging that they are doing so, and whose very collective nature allows for the deferral of responsibility. The power associated with innocence is precisely to be able to forget, to ignore, and to be unaccountable for one's actions. As Nietzsche suggests, forgetting is a way of protecting oneself from the poisonous secrets of a wound (Bhrigupati Singh 2010; on ressentiment, see Fassin 2013, 263). As part of this, I trace how the idea of "innocent victimhood" works as a strategy to absolve the powerful of responsibility, when they themselves claim to be victims.

Finally, I discuss how innocence gets called on today, not only in overtly white supremacist contexts, but in liberal movements and organizations such as feminist and immigrant rights movements. In these examples, I show how claims to innocence reveal the continuum between liberal and illiberal politics. I end by exploring how we might go beyond innocence and beyond liberalism itself, and how histories of oppression can be challenged by ethico-political concepts such as implication, complicity, and beneficiary;[4] and by political movements such as abolitionism.

White Ignorance and Colonial Unknowing

How is it that innocence enables the maintenance of certain hierarchies and inequalities, when innocence itself is defined as outside power? One way it is invoked is by professing a lack of understanding or knowledge about situations of injustice—and therefore, a lack of intention to do harm. One is innocent of *intention*. This not only blocks accusations of blame but allows for forgiveness. In this sense, innocence functions as part of a liberal, rationalist approach that believes that if people had the facts, they would surely act better (Bruyneel 2021). The two examples of blackface are particularly revealing; the men claimed that they did not know—they had not been taught its history—and therefore that they did not intentionally commit any offense. Now that they know, they have promised to adapt and change their behavior. Accountability is entirely erased due to the lack of individual knowledge and intention. They do not deny having done it, since evidence shows otherwise. Indeed, innocence is a strategy used to judge the *nature* of evidence, not its absence or presence: it is often summoned when photographs or videos depict harmful actions, and the question is how to interpret and adjudicate such actions.

So how does innocence work on the ground? In his famous tract about racism, *Black Skin, White Masks*, Frantz Fanon wrote about the nature of racism and how one comes to understand it, if one isn't directly subject to it: "The European knows and does not know" (Fanon 2008, 199). Dominant structures of knowledge work in wily ways to occlude histories of participation in oppression; certain common strategies—such as those responding to blackface—have developed to further both ignorance and claims to innocence. Many histories and analyses of racism and the institutions of slavery and colonialism have pointed to the inability or refusal of individuals and states to recognize enduring systems of violence. To be clear, individuals and states both act as legal persons in these cases, drawing on circumscribed moralized language. Yet how is it that white power and privilege have been maintained, in places with histories of slavery and in imperial and settler colonies, while asserting that we live in a color-blind or post-racial society? How is it that white people have maintained the unearned advantages they have accrued as a result of histories of oppression, without recognizing or acknowledging it?

Many have turned to the nature of epistemology to make sense of the maintenance of such power; in other words, as Foucault argued, certain forms of knowledge help reproduce power. As Proctor and Schiebinger write (2008), not knowing is not simply the absence of knowledge, or the loss of knowledge; as they say, ignorance, like knowledge, has a political geography, and this production of inattention can be made or unmade, for some and not others. "White ignorance," as Charles Mills (2007) describes it, is both a form of false belief and an absence of true belief in which race—white racism and white racial domination—plays a crucial causal role. White ignorance is a social epistemology; indeed, Mills suggests it is the corollary of "standpoint theory," which explains how epistemologies are located, and embedded in fields of power. While standpoint theory is usually evoked to characterize and recognize the particular viewpoints of those who are oppressed, in this case, we can use it to explain the way knowledge—grounded in experience—takes shape for the most privileged. In particular, feminist standpoint theories have suggested that vision can be clearer from below the powerful (Harstock 1983; Collins 1997; Anzaldúa 1987; Harding 1986), but perhaps most importantly, they have argued that knowledge is shaped by historically shared group-based experiences. For instance, Patricia Hill Collins suggests, "Standpoint theory argues that groups who share common placement in hierarchical power relations also share common experiences in such power relations" (1997, xx). While she is speaking about Black women who have been historically disenfranchised and whose perspective is shaped by struggle, giving them particular purchase on explaining how oppression works, there is no reason that this specificity of knowledge would not also be true for those who are privileged: they can shed light on their own experiences.

In this case, Mills suggests that a white epistemology is grounded in ignorance, meaning that the white delusion of racial superiority has been insulated from challenge. This is not necessarily based on bad faith; white ignorance can enable explicit racism, but it can also derive from mistaken beliefs because relevant knowledge is not taught or conveyed. So, for instance, people may believe that since the abolition of slavery in the US, everyone has had the same opportunities. This is not true; but to not know this is not simply an individual choice. It is a collective, structurally grounded form of knowledge (or ignorance). In this sense, Mills calls out the erasure of the long history of structural discrimination that has left white Americans with the greater resources they have today; "if originally whiteness was race, then now it is racelessness, an equal status and a common history in which all have shared, with white privilege being conceptually erased" (Mills 2007, 28). In other words, white ignorance allows people to deny the unearned advantages they have accrued as a result of white supremacy and to reject any responsibility for its continuation.

The question is *how* this knowledge is occluded. For instance, often the offending events or moments are located in the past and seen as irrelevant to the present: colonialism and slavery are said to have taken place a long time ago. But what other political, social, or cognitive mechanisms enable this disremembering? In addition to locating the problem in the past, Juliet Hooker (2017) suggests that attachment to white dominance operates at an unconscious level for many white people, including not recognizing themselves as "white"; this lack of recognition is what enables them to see themselves as committed to color-blindness. The management of memory is critical here. Without going into the rich field of memory studies, we can note that memory is selective; collective social processes determine what is deemed important to remember, and what is not. Mills suggests that white identity may require white amnesia—in the US, this has meant a whitewashing of the atrocities of slavery, and of the history of Jim Crow laws that enforced racial segregation, but also, the rehabilitation of certain histories over others. We have seen this in the case of monuments to Robert E. Lee, commander in chief of the Confederate Army. Those who defend the monuments to him erase the fact that he went to war to defend the institution of slavery and rehabilitate him as a neutral part of Southern history, identity, and heritage. The erasure of the history of Jim Crow makes it possible to present the current playing field as level, so that Black poverty can then be blamed on Black people themselves; similarly, monuments to the Confederacy suppress Black memory, and racial injustice.

However, recently, scholars have suggested that the idea of collective amnesia or omission does not go far enough in explaining how privilege is transmitted; this is not a passive act or a form of concealing that suspends culpability, even if sometimes ignorance can be about selective attention, or inadvertent neglect. Instead, they suggest that this ignorance is "aggressively made and reproduced"; this "colonial unknowing" is an epistemological orientation that "endeavors to render unintelligible the entanglements of racialization and colonization" in ways that attribute "finality to the events of conquest and dispossession" (Vimalassery et al. 2016, 2). It is a willful ignorance. Florida governor Ron de Santis's ban of African American AP classes in January 2023 due to their "lack of educational value" is a case in point: white identity requires an aggressive management and erasure of history. The Trump ban on all things considered "DEI" is based on the same logic.

Kevin Bruyneel (2021) suggests that "settler memory" produces both racial and colonial unknowing, and it is both a process of remembering and disavowing dispossession and violence. In other words, he suggests that settler memory produces a *particular* type of knowing, rather than an unknowing—rather than focusing on absence, he thinks about how it constructs a form of "settler common sense," as Rifkin describes it (Rifkin 2014, 7). The problem is not simply lack of memory—or amnesia—to which the solution would be to remember. This denies the imbrication of settler memory with dominant nationhood and the practices that secure state authority. In other words, memory is materialized and made into infrastructure, and cannot be easily willed away. It is baked into what we see as evidence, and who is a credible witness or a reliable narrator (Mills 2007).

Understanding knowledge as a particular conceptual grid is one way to explain this active unknowing or ignorance—a grid that in turn guides inference and judgment. This strategy is broadly applied in relation to race well beyond the US. Indeed, as the 2020 Movement for Black Lives or #BLM protests revealed very clearly, racism is global, and its strategies are globally shared, even if they are also more finely tuned by specific local histories and categories. In the case of the Netherlands, Gloria Wekker (2016) draws on Edward Said's idea of the "cultural archive," to think about how a deep structure of inequality in thought and affect based on race was installed in European imperial populations. She suggests that it is from this cultural reservoir that a way of being in the world was forged, one that comes with its own "structures of feeling," to use Raymond Williams's (1997) conclusive term. The cultural archive shapes what counts as everyday knowledge, and in the Dutch case, this includes understanding the Netherlands as a color-blind nation, one that serves as a leading moral force for other nations. The idea that it is free of racism is central, and yet, she says that a racial grammar structures all thinking: while it is often rendered in cultural or ethnic terms, the Netherlands is not free of police violence against young Antillean and Surinamese Dutch men, nor of racial profiling.

The controversial public debate about "Zwarte Piet" (Black Pete), a Black figure at the heart of a traditional Dutch festivity for children, illustrates this well. Black Pete is another version of the canonical racist form of blackface; he is a caricature with thick lips, an Afro wig, and golden earrings, dressed up as the Moorish servant of a white bishop from Spain, one who speaks with terrible grammar (as if dumb; but now also tinged with a Surinamese or Moroccan accent). In this Dutch tradition, the servant and his master visit at the end of each November, culminating in presents being given to children. The current incarnation of this figure appeared in a book in 1850, as the Black servant of Sinterklaas, when Dutch colonialism was ongoing. As many argue, it is a throwback to slavery, which had not yet been abolished in Suriname or the Dutch Antilles (de Abreu 2018). Despite protests of many kinds, starting in the 1960s but particularly since 2010—including a letter sent in 2013 by a human rights group from the UN (of people of African descent), a 2013 report of the European Commission Against Racism and Intolerance that showed how racism saturates life in the Netherlands, and a court case brought by one white Dutch and twenty-one Black Dutch plaintiffs against the year-end parade—the dominant Dutch public and the state refused to recognize that this tradition might be in any way grounded in imperial or racist histories (Wekker 2016). They called it "culture." They vigorously and aggressively defended this until 2020. It was only challenged after the killing of George Floyd and the global uprisings around the

Movement for Black Lives, when Prime Minister Mark Rutte—who himself had defended "Black Pete" and joked about his own experiences wearing blackface—admitted that the Netherlands has a problem with racism, and agreed not to feature this racist figure in their annual celebrations.[5]

Once again, blackface offers a good example to think with, since it is both an extremely public performance of racism—one with transnational resonance—and yet it is not acknowledged as such. In this way, it raises the question of the nature of knowledge itself, and what constitutes evidence. But also, as a transnational form, it comes with rehearsed responses, and forms of denial. Indeed, this form has served to hone the practice of racial innocence.

In the French context, we see a similar erasure or denial of race, despite a long, violent colonial history. There is no such thing as "race" in France—the French state does not legally acknowledge the category. The French state will not talk about it, count it, or collect statistical information about race or ethno-racial background because of the belief that this actually perpetuates divisions based on race, which it condemns as a misguided biologically based category. Instead, the French state's policies are based on a theory of "republican universalism," or a set of principles derived from the French Revolution of 1789 and its Declaration of the Rights of Man and Citizen. Specifically, it protects abstract individual rights but does not recognize collective identities in the public realm, beyond that of citizen. Republicanism has been renegotiated in each historical context, but it has been lauded both as an inclusionary, anti-racist egalitarianism, and as an exclusionary framework that leaves out women and people of color—what some call, for effect, "republican racism" (Scott 1996, 2018; Bereni et al. 2020; Dubois 2000). Indeed, we might say that in its aspiration to universal equality, this political ideology wants to will race out of being by ignoring it.

In this context, theories that take the history of colonialism seriously in relation to contemporary French racism and xenophobia—initially all labeled "postcolonial theory"—have regularly met with extreme resistance by both the French public and its intellectuals, condemned as imported from the US or from the UK, and labeled "le wokeism." The activist group that initiated public and intellectual discussions around French colonial afterlives in 2005, *Les Indigènes de la République* (the Indigenous of the French Republic), has faced deep antagonisms. Theories of French republican universalism frame colonialism as its negation, rather than as a central constitutive feature, despite many examples to the contrary: for instance, republican ideas about secularism, or "laïcité," have been implemented as bans against the veil and the burqa and against Muslims and the practice of Islam more generally. The French antipathy to the veil runs deep, and there are many reasons why, but these cannot be dissociated from France's colonial war with Algeria, where independence struggles to free Algeria from French rule were waged in part by Algerian women, hiding their weapons under their headscarves and burqas. Laïcité is steeped in and shaped by colonial violence, and a related Islamophobia.

France has its own histories of blackface and related colonial imagery that have similarly led to claims to colonial ignorance or unknowing; a painting meant to commemorate the abolition of slavery is, ironically, a case in point. In 2019, artist-scholar Mame-Fatou Niang was invited to the National Assembly to show her film *Mariannes Noires*, a documentary about Afro-French women. In the Palais Bourbon, part of the lower chamber, she saw a painting that, as she wrote, features "two huge black faces, with bulging eyes, oversized bright red lips, carnivorous teeth, in an imagery borrowing to [*sic*] Sambo, the Banania commercials and Tintin in the Congo." With white French novelist Julien Suaudeau, she started a petition to have it removed. The artist, a white French man named Hervé di Rosa, denied that it was racist, suggesting in particular that this was because his intentions were not racist; instead, he claimed, it was supposed to convey the exuberance of his anti-racist generation. He refused to recognize any of its colonial iconography. As Niang and Suaudeau (2022) suggested, it is irrelevant what he intended; he tapped into a larger set of racialized tropes, a cultural archive, intentionally or not—and, as the petition states, this is "a humiliating and dehumanizing insult to the millions of victims of slavery and to all their descendants."[6]

Ann Stoler (2016) calls this form of ignorance "colonial aphasia," which she defines alternatively as: an occlusion of knowledge, a disremembering, a difficulty speaking, the irretrievability of a vocabulary, a simultaneous presence of a thing and its absence, or a misrecognition of that presence.[7] She too suggests that amnesia is misleading as a way to explain the active dissociation from the history of French colonialism. What has been erased or forgotten or only partly remembered is the racial architecture of empire, and how this has seeped into and shaped modern France and its contemporary politics of immigration and xenophobia. As Achille Mbembe (2011) states, at base, race regulates the language and perceptual schema of empire. This is not to say that there have not been reckonings with difference or discrimination in France—just that they have most often been decoupled from empire. This is more than malicious intent, historical illiteracy, or the bad faith of individual actors. Rather, as Wekker suggested, such racialized regimes of truth determine what counts as recognizable frames of reference; it is the very nature of political thinking that determines who and what are made into "problems," and what constitutes common sense. These frames shape not just knowledge but affective sensibilities.

Racial Innocence

While colonial unknowing explains how knowledge can be filtered, rendering certain histories unintelligible, innocence does a different kind of work: it goes beyond simply not knowing or a problem of epistemology. It is about a lack of responsibility. That is, it makes the problem a moral one, which then enables the refusal of blame.

Charles Mills suggests that white ignorance also includes moral ignorance, meaning not just the ignorance of facts, but "moral unknowings, incorrect judgments about the rights and wrongs of moral situations themselves" (2007, 22). I am interested in how people not only make incorrect moral judgments but absolve themselves of the responsibility for racism and other forms of violence and exploitation. When innocence is claimed, the refusal to know becomes a refusal to repent; it manifests in a demand to be judged innocent. Shocked moral outrage functions to both reveal and prove the innocence of those who were supposedly duped, or ignorant.

I return now to Baldwin's *Letter to My Nephew*, mentioned at the start, to show that what he objected to first and foremost in white claims to innocence was their denial of culpability. Baldwin writes, "I know what the world has done to my brother, and how narrowly he has survived it and I know, which is much worse, and this is the crime of which I accuse my country and my countrymen and for which neither I nor time nor history will ever forgive them, that they have destroyed and are destroying hundreds of thousands of lives and *do not know it and do not want to know it . . . it is not permissible that the authors of devastation should also be innocent. **It is the innocence which constitutes the crime.**"* Baldwin condemns the innocence claimed by those in power to prop themselves up, while at the same time purifying or absolving themselves of the harm they inflict in the process. That is, a claim to innocence writes out responsibility. After all, in its Judeo-Christian interpretations—which continue to resonate today—the innocent were bound by divine authority; they could not act on their own. Only after the Fall, when Eve eats from the tree of knowledge, does human life acquire a will and responsibility of its own. How can people who did not know, who did not intend to do harm, to discriminate, be answerable for the harm caused?

When we view ourselves as innocent, as feminist scholars Fellows and Razack (1998) have stated, we cannot confront the hierarchies that operate among us. In this sense, innocence is a key strategy in the making of the dominant group; the reason Baldwin objected so strongly to such moral positioning is that the denial of culpability simultaneously forecloses any possibility of equality. In addition to the ways white ignorance or unknowing is produced—which are part of the process—innocence is solidified in several ways. First, as we have discussed, innocence is created by taking racism or oppression out of its structural and collective context, and making it an individual moral problem, dependent on malicious intent. For example, this describes racial innocence in the American post–civil rights courtroom, where racism is only located in the bad intentions of individual actors, obscuring the operation of racial power in penal practices and institutions. As we see in chapter 3, what Murakawa and Beckett call the "penology of racial innocence" begins with the presumption that everyone is race neutral—that is, not racist. In this sense, "racism" is only recognized if there is explicit individual intent to discriminate. What they argue is that this ever-narrowing definition of racism is accompanied by expanding definitions of crime and discretionary authority, and together, these drastically exacerbate situations of racial inequality (Murakawa and Beckett 2010).

Second, innocence is created by placing racism as a problem "over there"—externalizing violence (Inwood 2018). Thus, the French call the US and the UK racist, but suggest there is no such thing as racism in France. And third, innocence is part of a moral conceptual cluster, and often works in consort with concepts like victimhood, enabling the powerful to reconfigure themselves as the ones being harmed. In all of these, gendered, classed, and racial formations play in various ways, showing how innocence is a shape-shifting concept—its ability to be differently claimed and enacted is precisely what allows it such extensive reach and power. It is alternatively enhanced and diminished, depending on who and what it sits next to. I will focus on these latter two examples.

EXTERNALIZING RACISM: THE SOUTHERN STRATEGY

How is racism externalized to install or preserve innocence? Kirstine Taylor (2015) writes compellingly and persuasively about how racial innocence was created in the Southern US states by displacing responsibility onto a different population, creating a scapegoat. In particular, she shows how "white trash" was transformed to take the fall for the Southern elite's transition to a new race neutrality—but one which effectively maintained racial hierarchies. In this sense, innocence plays in the entangled relations between racial and class formations, shaping and informing both. From a category defined by biological deficiency—seen as "degenerate" and impure in the face of eugenics logics—Southern poor, rural white people were made into the vehicles of racism, violence, and backwardness. This substitution allowed the Southern elite to be produced as racially innocent—turning their story into one about rights, equal protection, individualism, and progress. "White trash" in the postwar period became a repository of intractable anti-Black violence and retrogression. That is, if before the 1940s, poor rural white people were simply "primitive," after the 1940s, they also became guilty—of anti-Black mob violence, lynchings, and white supremacy.

More specifically, after *Brown v. Board of Education* in 1954 rendered racial segregation of children in schools unconstitutional, and in the wake of the fall of Jim Crow laws that legalized racial segregation, a movement of wealthier moderates in the South decided to commit to a new way of being more in conformity with racial values in the North, including law-and-order, race-neutral state policies and "color-blind" progress. This movement— what Taylor calls the racial liberalist postwar New South movement, which was a form of racial liberalism—still valued racial segregation, and saw it as central to the stability of the South, but they turned their backs on the overt and blunt tactics of outward resistance. Instead, they preserved the benefits of white supremacy by opposing law to violence, and gentility to unruliness. Instead of enacting racial violence to maintain the full segregation of schools, they argued for orderly compromise; in reality, this translated into very limited desegregation. They cast the white mobs as violent, while they framed themselves as business-minded, and law-abiding; and rather than understanding the problem of racism in schools as one about integration versus segregation, they reframed it as a question of law versus violence. They thereby stripped themselves of blame, and reconstituted themselves as virtuous, and innocent. In this case, forms of racial knowledge and ignorance were specifically manipulated; the mechanism of racial innocence was indeed deliberate. "White trash" took the blame, and became synonymous with the Ku Klux Klan, as symbols of sickness in the nation, engaged in vigilante violence. But this focus on law and order also allowed the South to produce the Black civil rights movement as lawless, and disorderly. The claim to racial innocence served not only to render elite white people blameless, but in very crucial ways, it also broke up any hope of the cross-racial class alliances that had been forming in the early parts of the twentieth century. Instead, poor white people and Black people were both produced as guilty, allowing the elite to claim innocence in the face of racial injustice, even as they maintained legal forms of racial stratification. In this sense, innocence is manifest in an aesthetics of refinement and civility—that is, the attributes of class privilege are used to render complicity invisible and unrecognizable, and to cultivate a blameless purity.

This strategy of relying on law and order is still apparent, and serves to protect a version of white innocence; after the now infamous May 2020 murder (public lynching) of George Floyd, an unarmed Black man, by a white police officer who kneeled on his neck for 8 minutes and 46 seconds until he died, a Mississippi mayor, Hal Marx, blamed Floyd himself, saying "the video didn't show the resistance that got him in that position," and that he had likely died of an overdose instead. When asked by residents to resign for his racist statements, he said, "I will never surrender to that *mob mentality*" (my emphasis), and expressed outrage that he was being called racist, when all he wanted to do was get the facts straight before judgment was issued.[8] Once again, we see the language of law and order protecting white innocence against Black disorder. Needless to say, this kind of reaction jump started the global protests for Black Lives, the most important and significant protests since the 1960s, and possibly the most important in recorded history.

VICTIMHOOD OF THE POWERFUL

I want to turn now to the third mechanism by which innocence is produced: by coupling it with victimhood. If one of innocence's binary opposites is intentionality, another is guilt; in the previous case of the US South, the white elite could claim innocence precisely because the guilt was externalized, and the blame attributed elsewhere. Innocence refuses responsibility. If colonial unknowing and white ignorance might be addressed by changing how we know the world—countering it with what Mills calls "a genuine knowledge"—claims to racial innocence must be addressed by insisting on not just truth, but forms of responsibility and accountability. To be clear, a claim to innocence does not deny that harm may have been inflicted; the key is that it happened unintentionally. One did not know one was committing harm, and therefore cannot be blamed—indeed, this lack of knowledge diffuses the idea of harm itself, rendering it effectively irrelevant. Harm is divorced from its cause; and by harm, I do not mean or assume individual causation; this includes collective responsibility for perpetuating ideas of inequality. When accused of racism, or of upholding oppression, these so-called innocents may express shock—they may even be morally outraged at such accusations. Indeed, because the idea of innocence protects against moral responsibility, one of the responses by those claiming innocence has been to suggest instead that they are being attacked and wrongly charged—indeed, that *they* are the real victims. Racial innocence has produced claims to victimhood by the powerful. Innocence works as a strategy of power by making violence or harm into a moral problem, and then making moral responsibility impossible. This all-or-nothing response is encouraged by the structure of innocence: it is a moralized binary. There is no room for complicity or for any more complicated mix of partial guilt or responsibility, being a beneficiary of a system, or participating indirectly by being a member of a group. There is no room for accountability that is not moralized and rendered in terms of good and evil, but rather, part of a political process. And thus, if one refuses guilt, one must understand oneself as having been wrongly accused. This could not be more apparent than in the case of Israel's genocidal war on Gaza: there is no room for complicity or for the violent history of occupation leading up to the Hamas attacks on October 7th; Israelis are purely innocent victims, and their war is justified by the state as self-defense.

While innocence and victimhood are not identical, as we saw in the introduction, the focus on victims has made the language of innocence more politically salient. But perhaps more importantly, the connection between the two has made claims to victimhood a legitimate answer to charges of enduring structural racisms. It has suffocated other political and moral responses. In this sense, when white or other forms of dominance are threatened—when people are asked to take responsibility for the unearned advantages they have accrued as a result of white or Jewish or Hindu supremacy—they may mobilize a sense of victimhood, or what Juliet Hooker calls "white grievance" (Hooker 2017). This can happen at both the individual and state levels since both are subject to the same charge of either innocent or guilty; both take on the character-like qualities of moral individuals.

We see this slippage between innocence and victimhood in the French case; colonial unknowing can be willful and aggressive, especially when coupled with claims to innocence. Refusing any responsibility, the French tried to revise colonial history, to rehabilitate the colonial enterprise, and to suggest that the *real* victims were the colonizers, not the Indigenous. France's defeat in Algeria was massive, politically, morally, militarily; France had occupied Algeria for 150 years. As Achille Mbembe (2011) writes, the trauma caused by the French loss is almost impossible to measure; and indeed, while it led to practices of organized concealment and what he calls "willful colonial amnesia and melancholy," the counterpart of this, the part that enacts racial innocence, is a 2005 law that was instituted to explain "the benefits of a positive colonization." This included the idea that France brought enlightenment to the colonies; there is a heroic dimension. This law was passed by the National Assembly on February 23, 2005, and imposed on high school teachers to teach "the positive values of colonialism." To be sure, the French state is not a uniform body, and despite a collective attachment to the positive narrative, there are some who were more interested in and responsible for this historical revisionism—for the claiming of innocence—than others. President Jacques Chirac was in power when the law was passed, and then head of the center-right UMP (Union for a Popular Movement) party and pushed it forward, and future president Nicolas Sarkozy supported it, as did what many called a resurgence of the "colonial lobby"—a term used in the late nineteenth century to describe those in support of French colonialism, from businesspeople to scientists and politicians. After much debate, Chirac repealed the law in 2006, but the underlying feelings remain; many of the French unabashedly see themselves as victims—they feel they were being blamed for simply trying to help and do good. Some of this has translated into support for Marine Le Pen's ultra-right National Rally, and its violently anti-immigrant discourse.

When bound together, innocence and victimhood help reproduce dominant racial formations; but they do not do it alone. They work in the interstices of other forms of power. It is worth unpacking the mechanisms of the process. We can start with the May 2020 claims to racial innocence by Amy Cooper. Her now infamous reaction was part of what initiated the massive global protests against police violence and racism, along with the murders of George Floyd, Ahmaud Arbery, and Breonna Taylor. Amy Cooper, a white woman, refused to put her dog on a leash in an area of New York City's Central Park where a leash is legally required, when asked to do so by Christian Cooper, who is Black and who was there as a birdwatcher. Instead, in an angry and resentful manner, she threatened to call the police, saying she would tell them that "an African American man was threatening my life." Speaking calmly, he filmed her saying this, and then filmed her calling the police and changing her voice to a high-pitched, tearful, and panicked tone. Christian Cooper's video immediately went viral, bearing witness to the long history of white women in the US falsely accusing Black people—often men and boys—of crimes they did not commit, with very grave consequences. Perhaps the best-known case of this is Emmett Till, who was beaten, tortured, and killed in 1955 because a white woman accused him of making sexual advances—she later admitted this was not true.

While Amy Cooper weaponized her whiteness, after the fact, she claimed innocence: she said that the fallout from the incident had "caused" her to realize and recognize her privilege as a white woman in America (Blay 2020). But she also claimed victimhood, saying she had been afraid: "When you're alone in the Ramble, you don't know what's happening. It's not excusable, it's not defensible."[9] It is worth noting that in the context of New York City, by evoking the Ramble, she was conjuring a sense of uncivilized nature—a set of rambling pathways and forest or the "wild" area of the park where she supposedly had reason to be afraid; here, Christian Cooper becomes associated with dangerous, unruly nature. Her words reveal her claim to both victimhood and racial innocence. We might say her claims to ignorance were disingenuous; yet this is precisely how forms of unknowing and innocence work. Amy Cooper was at once oblivious and cunning. As Zeba Blay (2020), cultural critic, writes,

> What the Amy Cooper situation reveals to me is what instances of racism in America always reveal: There's a level of self-examination and self-awareness that white people are not doing that they *must* do. There's something that white people, even the ones who believe that they hold no biases, that they wield no power, must admit to themselves and begin to unpack. They are complicit—and even participatory—in the system of white supremacy. Individual white people may not believe they are, but their ability to tap into that system is always within reach.

But innocence—despite describing a state of purity—does not work in the same way for everyone, or even for the same people at the same moments. It gets honed and adapted over time, shifting as part of a Wittgensteinian family of resemblances, not as one unified concept. It is also constantly qualified by those who are in proximity, and can be drawn into its moral and conceptual frameworks. And indeed, certain subjects are better positioned to fit into its scaffolding. Gender configurations suggest that women are more easily understood as victims and as apolitical, and hence more easily interpellated into the role of moral purity. But these often-demeaning gendered attributes can be combined with the privilege of whiteness, paradoxically offering white women some of the most powerful and compelling claims to innocence. In this sense, Amy Cooper was more immediately able to configure herself as innocent than was Christian Cooper, who, because of the intertwined forms of racism and masculinity, immediately got interpellated into the category of guilty—something that Amy Cooper played and preyed upon.

The other figure in this triad was Amy Cooper's dog. Amy Cooper initially refused to put her dog on a leash, but when she did, at the insistence of Christian Cooper, in her anger and resentment she lifted her dog by the collar and dragged him around by the neck as she shouted at Christian Cooper, giving the impression that she was strangling the dog. The uproar about her treatment of Christian Cooper was only matched by complaints about her handling of the dog; indeed, sometimes, they were nearly conflated. On social media, people called her "an abuser of animals and people alike," but many simply focused on the dog, complaining that she had choked the dog, abused it, strangled it, and that she did not deserve to own it. Indeed, she was forced to surrender her dog to the rescue organization from which she had initially adopted it so they could check its health. The rescue did eventually return it to her, but many then expressed outrage at the rescue agency, repeatedly saying "shame on you" for not keeping the animal's best interest at heart, for not protecting the dog, or not caring for the dog's well-being: "that sweet dog deserves better."[10]

The rescue of Cooper's dog recalls the saving of poor women, innocent children: quintessential figures of innocence, quintessential victims. And like them, such animals are liminal figures, at the border of humanity. As almost, *nearly* human, they are more easily configured as innocent, recalling that innocence evokes both idealized purity, and a belittling lack of all the attributes of liberal personhood. In this first sense, animals are often—and increasingly, as we will see in chapter 4—claimed as innocent, configured as guileless and as requiring protection and care. This allows their abuse to be seen as the ultimate form of moral violation.

In this case, the dog becomes the key figure of innocence in the triad, sometimes lending credence to Amy Cooper as innocent victim, by being associated with her—she gets configured as an innocent woman who needs a dog to protect her from predatory men; yet clearly, at other times, the dog lends credibility to Christian Cooper, showing that Amy Cooper is indeed capable of violence and abuse, even (or especially) toward innocent figures. The visual evidence of her mistreatment of the dog confirms that she is also capable of being violent toward him. Interestingly, even as innocence seems to describe a fixed state, it has a contagious quality, either being transferred to or being harnessed by those in close proximity.

The Connective Tissue Between Liberalism and Illiberalism

Amy Cooper's case offers insight into the work done by the concept of innocence. While she now represents the particularly underhanded racism of white women, notably, she said she was not a Trump supporter; she said she voted Democratic and insisted that her behavior was not racially motivated. She said, "I'm not a racist . . . I think I was just scared."[11] Amy Cooper's claim to innocence after the fact—that she did not intend to harm Christian Cooper—reveals how innocence can function as and expose the connective tissue between liberalism and illiberalism. That is, liberalism works by creating and policing a line between itself and its Other; it foregrounds tolerance, but it makes good use of intolerance to police its boundaries—it is intolerant of other non-liberal regimes, for instance. The line between liberalism and its Others is a constant work of politics and power. It is muddier than many admit to, and as mentioned in the introduction, some argue that the projects of liberalism and neoliberalism have always embedded authoritarian tendencies (Maskovsky and Bjork-James 2020; Brown 2018; Toscano 2021). Another way to understand it, following Talal Asad (2015), is that liberalism embeds a moral conscience structured by innocence and guilt, while the illiberal is supposedly devoid of such morality; liberals may feel guilt about the (racial) violence they commit, but there is no inherent reason in liberalism to prevent such acts in the first place. That is, liberalism and illiberalism are not distinguished by acts of racism; liberal racism has a long history. Claims to racial innocence simply allow liberals to excuse themselves after the fact, denying intentionality or knowledge, and evacuating culpability at both individual and state levels. What I am suggesting is that we should read claims to racial innocence as exposing and accentuating the continuum between liberal and illiberal acts.

Specifically, Amy Cooper may have tried to absolve herself by a claim to lack of intention or lack of knowledge; but her actions nevertheless repeated and maintained a form of racism that assumes that Black men are inherently a threat, and that Black men are in prison in disproportionate numbers because they deserve to be. This reinforces a worldview based on racial types and hierarchies, one that also informs illiberal agendas. It is not accidental that many white people first assumed that Amy Cooper was a MAGA[12] supporter. As one tweet read, "Amy Cooper will probably receive an invitation to the White House and be awarded the Medal of Freedom from Trump. After all, she represents everything Trump loves: racism, hatred, lying and a dog hater."[13] Regardless of what she believed or intended, Amy Cooper's actions render visible, and facilitate, the connections and overlaps between the two.

Amy Cooper was treated as a guilty individual and punished—she was fired from her job and publicly shamed. But framing her actions in these terms does not help address the deeper currents of racism that informed her actions. Rather, it simply allowed others to harness the discourse of innocence, and to absolve themselves in turn: her company, Franklin Templeton, an investment firm for whom she managed their insurance portfolio, used her case to trumpet their own innocence. The firm put out a tweet, "We do not tolerate racism of any kind at Franklin Templeton"—a statement that they hoped would absolve them of past or future racist harms. This focus on innocence and guilt precludes a discussion of collective responsibility, one that locates Amy Cooper's actions in a long history of endemic structural racism. Christian Cooper pointed this out himself, in an opinion piece in the *Washington Post*, explaining why he did not want to press charges against her: "I've said all along that I think it's a mistake to focus on this one individual . . . Focusing on charging Amy Cooper lets white people off the hook from all that. They can scream for her head while leaving their own prejudices unexamined."[14]

This does not mean Amy Cooper was not culpable as an individual; but she is not alone, since the strategies and discourses she played upon are not only national, but global, as we see very vividly from the protests against racisms globally, kicked off by the Movement for Black Lives. These took shape in both specific and general terms across the world: in Europe (the UK, France, the Netherlands, Germany, Italy, Belgium, etc.), in Australia, and in Canada, pointing to the particular historical configurations of racism, all of which end in greater police violence against Black, brown, and Indigenous populations. In the Middle East, in places like Kuwait, the protests took place as "immigrant lives matter," and in India, as "Dalit lives matter." Even if "Blackness" is differently configured and defined, racism—and its origins in the racial capitalist forms of colonialism and slavery—has a transnational history (Robinson 1983; Du Bois 1920; Fanon 2008). Framing the problem as one of innocence or guilt allows responsibility to be eluded, and not only maintains these forms of power, but opens the way to the claims of the more illiberal, supremacist movements.

FEMINIST INNOCENCE

There are other liberal political movements and ventures that rely on innocence as well—capturing and using it to maintain and reinforce hierarchies of power. These, too, push into the boundary zone with illiberalism, and extend its reach into these political practices. As we saw with the Southern Strategy, some claims to innocence involve designating other people as guilty and separating oneself from them; another way is to combine innocence with claims to victimhood, turning the tables on who is seen as responsible. Yet another approach involves helping those who are seen as innocent, and using that to ignore or erase one's positioning in the hierarchies of power, and how one might be perpetuating inequalities in the process. Innocence can work by associating oneself with innocence, indeed, by creating an assemblage based on proximity to the innocent. As previously mentioned, innocence has contagious qualities; and these can occasionally be harnessed.

Humanitarianism is one example. As we saw in the introduction, innocence helps create a pure space for humanity; and humanitarian regimes regularly draw on the concept to both ground and enact their missions. Yet innocence ends up producing and enacting what Didier Fassin (2010, 239) has termed "hierarchies of humanity." Not only does it produce hierarchies among the people humanitarians seek to help or defend, enabling some to be prioritized over others; innocence also enables a distinction between those who help—such as humanitarian workers—and those they help. That is, innocence always brings with it the desire to protect and the impetus to take responsibility for those who—in their want of knowledge—cannot take care of themselves. As we will see with humanitarian photography in chapter 2, guilelessness evokes the need for care; innocents cannot take responsibility for themselves. But this means that it props up a feeling of control in those who care for the innocent; it assures them not only of their power but also of their knowledge, insofar as the innocent person is oblivious. It creates a class of saviors. As a space of purity, innocence itself appears outside history, and as such, it allows those who work as saviors to ignore the political and historical circumstances that created these victims.

This not only allows saviors to feel powerful or knowledgeable but also enables them to simultaneously *capture* innocence—to purify or absolve themselves. In other words, the concept of innocence also enables a savior class or subject, and they too make claims to innocence. If the people humanitarians are saving are understood as innocent, outside time and place, and one is intervening only to stop the suffering, how can this not be considered innocent too? While those inspired by humanitarian sentiments may try to bypass politics, claiming to act only as witnesses to injustice or in response to the immediacy of suffering, the political innocence they proclaim often ignores the privilege that allows them to act—it can masquerade as a refusal to acknowledge the structural inequalities that allow them to *be* humanitarians, witnesses, or saviors, and which are perpetuated by their actions.

Gayatri Spivak (1988) called out a gendered form of humanitarian action, or what I see as a form of liberal feminist racial innocence, fed by the comfort of superiority in knowledge and power: she called it "white men saving brown women from brown men." We could just as easily think about it as white women saving brown women from brown men. This is a flexible script that continues to have enormous appeal. As many will recall, US interventions in Iraq and Afghanistan in the 1990s and 2000s were justified in the name of saving their women. In an address to the nation, then First Lady Laura Bush justified American military intervention as a "fight for the rights and dignity of women." This warmongering is at the edge of the illiberal: in their imperialist zeal, such interventions insist on one way of being, and enforce it with violence. Scholars have shown that the US imperial interventions in the Middle East have been accompanied by hate crimes against Muslims in the US—they are two sides of one coin (Naber 2014). Indeed, one clear example of this is the tragic attacks on three Palestinian American students in Vermont in November 2023 by a white supremacist, in reaction to the war in Gaza, leaving one twenty-year-old a paraplegic.

The claim to help the women of Afghanistan functions as a deferral of responsibility, a way to erase US complicity in the imperial violence that created the Taliban regime, and the violence endured by those left behind. As Leti Volpp argues, the preoccupation with liberating Muslim women enables humanitarians and others to feel a transcendent moral purity, unburdened by their own complicity in military occupations—she too links this to a desire for innocence, in the sense of desiring the category of woman to be pure, but also in the sense of moral transcendence, wanting to be the savior of others, not the opposite: as blameworthy for their disenfranchisement (Volpp 2015).

Despite a large body of transnational feminist scholarship, perhaps most notably Lila Abu-Lughod's book, *Do Muslim Women Need Saving?*, the desire for violent rescue continues. The genocidal killings of Palestinians in Gaza by the Israeli state have been justified in part by the purported rapes and sexual violence committed by Hamas on October 7th against Israeli women.[15] In reference to footage of Israeli women on the 7th, US Senator Kristin Gillibrand said, "It takes your breath away at the sheer level of evil it depicts." She called the acts "barbaric," and insisted that Hamas be condemned as a terrorist organization that was committing "evil crimes against humanity."[16] In response, House Representative Pramila Jayapal argued that while such acts of sexual violence were horrible and unacceptable, thousands and thousands of women and children had since been killed by Israelis (the count is now over 56,000 people, a third of whom are children), which is also an outrage; yet CNN anchor Dana Bash insisted that what Hamas did was incomparable.[17] Violence against Israeli women justifies genocidal violence against Palestinians. And it feels superfluous to say that genocide fits the very definition of illiberal.

This is ultimately the same script, but rather than brown men attacking brown women, it figures brown/Muslim men attacking white/Jewish women. The special moral outrage we have witnessed resembles that of Black men accused of raping white women, which was used to justify the lynchings of Black men. To be clear, I join feminists who condemn all forms of sexual violence, whenever and wherever it occurs; but my goal here is to see how even the mention of violence is weaponized, and how innocence comes to play in this weaponization.

The purportedly feminist act of "saving" in these cases is a claim to racial innocence, one that slides into illiberal forms of violence and hate, against Muslims and Arabs in the US and globally. It is not unlike the racial innocence of white women like Amy Cooper, whose claims reinforce a regime of violence against Black men. As Nadia Abu El-Haj powerfully demonstrates, in the case of US imperialism, the innocence of everyday citizens is enabled by the American soldiers who go to war for them, taking the blame; but blame is evacuated for soldiers, too, by the category of PTSD, allowing them to be transformed into innocent, traumatized victims, not perpetrators or collaborators. This leaves no one accountable for nationalist and imperialist ventures (Abu El-Haj 2022). "White men (and women) who save brown women from brown men" are allowed to ignore their complicity in creating a category of people who need saving, and they need never ask whether these brown women actually want saving, since as innocents they are understood to lack desire or agency.

This type of action ignores the desire to feel morally upstanding; indeed, such moral claims can be pleasurable. As Sherene Razack (2007) writes in relation to the witnessing of pain, particularly in relation to racialized Others, identifying with the suffering of the Other can too quickly slip into feeling that one has *become* that sufferer, both erasing the actual suffering subject and displacing any sense of responsibility toward them. And as many transnational feminists and feminists of color have argued, this continued yearning for innocence can be found in certain strands of contemporary feminism—alternately labeled governance feminism (Halley 2019), carceral feminism (Bernstein 2018), security feminism (Grewal 2017), or femonationalism (Farris 2017)—grounded in the desire to save Others, such as Muslim women, and to not know about their complicities in the disenfranchisement of those they are saving (Abu-Lughod 2013; Volpp 2015).

Below, I give one more example of how contemporary movements that claim to be progressive or even anti-racist also use the capture of innocence in ways that ultimately serve to reveal and accentuate the connections to illiberalism, undermining their own stated goals.

IMMIGRATION AND CHILD SEPARATIONS

My second example of a liberal movement that perhaps surprisingly ends up both building and revealing the connections to illiberalism by way of innocence is the child separations or the "Zero Tolerance Policy" enacted by Trump in 2018. I am interested in the way the liberal reactions to Trump's policy actually work to reinforce his anti-immigrant stance, rather than undermining it—this is despite the fact that people protested vehemently against the separations. To summarize, hundreds of migrant children were separated from their parents at the US-Mexico border as of 2018 (and likely before), in order for their parents to be held in detention centers. This is because a 2015 court order, based on a document called the "Flores settlement," made it illegal to hold children in detention for more than twenty days. These children were forcibly and often surreptitiously separated from their parents, and placed in shelters, with the false promise that the US Office of Refugee Resettlement would then take care of them, placing them with families or sponsors; but the children remained in the ill-equipped conditions of the shelters for months, some even reporting that they were given psychotropic medications to subdue and control them. The parents did not know (and many still do not know) where their children were. There was an unprecedented uproar by the American public about these separations; it was framed as the most morally repugnant thing anyone could do.

First, I want to suggest that perhaps paradoxically, separating these children from their parents actually functioned to render them innocent, in a way that was not true when they crossed the border; and this innocence then rendered them deserving of care. The family separations did this, insofar as they also separated children from their larger, racialized contexts in which they (as immigrants, largely from Latin America) were regularly configured as suspicious and threatening. As we will see in chapter 2, Romantic images of the child—the images that have shaped our ideas of innocence—figure children alone, outside both time and place, outside history and context. Innocent children are, after all, figures that are understood to precede knowledge—they are promises of both the future and the past. Separating the children, then, allowed them to be framed as innocent. And the separations then evoked a response, calling on everyday Americans as saviors, required to step in not only for their parents, but for the state that abandoned them. Once in government care, they were fetishized in ways that respond to abstract definitions of innocence, not to their condition as real children. For instance, images of innocence specifically invoke the child's lack of sexuality; in the case of separated children, to protect this purity, they were not allowed to be touched—not allowed to be hugged or comforted. This is a strange, confused idea of sexual innocence that results in neglect.

Discourses of innocence regularly work to forge moral hierarchies and distinctions. This is because innocence comes into being in relation to its binary Others. In this case, it means that as the separated children were rendered innocent, their parents were condemned as guilty. In the case of the Dreamers—a category of young people in the US created by the Development, Relief, and Education of Alien Minors (DREAM) Act, first proposed in 2001, to provide a pathway to legal status for undocumented youth who came to the US as children—this idea has enabled the state to deport their parents, while taking the moral high ground to "save" the children, effectively stepping in as their guardian (see chapter 2); that is, giving rights to such innocent children (innocence here lies in the fact that they crossed the international border unknowingly) simultaneously infers the abdication of responsibility by their own parents or guardians, who are rendered irresponsible, neglectful, or simply criminal.

In past cases, this claim to protect children has enabled a racialized expansion of state power, with the state taking over guardianship of children. We have seen this in the US, with both Native American children and Black children. Child welfare workers removed Native children from their families for many years, often placing them far away such that they never saw their biological families again; this happened to such an extent that in the 1970s, between 25 percent and 35 percent of Native children had been stolen ("adopted") by the state. Thanks to a huge grassroots effort over the course of eleven years, this eventually led to the Indian Child Welfare Act, passed in Congress in 1978, but even this has not stopped the state from removing children from their families.[18]

In the case of the separated migrant children, the public questioned the state's guardianship, by showing moral outrage; but rather than fighting for the children and parents to be reunited to stay in the US, giving custody back to the parents, the public implicitly claimed "custody" themselves, insofar as the parents are still condemned as guilty. The liberal public took the moral high ground to save the children, with some offering to adopt the children, capturing innocence themselves in the process.

Second, then, the family separations have also functioned to render the outrage about the immigrant children innocent; it ignores and brackets out the other inequalities and forms of racism that ground this narrowly focused moralized upset. In particular, the intense focus on the children allowed Trump's alternate proposal to slip by almost unnoticed since it no longer purported to keep parents and children apart. The solution—as part of his challenge to the Flores settlement—was to detain children *with* their parents for indeterminate amounts of time. But because the outrage about children was felt as immediate and pure, it allowed people to ignore the fact that such exceptional acts of compassion are dependent on the belief that it is acceptable and normal to detain, deport, exploit, or contain immigrants in other circumstances. The outrage relies on the binary that *produces and accepts the parents as guilty*; and it brackets the fact that when children are reunited with their parents, they are once again rendered suspicious. The indignation erases the fact that these children are regularly forced to straddle the tender threshold between threat and care. Why else would this groundswell of outrage not be directed at the immigration system more broadly, but only mustered when lone children are involved?

Indeed, the "Title 42" policy reveals precisely this: it was instituted by Trump at the start of the COVID-19 pandemic but continued by Biden's administration. Title 42 largely suspended the right to asylum in the US, by way of a little-known health law, Section 265 of Title 42. This stopped individuals from crossing into the US in the name of protecting the territory from a communicable health disease. With COVID-19, Trump put this law into play, enabling CBP (the US Customs and Border Patrol) officers to shut down the border, expelling those who were at the US-Mexico border without giving them a chance to claim asylum. This happened even though CDC (US Centers for Disease Control and Prevention) officers argued that there was no public health rationale. This policy subjected both children and adult asylum seekers to detention, and expulsion to Mexico, or to the countries they were fleeing. The Biden administration continued this policy, using it to expel over one million people in 2021.[19] They did not continue it begrudgingly; they actually *defended* it. As Biden's Homeland Security secretary Alejandro Mayorkas said in an interview in March 2021, "The message is quite clear: do not come. The border is closed. The border is secure. We are expelling families. We are expelling single adults."[20] This contravenes the legal obligation the US has to allow individuals to seek asylum, having signed the International Refugee Convention. The only exception made was for unaccompanied children: the CDC issued an order exempting unaccompanied children from the policy.[21] Once again, children, when alone, outside their racialized context, may be configured as innocent, and worthy of care. Biden finally challenged Title 42 in 2021, and after a series of blocks and extensions, it was ended on May 11, 2023, when the federal government officially ended the national emergency related to COVID-19. But there was no major public outrage about the policy; and even as it was ending, Biden responded by shoring up troops at the US-Mexico border, rather than respecting the right to asylum. After ending Title 42, Biden worked to enact ever more draconian policies, from expelling migrants without asylum screenings—effectively re-enacting Title 42 without the public health rationale—to dramatically expanding immigrant detention and deportations.[22]

This response to the family separations and the exact opposite lack of concern about Title 42 cannot be understood outside the larger, endemic racial politics that criminalizes Black and brown people and assumes inequality as the baseline. As Neferti Tadiar writes, there is a commonsense notion that illegality constitutes an *ontological status*, which places migrant death and dying beyond the bounds of human sentiment or response (Tadiar 2022, 15). While liberal sentiments of protection, humanity, and rescue may fuel the desire to help the children, and while these may be noble and honest, when they assume the guilt of the parents, they reveal the intimate connections to illiberal sentiments about guarding the purity of the nation against immigrant contamination. They allow for practices that contravene the international legal order, and in this sense, open the way to more authoritarian rule. Racial innocence plays out at the intersection of liberalism and illiberalism, serving to undermine and redraw this line—and it can serve as the ground on which illiberal hate and resentment grows. My point here is not to attempt to shore up liberalism, but precisely to show how liberalism is inextricably intertwined with illiberalism, where innocence serves as a core, underlying thread; claims to innocence enable and strengthen their shared ground on issues of inequality and exclusion.

Toward a Collective Implicated Responsibility?

So, if innocence enables the maintenance of power, by first moralizing, then disabling or deferring responsibility for structural inequality, what other political concepts and grammars might we use to grapple with questions of justice and collective responsibility? How can we avoid strengthening the connections to illiberalism on the back of innocence, that is, how might we replace the liberal/illiberal continuum altogether? Can we use innocence to imagine a new political horizon?

In what we have seen, liberalism and illiberalism function almost as a Möbius strip; there is no clear cut between the two. They are connected by many things, including a shadowy infrastructure of white supremacy. The question is what is rendered visible, and what parts nevertheless carry on below, shrouded in darkness, ready to emerge when the strip turns and a new face is revealed. So how might the Möbius strip be undone, its connective tissue revealed? How can we think beyond liberalism and illiberalism? As it stands, responsibility is either embodied in and bounded by individuals, or located in institutions and states—which, despite being depicted as moral actors, cannot take responsibility without the individuals and groups that compose them. In the face of the very present afterlives of slavery and colonialism, state responsibility has been purely symbolic; monuments mark the place of violence, locating these in the past, as finished. They are part of our memories, not part of the present. Yet what if there were a different understanding of a responsible subject, one that is neither individual nor institutional, but rather collective, one that has both historical and contemporary breadth? What if this collective subject could occupy the unrecognized connective tissue that innocence sets up, between the individual and the structural, allowing for a different form of responsibility?

While collective guilt is one way to take responsibility—as the Germans have modeled, to atone for the Holocaust—this has been shown to produce more problems than solutions. It is still most often a form of moralized politics (which, in the German case, has created its own claims to German exceptionalism, where Germans claim the moral high ground about having taken responsibility), and creates deep forms of denial, defensiveness, and resentment (Krug 2018).[23] It has enabled a draconian policy in relation to Israel and Palestine, and the war on Gaza, where no form of critique of Israel is permitted: in this schema, because of Germans' resounding guilt, Israel has become the ultimate, untouchable innocent victim. In the name of protection of this pure victimhood, Germany has censured free speech, firing or disinviting scholars and journalists who dare to critique Israel's violence, whether they themselves are Jewish or not.[24]

In the perhaps most well-known rebuke of collective guilt as the way to handle the afterlife of a major injustice, Hannah Arendt (1968) distinguishes between collective guilt and collective responsibility, suggesting that we feel guilt for participating directly in harmful or violent events, but we remain captive to a communal responsibility by virtue of participating in collective life: "This vicarious responsibility for things we have not done, this taking upon ourselves the consequences for things we are entirely innocent of, is the price we pay for the fact that we live our lives not by ourselves but among our fellow men . . ." (1968, 157–58). Responsibility comes from the fact that we are social beings. In terms of guilt, she suggests that when all are guilty, nobody is—this exculpates those who are actually guilty, or liable.

While her analysis of collective responsibility is powerful, it is always circumscribed by the nation-state, which does not work for transnational political forms such as colonialism. Similarly, it does not allow for enough nuance in the form of responsibility taken; there is always a specificity to the subject position one occupies in a history of injustice. For instance, she suggests that refugees are always outside collective responsibility. Yet refugees are inevitably situated in the political communities they join; and they either benefit from or are harmed by the hierarchies of the society they now participate in—in this way, they inevitably become part of these structures of collective responsibility.

There are other positions available by which to think about relations of power and questions of justice that center collective responsibility and structural inequality: I will mention a few of these, starting with what I find to be the most compelling and useful concept, *implication*. We are all implicated in this system, even if differently so. What networks are we each implicated in, what activities do we participate in, even indirectly, that perpetuate the system? In a deeply insightful book, Michael Rothberg lays out this idea, explaining that "implicated subjects occupy positions aligned with power and privilege without being themselves direct agents of harm" (2019, 1). Implicated subjects include those who occupy the more obvious structures of racial privilege and white supremacy, but the concept involves more than that: the ways in which people are implicated are complex and often contradictory, and more importantly, these positions shift. Unlike innocence, implication is not an essentialized position—an ontological status—but rather, one that shifts in relation to different histories, communities, and presents. Of critical importance is that being an implicated subject does not assume intentionality or consciousness. We have seen that in order to recognize and legally condemn racism in the US, intentionality must be demonstrated. Being implicated is quite the opposite. In the US, white people are implicated in a system of racial hierarchy; and they all benefit from a lack of racial justice. This is true even if one fights against this system and disavows it—one is nevertheless implicated. This form of implication can shape how one acts to change the system, but it never renders one innocent. In the case of the child separations that I discussed, those who fight solely against child separations are implicated in reproducing larger systems of violence against immigrants. The idea of implicatedness allows us to see how we reproduce inequality, without necessarily intending to. Ideas of implication can direct how we struggle and what we fight for. It allows for a strategy other than labeling ourselves as innocent or guilty. We are not perpetrators of anti-immigrant sentiment if we fight to stop immigrant children from being separated from their parents; but nor are we innocent. Americans who work to "save Afghani women" are not perpetrators, nor are they guilty; but they are certainly implicated in the violence women may endure, and they may be perpetuating it.

This is not about personal failure or blame; it is about recognizing that one is part of a larger, collective set of structures, histories, and scripts. One way to understand this is as "common sense" (Gramsci 1971; Hall and O'Shea 2013)—a form of everyday thinking that offers us frameworks of meaning with which to make sense of the world. Common sense stitches together several often contradictory stories, creating a slowly sedimented, popular philosophy that grounds our actions. It works without most people even being aware of it. Differently stated, we are interpellated into and formed as subjects by larger systems of power. Judith Butler (2006, 2016) describes how this works through linguistic forms, in relation to gender: we act through speech acts, such as naming, but speech acts also act on us. Language acts on us well before we know how to act, before we even become subjects, shaping our gender performances before we understand what those are, but that does not mean that we in turn cannot alter language, and deviate from or refuse those norms in various ways. We can think about this in relation to racial or other collective formations. We are all subject to racialized collective scripts, sensibilities, and forms of embodiment. We are formed by these; we are not individually responsible for them, but we can also recognize them, change and queer them.

Each of these different relations imply different notions of responsibility. Implication is different from *complicity*, for instance, because complicity infers a causal and present relationship to the harm—the problem is that it does not allow us to think about attenuated forms of responsibility related to structural injustices, like the protracted fallout of racial capitalism. In addition to being an implicated or complicit subject, then, one can be a structural *beneficiary*; that is, even if one did not create the system, certain people benefit from it now, and inherit the advantages. This infers a particular temporal relationship to harm; that is, the harm is in the past, but one is still benefiting in the present. This could refer to white families who were not owners of enslaved people in the US, but who received material and social advantage from that regime, and continue to do so in the current one because there has been no form of justice or redistribution of material rewards (Meister 2011). In this case, responsibility should be assumed by these beneficiaries, which is precisely what the idea of reparations proposes to do.

Bruce Robbins (2017) has a different understanding of the position of beneficiary, and the related moral and causal relationships: he understands it as the way that one's well-being is related to and even dependent upon someone else's suffering or impoverishment. He juxtaposes this to a humanitarian logic, which assumes no responsibility for or relationship to the suffering that humanitarians respond to. Robbins refines this further to speak of the "well-intentioned beneficiary," such as liberals who live in city centers, and yet whose privilege often relies upon a whole set of processes that have left many dispossessed or abandoned. He is primarily concerned with economic inequality, and how privileged people, as beneficiaries, are not only responsible for this history, but also capable of rising up and changing it.

There are *perpetuators* (distinguished from perpetrators!) and *accomplices*, or people who are complicit. There are *descendants* (see Rothberg 2019; Robbins 2017; Meister 2011). These are all jumping-off positions to think about how to enact responsibility, in the face of the enduring systems of violence, oppression, and inequality. To think about perpetuators versus perpetrators, Rothberg offers the case of Israel-Palestine, and settler colonialism more broadly. Since the formation of the state of Israel as a settler state,[25] Israel has perpetrated violence against Palestinians, but the descendants of these settlers are not necessarily perpetrators. To be clear, there are contemporary perpetrators of genocidal violence; the Israeli war on Gaza, started after the Hamas attacks on October 7, 2023, is one clear contemporary example. While not every Israeli is currently a perpetrator, they are all deeply implicated. Similarly, the Jewish diaspora is implicated insofar as Israelis claim to speak for them, as the "homeland" of Jews, and so are Americans more generally, insofar as the US is spending billions of tax dollars on military aid and other forms of ideological support to enable Israeli violence. Americans are perpetuators of the system—citizens and taxpayers who bear political responsibility for US foreign policy—but not necessarily perpetrators. We are responsible, and yet not identical to perpetrators.

These are positions that are neither purist nor personalized, but allow for complicated combinations of debt, harm, and direct and indirect responsibility and repair that extend over time, from the past and into the future. They take into account communal responsibility by virtue of participating in a collective way of life. To be sure, political movements have proposed solutions to this problem already. Reparations are perhaps the most important strategy of redistributive justice being put forth, although this can mean many things, from literal cash payouts based on a liability model to the descendants of harms like slavery; to abolitionism, which offers a more positive program built on social connection, invested not only in dismantling the carceral system, but in reimagining the world based on forms of structural care. Reparations can be forward or backward looking, each with its own challenges. For instance, a backward-looking model is based on debt, and the debt accrued since the harm was enacted. In this case, one must find a clear starting point from which ill-gotten gains can be traced; this can prove complicated. But furthermore, capitalist society is built on debt; it is about accumulation and the constant deferral of debt. So the question of when to pay back becomes the sticking point; there is never a good time to pay back, never a good time for justice. Instead, Meister suggests a forward-looking model based on material equality; he proposes a system of property rights, held in a collective trust, that beneficiaries can sell whenever they choose. To be sure, in this model, one must still decide on who gets to be a beneficiary, and how one is related to the intergenerational harm.

If we think of reparations as redistribution and equality by way of shared property, not by way of shared affiliation, kinship, or emotion, this might also be imagined as a form of commoning. I discuss this more extensively in chapter 5, but as I mentioned in the introduction, commoning is often referred to as a struggle against private property, in addition to being a struggle against enclosures and exclusion. It can also mean the sharing of wealth and resources on the basis of collective decision-making. Could reparations be imagined in relation to the creation of commoning projects, which insist on redistribution, including the redistribution of risk? For instance, commoning might begin through a system of collective trusts, where those who have been excluded become primary beneficiaries, creating a more level playing field to start.

That said, even if property is redistributed, the question remains of how people should live together (or apart). If the answer is as part of commoning projects, how can we do this well? As Ta-Nehisi Coates (2014) writes in his argument about reparations, reducing poverty and ending white supremacy are not the same. Transitional justice institutions have attempted to deal with the affective aftermaths of major wars and conflicts. These include Truth and Reconciliation Commissions (TRCs), which center forgiveness but not justice. They are built on the principles of human rights, and the sentiments they mobilize are about postponing large-scale redistribution; they work on acknowledging harm, and moving on. So what affective dimensions accompany the creation and enactment of a trust? What moral grammars? If innocence creates a moral grammar of judgment based on purity and deservingness of individuals, what grammar would replace it as a way to parse and to evaluate collectives? What affective grammars would accompany a political vision of egalitarianism? In German, guilt and debt are the same word. Debt has an infrastructure, which is guilt—this enables debt's deferral. Even if we decide that we do not want to follow a model of reparations based on debt, we still have the infrastructure of guilt on which capitalism is built. There is white guilt, for instance. Will a transfer of property necessarily rid people of guilt and its poison? How do people transform and transfer it to another social and affective form? These are the questions we need to attend to. What kind of collective subjects should be cultivated? This is something I take up again in chapter 5.

There are other models of repair and reparations. Several scholars have made arguments about reparations for colonial harms that involve allowing all those from former colonies to migrate to the former colonial metropoles, as a form of compensation for colonialism (Achiume 2019; Nevins 2019). While this is an interesting and provocative idea, there are also a few serious problems that would need to be addressed before taking it forward: for instance, it relies on the idea that one would want to move to Europe or the metropole, and that a form of European citizenship is the ultimate prize. It also assumes an individual model of reparations, migrant by migrant. This idea gets even more complicated when the conditions into which migrants move are exploitative and dangerous (which is the case right now with migration all over). The question is how to create the conditions for fair movement of people, when the movement of people is part of the very strategy to create equality and redress injustice.

Finally, abolitionist programs of social justice offer another possibility: they work to redistribute resources, and undermine and remake the systems that were put in place to enrich some by subjugating others, from slavery to colonialism, policing to prisons. But abolitionism does not just work by dismantling institutions: it is a world-making and world-building project. It includes the creation and institution of universal healthcare, universal education, affordable housing, and so on. As Ruth Wilson Gilmore has said, "Abolition seeks to undo the way of thinking and doing things that sees prison and punishment as solutions for all kinds of social, economic, political, behavioral and interpersonal problems. Abolition, though, is not simply decarceration, put everybody out on the street. It is reorganizing how we live our lives together in the world" (Gilmore 2020).

A different, more egalitarian political life requires we understand ourselves as collective beings who are always implicated and responsible in some fashion. We are all situated in relation to historical injustice and inequality: no one is innocent. Why not create or join forms of future-oriented collective action to repair these? Everyone will benefit from living in a society where fear, resentment, and guilt do not take center stage.

[CHAPTER TWO]

The Innocence of Inequality

Defining the Refugee-Child

The now-iconic image of Alan Kurdi, the three-year-old Kurdish-Syrian boy whose body washed up on a beach in Turkey in September 2015, grabbed the world's attention, eliciting sympathy rather than the usual mix of fear and indifference toward those who have left their homes to land on European shores. The photo gave what some call the "refugee crisis" and others call the "long summer of migration" a new face: innocence. Many have suggested that the image of Alan Kurdi, lying face down, drowned in an attempt to get to Europe from Syria with his family, served as a moment of reckoning in the long summer of migration, countering the wave of immigration policies based on fear, indifference, or hatred. The EU immediately reviewed its refugee policies; Chancellor Angela Merkel decided to admit more refugees to Germany. While the attention and goodwill was short-lived, and ultimately counterproductive, it nevertheless reframed the terms of the debate. In this new debate, refugees were reconfigured as childlike innocents; Kurdi became the new face of "the refugee."

What no one mentions is that as part of this reframing, migrants were increasingly portrayed in the media and in policy discourse as wily, deceiving their way into Europe's welfare and other beneficiary systems and undermining not only European security but European values. They were blamed for insecurity, violence, and unrest: from the sexual assaults by "foreign men" on New Year's Eve of 2015–2016 in Cologne, Germany, to the ISIL attacks on November 13, 2015, in Paris that killed 130 people. In fact, the tragic and yet far-too-predictable death of Alan Kurdi, like so many others before and after him, shored up a distinction that had been in the making for at least the past fifteen years: that is, the concept of innocence has been used to create a principled, moral distinction in both American and European public discourse between "refugees" and "migrants." *Real* refugees are seen as innocent—fleeing well-founded fears of persecution.

They are understood as passive, vulnerable, and in need of saving. Migrants, however, are seen as illegitimate, surreptitious, untrustworthy and, ultimately, criminal.

In the US, this same set of moral distinctions grounded by innocence helped shape the case of the Dreamers (undocumented youth) and their parents. As mentioned in chapter 1, the DREAM Act was first proposed in 2001, to provide a pathway to legal status for undocumented youth who came to the US as children. While at least ten versions of the DREAM Act were introduced in Congress, it was never made into law. In the face of this, the Deferred Action for Childhood Arrivals Act (DACA) was enacted as Executive Order in 2012 under President Obama, in order to provide temporary relief from deportation and work authorization for certain undocumented youth brought to the US as children. As a special category of immigrants, Dreamers and DACA recipients are set apart, as innocent; the justification for helping them is that they came unknowingly, as very young children. As such, they are considered innocent of everything—they came to the US without adequate knowledge, will, or autonomy. In this frame, which as I will show always creates a binary Other, their parents are condemned as the ones who acted "illegally"; they chose to cross an international border without authorization. As such, the parents and other adult family members are rendered guilty, and hence deportable.¹ The parents are migrants; the children hew closer to the figure of the refugee.

The focus on helping the innocent—whether children or vulnerable adults—may appear generous and humane; it responds to the request to lend a helping hand, to rescue those in need, particularly those who cannot help themselves. The International Refugee Regime itself, instituted officially in 1951 with the UN Convention Relating to Refugees, is framed as benevolent and humane. Indeed, according to many governments today, it is far *too* generous. After all, it was instituted after World War II and some of the worst mass atrocities that the world had witnessed, in part as a gesture of contrition and caution; it was a way to say "never again." However, as I will suggest, in practice, the refugee regime is not generous at all: it functions to radically limit the numbers of people given legal status by selecting a few exceptional cases and disqualifying the rest. It is built on moral hierarchies. Innocence is held out as the gold standard; and yet, to be clear, while used as a distinguishing criterion, innocence is not a status or condition that most people can or even want to claim in their everyday lives, as it revolves around lack: lack of knowledge, lack of desire, lack of agency, lack of will, lack of guilt. Indeed, those who are designated innocent are only precariously included in the category of (liberal) humanity, because they are not considered rational or autonomous. Whether we agree with the liberal definition or not, it is hegemonic in the realm of rights, and in this sense, innocence acts as the boundary of humanity that is constantly drawn and redrawn, where this constituent outside is simultaneously idealized and denigrated. To be included in a polity by virtue of innocence is to be included on perilous terms, as not-quite-equal (sometimes greater than, sometimes lesser than, the rest).

To be sure, as we saw in the introduction, the concept of innocence does not work alone to make distinctions; it is part of a cluster of moral concepts from victimhood to purity and vulnerability, and as such, it shape-shifts and can mean multiple things at once. Deservingness is a concept that also figures prominently in this cluster in the case of migrants and refugees. Originating from the Latin "to serve well," deservingness measures moral worth; it means to be worthy of merit, or to be entitled to something because of good service. In the US, the discourse of deservingness is harnessed in many ways to mark the most valuable members of society; those who are hardworking and law-abiding are singled out as part of a larger discourse of meritocracy. Immigrants are divided up as good and bad, deserving or not along the lines of whether they are seen as contributors to society through hard work and education, or whether they are considered economic burdens or freeloaders; the label of "undeserving" includes racialized claims of criminality, low morals, threat, and disease. In this chapter, I am interested in how deservingness—along with other concepts such as victimhood and vulnerability—have so often come to be connected to, or measured by, innocence in contemporary political discourse.

More broadly, I am interested in how claims to innocence help create and legitimize moral distinctions, which in turn work to institute or maintain structural inequalities. That is, the concept of innocence—rather than enabling generosity, fairness, or equality—is a crucial player in the way moral distinctions, political hierarchies, and inequalities are made and perpetuated. This has important political consequences in many realms, from the politics of migration to criminal justice, from environmental justice to reproductive justice. Ultimately, in this chapter, I look at how, as one incarnation in its family of resemblances, the concept of innocence works by enabling ontological distinctions, or different "humankinds": some innocent, some guilty. These ontologies both build on and perpetuate forms of inequality based on socio-political categories like race, class, and gender. When one does not qualify as innocent, one may be excluded from protections, benefits, and sometimes, from the very category of humanity.

I focus on the category of refugee because it puts this set of moral distinctions into particular relief; the history of the refugee regime is one critical site where moral grammars begin to supplant political ones, opening the way for innocence to play a role in the world of politics. But since the refugee *child* is the archetypal figure of innocence, this also raises the question of the role of the child in contemporary political imaginaries, and I am interested in the relationship of innocence to the idea of the child as universal figure of liberalism (Edelman 2004). To be sure, the figure of the refugee and that of the child have separate configurations and genealogies, so I tack back and forth between them with the goal of dwelling on their moments of co-constitution and intersection, not on giving a complete account of either.

First, I demonstrate how the concept of innocence works to create moral distinctions and inequalities between refugees, migrants, and others. Second, in thinking about how innocence gets associated with the refugee/child, I analyze the role of aesthetics in producing innocence. Images of innocence not only represent innocence, but inform the very concept; in late modernity, innocence is in fact a visual construction (Higonnet 1998; Fischel 2016). I examine how this works first by way of images of children, and then through humanitarian photography, arguing that coupling suffering with innocence helps produce it as a particular moral concept. Third, without promising to give a comprehensive account of the genealogies of innocence as a political concept, but rather, taking more a conjunctural approach (Hall et al. 1978), I explore one of the histories that have led innocence to play a leading role in so many political realms. Specifically, I look more closely at the International Refugee Regime to help us understand how vulnerability and persecution become central to our political worlds, which in turn open a central role for innocence. Overall, this chapter is guided by the argument that both history and aesthetics enable the concept of innocence to do important work in shaping moral and political hierarchies; I take us through some of the stories to show how this works, and how it was enabled.

Parsing Innocence, Reproducing Inequality

INNOCENCE AT THE INTERSECTIONS OF INEQUALITY

I turn again to the case of Alan Kurdi; its iconicity makes it revealing in various ways. Kurdi's death occurred as migrants and refugees fled a growing number of wars and conflicts. These conflicts have been fueled by US, European, and Russian imperial interventions in places like Syria, Afghanistan, and Iraq, but European nation-states have taken no responsibility, reacting to the people-on-the-move with fear and nationalist panic, hastily closing their borders. Hungary initiated a razor-wire barrier on its borders to keep refugees out, first with Serbia and then with Croatia, and threatened to erect a fence along its border with Romania. Austria constructed a four-kilometer fence at its border with Slovenia and deployed armed forces.[2] But then in September 2015, photographs of the three-year-old Syrian-Kurdish Alan Kurdi spread across the world. In the most circulated image, he was lying face down on a beach, where the water meets the sand in the Turkish town of Bodrum; he had drowned as his family was trying to reach the Greek island of Kos, twenty kilometers away. He and his family had fled to Turkey from a Syrian town under attack by the Islamic state. His brother and mother also drowned when their boat capsized; his father survived. The photographs generated immediate outcries of sympathy, pity, and compassion around the world. They also produced public expressions of shame that the world was letting children die. Portrayed as vulnerable, dependent, unknowing, in need of rescue and protection, political leaders emphasized Kurdi's innocence, and the media obliged. He was used to call out Europe and the Global North more generally for their lack of benevolence and humanity. Days after the image of Alan Kurdi appeared in media outlets, Germany, France, and the UK increased the numbers of refugees they were willing to accept.[3] New York City mayor Bill de Blasio held up a photo of Alan Kurdi to support the idea of accepting more Syrian refugees in New York, saying, "This is the cost of not bringing in people who are innocent victims of a humanitarian crisis."[4]

Yet the deaths involved in the refugee crisis were not news. There had been report after report of people dying in the sea. In the same year that Kurdi died, around one million people-on-the-move reached Europe. So why was Alan Kurdi noticed? How did his image shift the epistemic terrain to evoke innocence rather than threat? There are several factors at play here in determining who is deemed innocent and worthy of protection or of being mourned, and they work together, in clusters, cross-cutting and shaping what counts as innocence, just as innocence gives meaning to categories like "childhood" and "whiteness," and non-innocence helps inform categories like "terrorist." First, there is the issue of class. As Charles Homans argued in the *New York Times*, his appearance—including his shoes, shorts, and red shirt—made him look like a Euro-American middle-class child.[5] He looked like "one of us." In addition to making Westerners think of their own children, this class position helped render him innocent; historically, childhood innocence has been represented by cleanliness and lack of want, which in turn is associated with a certain middle-class status (Higonnet 1998). The middle-class child is allowed to be naïve; they are protected from knowledge.

But the process of racialization, too, is critical; indeed, childhood innocence was from the very beginning racialized as *white* in the US (Bernstein

2011), and as we will see, this configuration is true transnationally, albeit in slightly different forms, against different notions of Blackness or brownness. Insofar as Kurdi was a white-presenting child, it was easier for him to be noticed and claimed by dominant media sources. There have been reports that smugglers know European preferences and have instituted a racial hierarchy on the boats that carry migrants to the borders of Europe. Lighter-skinned migrants are given priority on the safer upper levels, in the hope that whiteness will translate into rescue, rather than death or deportation. The Ukrainian crisis could not have made this racial regime more explicit. When Russia invaded Ukraine in February 2022, the Global North uniformly opened its arms to Ukrainian refugees, while keeping the borders closed to others from the Global South, continuing to deport, detain, and beat Africans, Arabs, and Asians. The EU implemented an unprecedented Temporary Protection Directive for Ukrainians, giving them the right to work, live, and go to school in the EU for three years without asylum approval. This differential treatment was justified by Bulgarian prime minister Kiril Petkov, who stated, "These are not the refugees we are used to . . . These people are Europeans . . . These people are intelligent, they are educated people . . . This is not the refugee wave we have been used to, people we were not sure about their identity, people with unclear pasts, who could have been even terrorists" (Esposito 2022). Racism and Islamophobia are explicit; a former deputy prosecutor general of Ukraine told the BBC that "it's very emotional for me because I see European people with blue and blond hair . . . being killed every day."[6]

From Petkov's words, we see that racialization works in relation to other factors, like religion or "civilizational" status. Those associated with Islam are racialized in such a way as to designate them as non-innocent or "terrorists" (Asad 2007). Kurdi's appeal was no doubt enhanced by his Kurdish background: the Kurds have been US allies, enlisted to fight against ISIS in Iraq—allowing him to be seen as one of "us" on another front. In this sense, innocence produces and enables distinctions between all kinds of children—the concept is at play wherever liberal and illiberal regimes are being distinguished—innocence is crucial in helping draw this line. Palestinians are a case in point. After the October 7, 2023, Hamas attacks on Israel, and in the middle of the subsequent Israeli genocidal violence in Gaza, liberal-centrist Israeli politician Meirav Ben-Ari said that "the children of Gaza brought this upon themselves"[7]—refusing to understand all children as equally undeserving of suffering and violence. This kind of statement about Palestinian children—and certainly, adults—has become commonplace, serving not only to excuse, but to justify ethnic cleansing. At the time of writing, more than 17,000 Palestinian children have been killed in Gaza, and many thousands more have been wounded.[8] The impossibility of innocence for Palestinians is well known (Allen 2021; Shalhoub-Kevorkian 2020): we can look at Ahed Tamimi, the sixteen-year-old Palestinian girl who was arrested by Israeli soldiers in December 2017 for trying to protect her little brother from being taken by a soldier. Rather than seeing her as a child, the Israeli soldiers in turn accused her of assaulting them and sentenced her to eight months in prison in 2018. Innocence helps distinguish and patrol the boundaries of liberalism, ejecting certain people as irrevocably illiberal and, as such, less than human, insofar as humanity is a secular category. Palestinians have been designated as illiberal—terrorists—in relation to the type of violence deployed (seen as barbaric, gratuitous), a point to which I will return at the end of the chapter.

Still other elements come into play, in addition to the way innocence shapes and is shaped by processes of racialization, class, and religion/civilizational status. These processes include spatial distinctions, such as proximity and distance. Humanitarian organizations regularly figure African children on their home pages and in fundraising materials to elicit support for those considered most vulnerable. The question of distance is critical here; distant suffering (Boltanski 1999) elicits pity and sympathy, but when this suffering gets closer to home in the Global North—physically and symbolically—innocence transforms into threat. It seems that there is an invisible line (in the ocean, in the sand) which, when crossed, makes sympathy evaporate for certain people, and we cannot understand this without thinking of racial formations; yet race by itself is never fully determining of innocence.

The photograph of Alan Kurdi reveals how these many factors work together to configure innocence, as well as non-innocence. In other words, innocence is established by way of its opposite; it produces a distinction, and often, a binary other. Sometimes the non-innocent are considered guilty; sometimes they are seen as too knowing, and framed as manipulative or threatening. Other times, they are seen as too sexual, and hence immoral. In the case of refugees, innocence serves to manage the border between worthy and unworthy. For every Alan Kurdi, there are many others who are deported, detained, or left to die. That said, the binary opposite of innocence is an unstable position; it shifts and is mediated by historical and identity characteristics in conjunction with forces such as proximity, place, and geopolitics. With certain racial contours, proximity can change the same figure from one of innocence into one of threat. But in each case, innocence, in combination with other qualifying elements, is used to create moral hierarchies, often with life-and-death consequences.

The Dubs amendment to the UK's Immigration Act 2016 is another example of the making of non-innocence: this time, we see the critical role of both gender and age in relation to other regimes of identity and power. The Dubs amendment was an attempt by the British government to respond to the "refugee crisis" in Europe, by accepting responsibility and caring for some of the unaccompanied children detained in these camps. Lord Dubs, the author of the amendment, was himself part of the Kindertransport from Nazi Germany—the initiative that saved about 10,000 Jewish children from the Nazi death camps by transporting them, alone, to Britain. The focus of the amendment was saving children from the "Jungle" camp in Calais. People-on-the-move claimed the area starting in 2015 as a place they could live for however long it took them to cross over to the UK, by way of trains or ships or trucks; they made a home of it, created communities. While, as we will see in chapters 4 and 5, its location as a place of freedom or imprisonment was contested, images of children in the camp in Calais were particularly prominent in the British media, and the Jungle itself was figured as decrepit. Manuel Valls, French prime minister at the time, eventually used this excuse to close the camp, displacing the many in it. The photos of the unaccompanied migrants in the media highlighted their childlike features: smooth, baby skin, large eyes, and small hands; these were often accompanied by images of teddy bears and abandoned shoes (McLaughlin 2018). The rescue of these children was presented to the public as a moral imperative, and images of their innocence helped make the argument. Across the spectrum, the media depicted them in distress, as vulnerable and helpless.

But when they arrived in the UK, the migrant children's legitimacy was immediately questioned by the very same media, and by the public who seemed to have supported them. This happened in large part by calling their age into question. Their physical attributes were commented upon, with reference to facial and body hair, burly size, and height. The references to their physical maturation rendered them suspicious as children. As Rosen and Crafter (2018) note in their media analysis of the amendment, the British media commented on their "hairy arms" (*The Sun*, October 24, 2016) and "stubble" (*The Mail*, October 19, 2016), pointing to characteristics that signify adulthood, and more specifically, adult masculinity.

To be sure, age assessments of migrants have been common for some time now; with the growing number of unaccompanied minors, governments are increasingly insisting on such assessments to determine who is worthy of certain protections and rights. This occurs despite acknowledgment of their medical inaccuracy. Assessments include dental examinations and measurements like the wrist and hand bone, to check form, size, and development by way of ossification. Psychological assessments and other biometric technologies are also used. That said, reports acknowledge that these measures are all subject to other variables, from nutrition to gender and ethnicity (Schumacher et al. 2018). This is another example of the suppleness and instability of the category of childhood, and international borders seem to be an especially important set of sites for its contemporary reworking.

The media compared the children coming in under the Dubs amendment to the "genuine," innocent children of the Kindertransport; this history allowed the British to claim the moral high ground, and to posit this as the standard for "real" refugees. Despite evidence that those on the Kindertransport were varied in age, the most circulated images depicted these children as very young, and as uniformly "vulnerable" and "innocent." The comparison establishes a particular politics of memory, with these victims as blameless, against which the children from the Jungle were judged. The media reports suggested that unlike the children in the Kindertransport, who required the help of adults to put them on the ships and to receive them on the other side, these migrant children had traveled alone, which threw into question their status as "real" or vulnerable children. Autonomy disqualifies one from the category of innocence. It opens the way for children *at* risk to become the *source* of risk.

Further illustrating how children straddle the tender threshold between threat and care, the migrant children from the Jungle were depicted as wearing "hoodies" (*The Mail*, October 19, 2016; see Rosen and Crafter 2018, 73), signifying a racialized, predatory masculinity. The word "children" in the media and public discourse was quickly replaced by descriptors like "youth" and "minors" and "lads" (McLaughlin 2018). As noted in the introduction, Liisa Malkki (2010) has argued that when children occupy positions that do not fit the idea of innocence—like child soldiers—there is an attempt to use alternate terms, such as "youth" or "teens," to set aside and protect a time of childhood innocence, when they are still unworldly and untainted. In other words, innocence not only draws attention to children, but works to determine who counts as a child, and therefore, who gets recognition, attention, rights, or aid. As this example illustrates once again, racial regimes in conjunction with factors like gender and age are critical in determining who counts as a child, and who qualifies as innocent. While Jews were not always considered white (Brodkin 1998), today the images of the Kindertransport are viewed through the lens of whiteness. In contrast, as feminist theorist bell hooks has noted, Black children in the United States, particularly Black boys, are still never allowed to be children (hooks 2013). We need only think of Tamir Rice, the twelve-year-old who was shot dead by the police in 2014 in Cleveland, Ohio, for holding a toy gun. But this is also true for Black girls, who, starting as early as five years old, are treated as more adult than their white counterparts, with presumed knowledge of topics like sex.⁹ The 2023 case of nine-year-old Bobbi Wilson offers yet one more example: Bobbi was looking for spotted lanternflies in her hometown in New Jersey, to help in the effort to exterminate an invasive species. She was walking around with soap and water to spray them, when someone called the police and reported her as "a little Black woman, walking and spraying stuff on the sidewalks and trees."¹⁰ Framed as a "little" adult rather than a child, she was immediately incorporated into a regime of life deemed suspicious and threatening.

Racial regimes mean that Black and brown children are never allowed this period of untroubled and ignorant life; they are immediately inter-pellated into the structures and hierarchies of society, which render their knowledge suspect. As previously mentioned, historian Robin Bernstein (2011, 30–35) argues that childhood innocence was from the very beginning racialized as *white* in the United States; it came into being in the second half of the nineteenth century in relation to its Other, the Black child, who was constructed as a nonfeeling, non-innocent, juvenile worker. In this sense, childhood was forged in the context of capitalism and slave labor—and in-nocence worked to mark the boundary of allowable, exploitative, racialized labor. We can add labor to the factors that work to shape innocence.

Insofar as the figure of the child is a universal signifier for a liberal social order—standing in as hope for the future (Edelman 2004)—there are high stakes to who counts as a child, as they are endowed with the task of repro-ducing the social order. What the examples have shown is that when one is a non-innocent child, one is no longer a child—one is simply expelled from the category. In this sense, innocence produces and regulates ontologies of humankinds.

CASCADING MORAL HIERARCHIES: CONDEMNING PARENTS AND TRAFFICKERS

As we have seen, the act of labeling someone as innocent produces a moral distinction and hierarchy between them and the non-innocent Other, with moral qualifications such as predacious and delinquent for the non-innocent. It can also produce them as different categories of being: child versus adult, or refugee versus migrant.

Such ontological distinctions are produced on multiple fronts in asylum and immigration discourses, and these have cascading effects: the primary ontological distinctions produce subsequent moral hierarchies. First, there are moral distinctions forged between children and parents. Not only are precarious distinctions made between who counts as a child and an adult; if one is considered an innocent child—as in the case of Alan Kurdi—this opens the way for the parents of the innocent child-to-be condemned as guilty. The parent-child binary is also ripe for moral qualification. In the US, migrant families are regularly described in both liberal and conservative press as bringing their children over in irresponsibly dangerous conditions. In the case of Dreamers, for instance, immigrant parents have been denounced for having put their innocent children in harm's way; they are said to have made "poor choices," condemning their own children to illegality. This enabled a political discourse that forgave Dreamers but rendered the parents deportable, inferring the abdication of responsibility by the parents or guardians, and framing them as neglectful at best, criminal at worst. Such a framing in turn enables the state to take the moral high ground, working to save or rescue those who are innocent and unable to care for themselves. This move by the state has been described as a "double colonial paternalism," portraying the Global South as childlike and in need of assistance from the Global North, and at the same time, depicting the Global South as unable to care adequately for its children (Manzo 2008; Adler-Nissen et al. 2020).

In Alan Kurdi's case, his father, Abdullah Kurdi, enters the frame in the media and in public discourse only insofar as he is blamed for his own son's death. He was held responsible for subjecting his sons to a dangerous and potentially lethal journey; as part of this, a Turkish court accused him of organizing the smugglers who helped them make the lethal trip.[11] Some said he was driving the boat when it capsized. But this set of accusations and the label of "guilty" push the rest of the story out of the frame, including how Abdullah Kurdi and his wife tried everything to take care of their family: they applied for refugee status in Canada, but the Canadian government denied them legal status, even as they were fleeing the proxy war in Syria. They were living in Turkey with no rights, as Syrian refugees and as Kurds, both of whom are already persecuted by Turkey. The frame of innocence or guilt does not allow for complex structural realities. Perhaps ironically, depicting Alan as innocent works to muffle and erase his father's grief.

Once again, innocence inevitably produces a binary Other; when it is not the parents, another discernibly guilty party must be found to maintain the innocence of the child as well as of the savior—in this case, the state. In this sense, we can discern a second set of moral distinctions: this time, between refugees and smugglers or traffickers.[12] As was just mentioned, Alan Kurdi's father, Abdullah, was not only depicted as an irresponsible parent; stories appeared in the media about him as a "people-smuggler," conflating these two figures.[13] That is, rather than take responsibility for the conditions that people are fleeing, European states have blamed smugglers—framed as and conflated with coercive, immoral traffickers—for the flight of refugees and for their deaths in the Mediterranean; the argument offered is that traffickers take advantage of people who are vulnerable, extorting money and transporting them in horribly dangerous conditions, encouraging them when there is no hope. The deaths of 360 migrants off the coast of Lampedusa in October 2013 was one particularly notable and horrific occasion. Italian president Giorgio Napolitano called the drownings a "slaughter of innocents."[14] This begged the question of who committed the "slaughter"; that is, this focus on innocence and vulnerability immediately invokes a simultaneous slot for—and criminalization of—the guilty. Libyan, Sudanese, and Somali traffickers were held responsible, having charged migrants $3,000 each for the passage across. Rather than attending to the conditions driving the people-on-the-move to leave their homes or the conditions that make smuggling a choice for both smugglers or smuggled, the state focused attention on criminalizing the traffickers, with the insincere argument that if they disappeared, migration would stop.

Smugglers may indeed be part of criminal or drug-related gangs, but they may also be family members, friends, or part of migrant communities, in similar situations as the migrants themselves; people-on-the-move must solicit help to cross—it is not a simple situation of the innocent being preyed upon by the guilty. Indeed, it is effectively impossible to enter the Global North to make a claim for asylum now without a smuggler's help (Hathaway 2008; Keshavarz and Khosravi 2022), but this is primarily the consequence of the varied militarized security apparatuses that have grown exponentially at borders all over the world—the border security industry is enormous and hugely profitable (see Miller 2019; Aizeki et al. 2021; Ticktin 2022). Furthermore, as migrant rights groups have shown, countries like Italy use techniques such as anti-mafia laws to criminalize asylum seekers and use them as scapegoats, offering money and other incentives to migrants to testify against boat drivers and say they are smugglers. In fact, boat drivers are often migrants or asylum seekers themselves, who take up the job if they don't have enough money to pay their way.[15]

I will provide one more such example, from the US, to show the way smuggling is used to deflect from the conditions that produce migration and ultimately condemn so many migrants to death. In June 2022, fifty-three migrants were found dead in an abandoned tractor-trailer, smothered to death by the heat in the truck, where they had no air-conditioning or water. The tractor-trailer was found near San Antonio, Texas. Biden stated, "This incident underscores the need to go after the multibillion-dollar criminal smuggling industry preying on migrants and leading to far too many innocent deaths."[16] And yet, in the same article, we hear that migrant deaths are increasing at the border because it has been closed due to Title 42, a little-known health clause that Trump instituted during the pandemic, and which Biden explicitly chose to leave in place; it suspended the right to asylum in the name of protection from a communicable disease, despite this being medically unfounded (see chapter 1). The migrants who were found dead, mostly from Central America and Mexico, have been shown to be more likely to be expelled or detained due to Title 42, hence their need to find other routes into the US. But rather than look at his own US immigration policy, Biden blamed the smugglers for these "innocent deaths."

The emphasis on smugglers and traffickers by state and media actually furthers the criminalization and securitization of borders, which in turn leads to more deaths—all the while exempting states from responsibility. It does not help or save "the innocents." Innocence is an unstable category; it requires an Other, but the site of Otherness can have multiple occupants, and can shift between them. Insofar as innocence works by creating binary Others that then become structured as moral hierarchies, it undercuts any discussion of larger, more complex structural causes or explanations for people-on-the-move. It not only renders structural and political inequalities invisible, but the search for individual blame or guilt helps reproduce inequality by misconstruing the causes as individual.

The Aesthetics of Innocence

Innocence produces clear demarcations between humankinds, even as these categories themselves may change over time. To further explain how this works, I will suggest that innocence is not only a theological, philosophical, or political concept: it is an aesthetic one. Innocence functions on a visual level. We have seen already that images are central to questions of innocence, from those of Alan Kurdi to those in the debates around the Dubs amendment. More specifically, innocence is not simply represented after the fact; rather, images have served to produce the very contours of what we understand innocence to be. I explore how this works, by continuing the analysis of the iconic photo of Alan Kurdi. I first trace the building blocks of the aesthetics of childhood innocence, and then turn to the way innocence has taken a slightly different form in relation to humanitarianism.

THE VISUAL BUILDING BLOCKS OF INNOCENCE

Images work in different registers than words; they invoke a powerful range of emotions, in part by bundling several emotions together (Adler-Nissen et al. 2020) and in part by circulations of affect (Ross 2014). They can also

activate a deep register of moral response. I lay out some of the formal aesthetic characteristics of the concept of childhood innocence, in order to
think about how these have produced innocence as a concept.

First, innocence is most effectively marked by singularity—that is, by
representing individuals outside of any context, outside time itself. In the
Romantic tradition, innocent children are figures that are understood to
precede knowledge: they are promises of both the future and the past. This
otherworldliness has been accomplished in significant part through the
framing of images. To illustrate, I turn again to the images of Alan Kurdi;
there were several photos of him, taken by Turkish photojournalist Nilüfer
Demir. In one, Kurdi was lying face down on the beach. In a second photograph, there was a man in uniform looking down at him, and in a third,
we see the man in uniform carrying Kurdi. But in most reproductions of
the photo, Alan is figured on the beach alone, without this uniformed figure, and without parents or other guardians. Photographs of the migrant
children in the Jungle who were to be rescued by the UK government also
show them alone, devoid of parental protection (e.g., articles in *The Independent* on October 10 and October 15, 2016). Not only does this emphasize
vulnerability, helplessness, and lack—all characteristics of the concept—
but this interpellates the viewer into the position of carer for the vulnerable. It urges them to take responsibility, creating a direct relationship to
the innocent.

In contrast to this individual figuration, we regularly see people-on-the-
move photographed in groups, faces indistinguishable; as such, they are
constituted more as threatening masses. Here, we see individuality juxta-
posed to the mass, and a moral hierarchy set up between the two. As Liisa
Malkki noted long ago, there is a visual regime to refugees in which "Black
bodies are pressed together impossibly close in a confusing, frantic mass"
(1996, 387). This "sea of humanity" erases all distinguishing personal characteristics: names, histories, connections. Reduced to an undistinguished
mass of bodies rather than individuals, these refugees, Malkki argues, represent a humanity stripped of dignity. On the one hand, what Allen Feldman
(1994, 407) calls an "anonymous corporeality" can evoke pity and helplessness. But on the other hand, as he states, the "anonymous corporeality
functions as an allegory of the elephantine, 'archaic' and violent histories
of external and internal subalterns." The racialization of the mass of bodies
gives it a different quality; such images can be used to shift from menaced
to menace. We can see this same affective orientation in relation to collectivities, such as crowds or mobs; I will discuss these as potential political
subjects in chapter 5. This is in contradistinction to the singular, human-
ized, innocent subject.

Second, images of childhood innocence are rendered more powerful by the ways in which distinctions between children and adults are foregrounded: for instance, an emphasis on children's roundness, their pudgy quality. But this focus on roundness is an effect of aesthetic histories that helped produce the very notion of Romantic childhood as an ontology or way of being, distinct from adulthood (Higonnet 1998). Childhood innocence is a physical, embodied state, but from the Romantic period onward, when ideas of childhood were constituted as Edenic and pure, images of innocence emphasized the parts of the body least closely associated with adult sexuality: downy cheeks, dimpled hands, tiny bare toes (Higonnet 1998, 15). In many ways, innocent children are figured as genderless, although art historian Anne Higonnet claims that over time, as elite paintings transitioned to commercialized photography, childhood innocence was increasingly feminized. This is because after the Romantic period, childhood continued to be connected to the sentimental, but sentimentality became associated with women. But across these periods, childhood innocence is figured against adult sexual passion. This is one reason that childhood innocence is captured and configured at a very young age, as these baby-like descriptors are more marked. In addition to thinking of how this played out in the debate about the Kindertransport and in relation to children from the Jungle, we can take the example of Omran Daqneesh, also a child from Syria, a victim of the war in Aleppo a year after Alan Kurdi (see figure 1). The video of five-year-old Omran Daqneesh went viral in August 2016: he was pictured as dazed, covered in blood and dust, sitting in an ambulance in the aftermath of an airstrike in Aleppo. Daqneesh appears confused, unknowing, alone, and vulnerable, even as he looks straight at the camera; these characteristics produce innocence, but the roundness of his face and his big eyes work to confirm it. His image was used to generate shame about the ongoing war in Syria, and to mobilize publics. In response, US Senator John McCain issued a statement, saying that "images of the carnage in Syria must do more than inspire shock and outrage; they must compel us to action" (statement from 2016, cited in Al-Ghazzi 2019, 3231). Innocence is produced here as a distinct ontology of childhood.

Third, innocence is perhaps most vividly figured in death, the state of absolute nothingness—no thoughts, no desires, no longings. It is visualized as a specific kind of lack. Alan Kurdi both produced and exemplified the pure innocence of refugees after he washed up on the Turkish shore. This emptiness—or blank slate—allows adults to project whatever fantasies they want onto the children, whether they are fantasies of saving and protecting, or darker, sexual fantasies, evoked by sexual purity. As Anne Higonnet states, images of Romantic childhood are always haunted by death—that

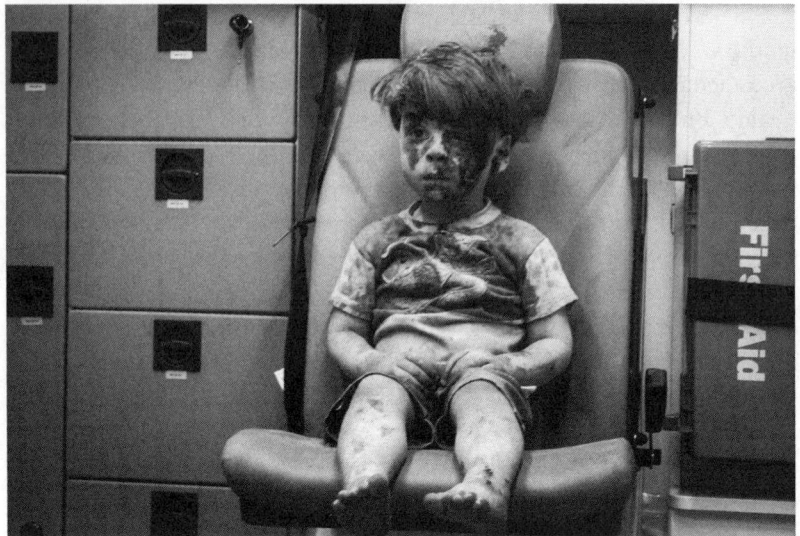

FIGURE 1. Omran Daqneesh, Aleppo, Syria, 2016. Photo by Anadolu, licensed by Getty Images.

is, childhood innocence always ends in loss—whether the death of the child, or the loss of innocence as the child grows up and enters into the impure, corrupt social and political worlds of adults (Higonnet 1998, 30). As in death, innocence is understood as passive; those portrayed as active or agential do not fit the frame, and when innocence serves as the ground for moral or political decisions, those who are too active are disqualified from consideration.

SHIFTING THE FRAME: INNOCENCE'S OTHERS

One of the important characteristics of images is that they are polysemic and allow for multiple interpretations (Barthes 1977). They can be reappropriated to mean many things. The fragility of the concept of innocence is actually built into the tenuousness of the image itself: What if one were to widen the frame, to include more context? What if the photo of Alan Kurdi had been of his brother, instead, who died in exactly the same way, on the same day, but was a few years older and appeared less childlike? That is, innocence is an ephemeral position, which easily slips into its opposite; in this sense, we can how see innocence's "Others" are evoked and produced by the image itself. This can be seen very clearly in the appropriations and remediations of the image of Alan Kurdi. As mentioned, the photograph has turned into an icon, easily accessible to a global audience, and the appropriations have helped in this process, mobilizing political memory to new ends, and offering competing interpretive frameworks. Within days of the publication of the photograph, the imagery was shared on social media sites and under many hashtags. #humanitywashedashore was only one of these, and in the first few days, 1,634 images were shared under this hashtag. According to Mortensen (2017), 656 of these were appropriations; some of these decontextualized the image, isolating the figure of the drowned child. Others recontextualized him, inserting him into a new context to make a different point. These appropriations took multiple forms: cartoons, murals, graffiti, photographs, and collages.

I want to explore two of the most controversial appropriations of the image to think further about innocence, and how quickly it can be turned into its often morally repugnant opposite. That is, I use these to further demonstrate how moral hierarchies are embedded in and produced by the aesthetics of innocence. First, I turn to Chinese artist and activist Ai Weiwei, and his appropriation of the image by posing as Alan Kurdi, lying face down on a beach, at the water's edge, on the Greek island of Lesbos.

This photograph was taken in January 2016 for *India Today*, "to raise awareness about the plight of refugees" (Biri 2016; Mortensen 2017).[17] The photograph was not well received. Ai Weiwei was accused of many things, from benefiting from the suffering of refugees, to aestheticizing violence, to colonizing the space of the refugee, leaving no space for them to speak; and finally, to decontextualizing the image. The photograph was called "sickening" and "crass."[18] Much of the commentary focused on how his middle-aged, burly body compromised the power of the image, almost mocking it. While he had said that as a refugee himself, he wanted to pay tribute to Kurdi and to all refugees who have drowned in search of better lives, he also said he wanted to physically enact this position—to embody it, in order to understand it. His attempt points to the impossibility of embodying the sentiment at the heart of the image; the image was not about the refugee, or even death itself. It was about innocence. The photograph of Ai Weiwei inadvertently reveals that the power of innocence is only open to a few, at the expense of everyone else who may suffer similar fates of poverty, violence, displacement, loss, or death. Ai Weiwei was treated as morally bankrupt for trying to occupy this space of purity.

Putting other bodies into the frame of innocence reveals the moral distinctions that lurk in and around the concept—these are its constituent outside. First among these are gendered and racial distinctions. In some ways, we should not be surprised by the reaction to this image of Ai Weiwei, since grown men of color rarely, if ever, qualify as innocent, regardless of whether they are famous or wealthy. To be clear, white men may succeed in claiming

innocence in certain circumstances—claims to racial innocence, in particular, are open to them, as we saw in chapter 1. But the only time men of color
are afforded even a hint of innocence is when they are seen as somehow
without choice or agency (see chapter 3), or when they are almost conflated with children. To this second point, historian Robin Bernstein (2011)
writes that white children's innocence often works by being transferable to
surrounding people and things. In the contemporary US, people-on-the-
move crossing into the US from Latin America have received very little
sympathy, but a photo in June 2019 of Óscar Alberto Martínez Ramírez with
his twenty-three-month-old daughter Valeria also produced an unchurac-
teristic outpouring of grief (see figure 2).

They had washed up dead on the shores of the Rio Grande, both lying
face down, her tiny head tucked into his T-shirt. The photo emphasized
Valeria's innocence, by way of her smallness compared to her father, and
once again, by figuring her death. Her innocence translated at least in
part to her father, whose efforts to protect her were visible in the photo:
he had had her on his back, under his T-shirt, as they crossed, and they
washed up together, bound by the T-shirt. But her arm was also thrown
over him, raising the question of who was protecting whom. It seems that

FIGURE 2. Óscar Alberto Martínez Ramírez and his nearly two-year-old
daughter Valeria lie on the bank of the Rio Grande in Matamoros,
Mexico, Monday, June 24, 2019. Photo by AP Photo/Julia Le Duc.

the physical proximity allowed for the innocence to effectively wash onto him. But again, the most important aspect here is that Martínez Ramírez was also dead—he could no longer be a threat. Innocence is constructed in and through lack. He occupies the space with his child, rather than usurping it, as did Ai Weiwei.

If Ai Weiwei's remaking of the Kurdi image reveals the racial and gendered hierarchies and inequalities built into the aesthetics of innocence—in this case, racial and gendered attributes determine who can be figured in such an image of moral purity, where life is both given value and mourned—I turn now to the second appropriation of the image of Alan Kurdi, in the cartoon by *Charlie Hebdo*, the French satirical weekly, to probe further into the hierarchies that images of innocence enable and produce. *Charlie Hebdo* published a series of cartoons in September 2015 and January 2016. The most offensive of these showed pig-faced men running after women with the caption "What would little Alan have grown up to be?," and the bottom caption read, in response, "Ass-groper in Germany." This was a reference to the series of sexual assaults on New Year's Eve in Cologne (2015–2016), blamed on "marauding" groups of people of North African origin. *Charlie Hebdo* is well known for its caustic jokes, often in bad taste and regularly racist and Islamophobic. The magazine has been accused of hate speech, the most significant charge of which resulted in a deadly attack on their offices, in January 2015. This satire of the Kurdi image was also condemned as nearly sacrilegious; Alan Kurdi's father called the cartoonists "inhuman and immoral."

I do not disagree that this is a deeply racist, callous cartoon, and this is precisely why I focus on it here, to bring attention to the hierarchies built into the visual concept of innocence. Alan was initially presented as a near-deity—his innocence was configured as the savior of Europe, indeed of humanity. Humanity is at once the Other to the photo—corrupt, depraved, unable to see or respond to human suffering—and the witness, the spectator, provoked and shamed into reclaiming its own innocence. But the failed project of a unified, moral humanity is conjured by the *Charlie Hebdo* image, which renders visible the profound racialized structures that divide "humanity" and haunt Europe. Arguments against colonialism have long exposed humanity itself as exclusionary and racist; as Frantz Fanon (1963, 312) writes in *Wretched of the Earth*, "When I search for Man in the technique and style of Europe, I see only a succession of negations of man, and an avalanche of murders." While Fanon argued for replacing this restricted colonial humanity with a new and better version, as we will see in chapter 5, this is a contested project. The image plugs into the larger discourse about migrants, where childhood innocence always has as its double the racialized, criminalized Other—the flip side of innocence is usually guilt, and the pendulum can swing quickly between the two. As Muehlebach (2016) suggests, after the sexual assaults in Cologne by those named as "foreign," Alan could not be thought about apart from the man people thought he would have become: a rapist, a criminal, violating not only women but the German state, or oppressing women, forcing them to veil themselves. Racial difference is transposed into a set of moral distinctions—racialized masculine Others are guilty, criminal, sexist, homophobic, evil—and *Charlie Hebdo*'s cartoon reveals that these are part of the image of innocence—its binary Other, either just outside, or encroaching into, the frame.

Nothing could show the racialized binary that the concept of innocence relies upon more clearly than the reactions to the horrific November 13 ISIL attacks in Paris, where 130 people were killed in three different locations, including ninety people at the famous nightclub the Bataclan. The Islamic State claimed responsibility. After initially promising greater generosity to refugees in the face of Alan Kurdi's drowning, France immediately closed its borders, collapsing refugees with the Islamic State, creating one big racialized, undesirable, and criminal Other, even though Alan Kurdi's family, along with countless others, were actually *fleeing* the ISIL and other warring factions. France set up a state of emergency that suspended the rules of the Schengen Agreement—which, in 1985, abolished internal borders across an area of twenty-five EU members and four non-EU members—closing its borders in a bait and switch that rendered refugees guilty for the attacks; the US and much of Europe followed suit. From innocent to guilty in the blink of an eye. This frame careens between identifying with the innocent to making them into a distant and barbaric Other. The aesthetics of innocence allow for this instability that translates moral and political panics into sedimented racial hierarchies.

INNOCENCE AS SUFFERING:
HUMANITARIAN PHOTOGRAPHY

While the concept of innocence is shaped by an aesthetics of childhood, it also builds on and overlaps with other aesthetic traditions. For instance, Sianne Ngai (2005) describes the aesthetics of cuteness, and suggests it accentuates helplessness and vulnerability. Innocence shares many formal signifiers with cuteness, organized around small, helpless, abject, or deformed objects: for instance, large eyes that evoke distress. These induce both the desire for mastery as well as the desire to help and to cuddle. Indeed, innocence, like cuteness, seems to name an aesthetic encounter based on an exaggerated difference in power; it works in relation to a socially disempowered Other.

But I turn to another aesthetic tradition that has profoundly shaped the meaning of innocence—that of humanitarian photography. Humanitarian aesthetics has linked the concept of innocence to suffering in an unprecedented way, bringing the concepts of vulnerability and victimhood with it into a tighter moral cluster.

Photos of Romantic childhood, which helped invent the idea of "childhood innocence" just 200 years ago (Higonnet 1998), do not necessarily involve suffering; this seemingly natural, unchanging childhood state was illustrated by a singular child, visually distinguished from adults. The children were in costume, either dressed as little adults, as the portrait of Penelope Boothby by Joshua Reynolds suggests (see figure 3), or in oversized and fluffy clothes to draw attention to their smallness. Another strategy was for them to pose with pets, to make them seem less human, more at one with nature. One of the goals of such images of innocence was to help people forget the problems with adult society (Higonnet 1998).

FIGURE 3. Penelope Boothby, portrait by Joshua Reynolds,
1874. National Portrait Gallery, London.

But starting in the 1970s, humanitarian imagery and its partner, atrocity photography, developed into more popular and widely circulated genres, driven by a reckoning with the horrors of the concentration camps in WWII. In the humanitarian genre, innocence was increasingly pictured in relation to suffering; images were created to teach a moral lesson, cultivating a moral imperative to act. Humanitarian photography responded to a perceived need to witness suffering, even at a distance, in order to prevent future crimes. In 1986, Bernard Kouchner, cofounder of MSF, published *Charité Business*, arguing for the critical role of media in humanitarian work. As with documentary photography, there was an implicit assumption that seeing pictures would result in people taking action. In this sense, images of innocence became a political project, even while masquerading as simply a moral one.

To illustrate humanitarian aesthetics, I turn to another iconic image: a photograph of an emaciated Sudanese child, too weak to stand up, being preyed upon by a vulture (see figure 4). Taken in 1993 by Kevin Carter—who subsequently won a Pulitzer Prize for the photograph[19]—it quickly came to signify the South Sudanese famine and served as an early example of the humanitarian call to action, driven by pity and shame. In the photo, the moral imperative to help eclipsed the political reasons for the suffering, helping initiate the form of humanitarian innocence.

FIGURE 4. "The Vulture and the Little Girl," *New York Times*, March 26, 1993. Photo by Kevin Carter, licensed from Getty Images.

In the photograph, we see the child, in a moment of profound suffering; it is hard to tell if it is a boy or girl—as already noted, genderlessness is a feature of photographs of innocence (it was later discovered that the child was a boy), although the tendency to feminize vulnerability is revealed by the title of the photograph when first published by the *New York Times* on March 26, 1993: "The Vulture and the Little Girl." The child's head is bowed, he is too weak to keep it up, or perhaps he is in pain. His vulnerability is shown by his emaciated body, but it is amplified by the vulture lurking in the background. As the figure of death, the vulture represents the darkness of the world, against the innocence of the child. As with other images of innocence, the child is pictured alone; we do not see the cause of his suffering—that is outside the frame. He is a victim of extreme hunger and malnutrition, but there is no indication that the famine is part of an ongoing civil war in Sudan.

We learned later that Carter was being escorted by soldiers when he took the photo, and the child was on his way to a United Nations Feeding Center, but the war is kept out of the frame, to allow for the viewers to be called to action to save the child. That is, spectators are not being interpellated to fight in the war, or to engage with the histories that informed the war, but to give money to stop the famine, to effectively reach in and stop the vulture—it is framed as a moral challenge of the human condition, without a clear or named cause, and the photograph empowers the spectators (or witnesses) to act. The image of innocence precludes politics; when coupled with suffering in this way, innocence is configured as a timeless, moral condition. To be clear, this photograph, like much humanitarian imagery, is deeply racialized; the image was published by the *New York Times*, and the victims are in Africa, and it reinforces the belief that Africans live in "primitive" conditions, unable to manage the challenges of life. Once again, there is no hint of the civil war, nor of the colonial histories that shaped the lead-up to war, where the north was governed differently from the south. We return to the notion of "double paternal colonialism" (Manzo 2008), where the Global South is portrayed as both childlike and incapable of caring for its children.

Humanitarian photography overlaps with atrocity photography in various ways, but most significantly, humanitarianism does not center violence or injury. To be sure, violence consistently haunts the images, even if it is not directly pictured. Atrocity photographs (such as those from Abu Ghraib prison) are controversial for many reasons, including that they risk trafficking in voyeurism or a form of pornographic pleasure, compassion fatigue, and (re)traumatizing spectators (Sontag 2003; Linfield 2012; Butler 2009; Dean 2015). However, I want to take seriously another claim about atrocity photos: that they interpellate the spectator as complicit in the violence or murder pictured in the photographs (Dean 2015, 242; Schoenberner 1960, cf. Sackett 2006). They do not let spectators off the hook—to look is to be involved or complicit. To be sure, as with all images, there is no one interpretation or response, and there are variations as to how people react to being interpellated. Some may feel outrage and shame, others may feel satisfaction; it may depend on the context. The video of George Floyd being murdered elicited a global cry of outrage; it was an acknowledgment of complicity in a racial regime and subsequently an insistence that it be stopped. But other such videos of police violence have not prompted the same response or set of feelings.

If we compare this to humanitarian imagery, which focuses on the suffering of the innocent, not the violence itself, we can see that humanitarian imagery leaves more space for spectators to understand themselves as potential actors or rescuers, not as actually complicit in the suffering; while some may experience these images through the lens of powerlessness, humanitarian imagery largely works by invoking a moral imperative to act. As Robert Meister (2011) suggests, humanitarian imagery works by eliciting compassion, and this compassion in turn makes one feel that *if* one had been there, one surely would have acted—and this then leaves one feeling good, or morally righteous. The humanitarian image channels this feeling of moral superiority, related to a sense of rescue. It does not allow room to feel complicity. And while atrocity photographs may activate people to respond to the atrocities, I am suggesting that humanitarian imagery does not cultivate a sense of shared involvement or collaboration.

The suffering of those pictured—for instance, the Sudanese child, or Alan Kurdi—posits vulnerability and need; it creates a hierarchical relationship between the innocent figure in the photograph and the spectator. The spectator has power; the photographed subject is pictured as powerless. In this sense, it both produces and depends on a hierarchical relationship. Innocence is figured as a form of weakness, vulnerability, and victimhood, which requires a moral response—not a political one, since the political world is rendered invisible. Indeed, these photographs play on the indignity of those who are powerless. Carolyn Dean (2015) helps render the relationship between hierarchy, indignity, and innocence clearer. As she writes, the indignity of maimed or violated bodies is critical among the many reasons that atrocity photographs make people feel uncomfortable. She suggests that dominant ideas of dignity assume wholeness; to show maimed bodies is to signal weakness and vulnerability. She argues that dignity and human frailty do not need to be considered opposites; vulnerability does not need to evoke contempt, and power and powerlessness do not need to be fully incommensurable. She wants to shift the contours of the concept of dignity—a concept I discuss in more depth in chapter 5. I draw on her insights here to suggest that photographs of innocence work as moral imperatives precisely because they rely on this hierarchy—that those who suffer are not human in quite the same way—they lack dignity. They elicit not just compassion, but pity. In the case of humanitarian images, this indignity is palatable because suffering is shown in the form of a racialized child or a woman, who, in most dominant imaginaries, are already considered weaker. As I have stated, innocence marks a position at the border of humanity: one that is simultaneously included and excluded, disparaged and romanticized.

In humanitarian photography, innocence's co-imbrication with suffering renders innocence a moral concern with real emotional power—but it always keeps politics outside the frame.

The International Refugee Regime

The concept of innocence emphasizes moral ascriptions over political ones, describing situations in terms of right or wrong, good and evil, as opposed to engaging more nuanced and complex political concepts such as justice. While aesthetics helps shape the contours of innocence and fill out its structures of feeling, how has the work of innocence become so politically salient? I traced the role of the new humanitarianism and victims' rights movements in the introduction, and still, without pretending to offer a comprehensive history of how innocence came to be so central, in this third section, I briefly discuss yet another intersecting history of this concept: I trace the shift from the political to the moral, arguing that it was encouraged by the institution of the current refugee regime. More specifically, I suggest that the refugee regime helped set up the system by which vulnerability and persecution became central to our dominant political worlds, opening the way for innocence to play a key role. This is in part because the Refugee Convention and the UNHCR (United Nations High Commissioner for Refugees) played a central role in the development of both human rights and humanitarian regimes, cultivating and circulating the role of innocence.

A refugee, by legal or UNHCR definition, is someone fleeing a well-founded fear of persecution, for reasons of race, religion, nationality, political opinion, or membership in a social group. But the category has always exceeded its legal core. Political persecution was seen as the exemplary form of persecution. The classic image of the refugee—often also understood as an individual in exile—centered the trope of hero; he was a freedom fighter, perhaps a revolutionary. Indeed, the ideal subject of the United

Nations Refugee Convention, which was created at the very beginning of the Cold War, was that of the Soviet refusenik—the individual attempting to flee communist regimes. This was the heroic figure of bourgeois individualism. But the longer tradition of refuge or sanctuary includes people who were petty criminals, subversives, outlaws, or otherwise forced to flee the polis. A refugee was an active, not passive, figure, even when this was romanticized. But over the past fifty years, the category of the refugee has shifted in meaning. Hannah Arendt ([1943] 1996) describes this change in her short but prescient essay "We Refugees." She writes, "Now, refugees are those of us who have been so unfortunate as to arrive in a new country without means and have to be helped by Refugee Committees" (110). Stated otherwise, the category of the refugee now evokes misfortune, pity, and helplessness. How did the figure of the refugee shift from heroic to pitiful? How did it become focused on suffering and victimhood?

The International Refugee Regime was formed in the interwar years, culminating in the 1951 United Nations Refugee Convention. The formation of this system opened the way for the concept of innocence to enter into politics in unprecedented ways. This was shaped by the political situation that resulted from World War I, which in turn led to World War II. As Hannah Arendt (1951) writes in her famous work *The Origins of Totalitarianism*, the interwar years created the problem of statelessness; from the breakup of the Ottoman Empire to the Russian Revolution, the international system radically changed, producing millions of displaced people, many of whom were subsequently denaturalized by totalitarian regimes. The League of Nations tried unsuccessfully to manage this by way of the Minority Treaties, which were mandates that gave minorities the right to appeal directly to the League of Nations or the UN General Assembly rather than the (often newly formed) nation-states in which they found themselves, but governments increasingly ignored these mandates, and they collapsed in the 1930s. The Nansen passport—designed as an internationally recognized refugee travel document by the League of Nations—was another strategy to allow those without nation-states to travel temporarily, but it was only available to Armenians (rendered stateless by the fall of the Ottoman Empire) and Russians (who fled or were rendered unwelcome by the revolution). It functioned from 1922 to 1938, and as legal scholar Berhman (2015b) argues, it was used more to track and surveil refugees than to enable their mobility.

As Arendt argues, during this time, the state became an instrument of the nation, effectively undermining the nation-state form whose goal was equal protection under the law; instead, the new nations were circumscribed by ethnicity or blood, leaving millions of people who did not belong to the majority nation or ethnicity without a home. While mass displacement was not new, what was different was the inability to find a new home, and the complete loss of governmental and legal protection that accompanied this new status. In this political landscape, a new figure appeared: the "apatride" or stateless person, or what Arendt calls "a legal freak." Naturalization did not work for these stateless masses, as the process was put in place for individuals, not populations. Similarly, those who were displaced could not be repatriated, as their homes no longer existed: for instance, Armenia had been swallowed up into the Soviet Union.

This set of political upheavals worked to undermine the ages-old informal tradition of asylum. While it certainly varied across geographies and cultural traditions, this informal tradition offered a safe space or sanctuary for those fleeing persecution of some form or another, and this was as true in the Muslim world as it was in the Indic and Christian worlds. It was considered sacred in many ways, outside the political realm, and inviable by armies or sovereigns. It may never have been meant for masses, but it did presuppose people fleeing for religious or political convictions (Berhman 2015b). By contrast, in the interwar era, the stateless were not fleeing because of their convictions, but because of who they were presumed to be—it was about their identity (as Jews or Armenians, for instance), not their actions. A 1933 Convention and a subsequent 1938 Convention both attempted to address the situation of stateless people, without success; the result, as we know, was mass extermination of many of those rendered stateless. While it built on these earlier attempts and conventions, it was only after the wars, in 1951, that the International Refugee Regime was finally instituted; while some might say that the impetus was to make a better world, there was also a pragmatic need to manage the fallout of the world wars.

As I read this history, a few important shifts in this 1951 Convention stand out to me as opening the way for the primacy of innocence. First, the regime instituted persecution at its heart: it requires a victim. Second, it embeds a focus on protecting individuals subject to persecution, not displaced populations. And third, an extremely circumscribed version of politics got built into the definition of asylum, effectively criminalizing politics and making asylum about suffering. Ultimately, the regime was put in place to safeguard the new liberal, democratic nation-state order from refugees; it was not put in place to protect refugees. Indeed, initially it was only for those "displaced by events in Europe," not for those fleeing colonial violence or any other kinds of persecution—those people simply did not count. Only in 1967 did it get amended with a Protocol to universalize its geographic range (Aleinikoff 2019). I briefly elaborate on each of these emphases in the Convention.

Persecution is the key to the definition of the refugee in the 1951 Convention. It puts the victim figure front and center, subject to injury or oppression. But not only is a victim required; there can be no refugee status without an active persecutor who targets the asylum seeker or victim. In this sense, victims of larger systemic collapse—such as civil war, poverty, or natural disaster—cannot claim refugee status. This refugee/victim figure must show a particular fear of persecution, not a generalized fear of violence (Behrman 2014). To shore up this idea of persecution, the Convention insists on proof that the person is a refugee so defined—when this was instituted in the 1938 Convention, it was the first time that evidence was asked before offering help. "Real" persecution was set apart from moving for "reasons of purely personal convenience" (Behrman 2015b)—for instance, Jews who chose to leave Germany before the official campaign of extermination began did not qualify, even though they left because the Nazi regime was not friendly to them. Indeed, Gil Loescher (1993) claims that the term "economic refugee" was used for the first time to describe such Jews leaving in the 1930s, and to distinguish them from real refugees. In this sense, the moral qualification we noted at the beginning of this chapter between "refugees" and "immigrants" was built in from the start, even though it has been differently emphasized over the years. Suspicion grounds the definition of refugee: the Convention sets up a distinction based on whether the adjudicators think someone is lying or not—whether they're genuine or "bogus." The basis of suspicion grounding the claim, and the fact that evidence had to be gathered, meant that the police were immediately implicated. This had precedents: as Arendt writes (1951, 285), in the interwar years, as the number of stateless people grew, so did the power of the police, since many of the laws did not apply to stateless people. Giving authority to the police over stateless people/refugees transformed their status into criminals, rather than as people who were simply without a home, and without national rights.

Second, the individual victim of persecution is at the heart of the Refugee Convention. People must show how they are *individually* targeted—the convention imagines the refugee as an individual, not as a population; protection was no longer provided to groups on the basis of nationality as had been the case prewar, for instance, for Russians fleeing the Bolshevik revolution (Aleinikoff 2019). In a Cold War sense, the West won out, instituting the individual subject of political persecution rather than the collectives suffering from a deprivation of socioeconomic rights. Once again, this excludes a vast number of people forced to flee their homes for reasons such as war or environmental destruction; it even excludes those who experience the secondary effects of persecution—that is, land taken away from a specific ethnic group, which then leads to poverty or famine. This individual approach continues to this day, shored up by the ever-growing, convoluted administrative and juridical infrastructure assessing asylum claims in the Global North, where individuals have the burden of showing their own specific and personal reasons for fearing persecution.

Finally, perhaps the most significant aspect of the Refugee Convention for my interest in how innocence later gets instituted at the heart of this regime is the way it embeds an impossibly narrow definition of what constitutes politics; the result is that the "real refugee" must be someone outside of politics. In particular, Article 1F of the Convention sets the parameters for politics as political exception, through its so-called "exclusion clause." Under this Article, to receive asylum, one cannot have been found guilty of a war crime or a crime against humanity, or serious nonpolitical crimes. But more relevant is that it excludes those prosecuted for violent acts against a state, repressive or not: Article 1F has been used to deny asylum to Islamic militants, Hamas activists, and Mexican guerilla fighters (Kaushal and Dauvergne 2011; Behrman 2014). According to Kaushal and Dauvergne (2011), this has created a criminalization of politics, which renders illegitimate the actions of anyone outside the sphere of liberal politics; one cannot commit a crime of violent resistance, as violence itself is cast as irrational—always outside the realm of the political. Anarchism is a case in point. We can return to Talal Asad (2007) to understand this condemnation of violence in politics as a distinguishing feature of liberalism, which pretends that it is radically separate from violence; the liberal state's job is to excise violence from the arena of politics and put it in the domain of war, and to incarcerate those who commit political violence outside of "war," labeling them as criminals, not political actors. However, as Asad demonstrates, liberalism is inherently about mortal violence, with the significant distinction that liberals feel *guilt* after committing "necessary" violence. This is understood as a sign of grace, and what distinguishes liberals from illiberals, or "terrorists." In this sense we must understand the International Refugee Regime, and the innocence it installs and relies upon, as a critical part of the liberal project.

Together, these three critical elements of the Convention paved the way for the apolitical, innocent victim to inhabit the heart of the refugee regime—which in turn served as a model and precursor for the broader human rights and humanitarian regimes, which have dominated much of the liberal political world since the 1970s (Moyn 2010; Fassin 2011; Barnett 2011; Slaughter 2007). The majority of refugees end up having to inhabit the space of the pathetic, passive victim, and a contradictory one at that, as it requires heroic efforts to even be acknowledged as a legal subject—that is, to simply get the right to prove one's persecution. Arendt describes the figure that gets created by the new human rights regimes, over the two world wars. Rather than active enemies, she describes the stateless—potential refugees—as people who appeared to be "nothing but human beings whose very innocence—from every point of view, and especially that of the persecuting government—was their greatest misfortune. Innocence, in the sense of complete lack of responsibility, was the mark of their rightlessness as it was the seal of the loss of their political status" (1951, 292). While she is suggesting that these stateless people are innocent and therefore rightless, in fact, it is precisely this figure that gets instituted as the subject of the refugee regime and the subject of rights after the wars are over. It is no wonder that the system of rights that grounded the 1951 Refugee Convention gradually transformed into a system of humanitarian assistance, where states are not obliged to deal with the causes of displacement, nor to include refugees as full members of their polities, with rights and entitlements (Aleinikoff 2019). And, we have seen how humanitarianism is grounded on innocence, and its forms of government.

∴

The history of the refugee regime is one among a series of histories that converge to center innocence in our political worlds. What is clear is that hierarchies and inequalities are a profound part of these histories and the visual regimes—racial, geopolitical, gendered, class, religious, and so on—and yet I have tried to show how these get eclipsed or concealed. Either they lurk outside the visual frame or they are rendered invisible by a blinding focus on the moral imperative to save innocents. The concept of innocence relies on the externalization of all that isn't pure or morally good—but the process of parsing what is "good" is simultaneously a process of creating and demeaning what is "bad"—and this produces a world full of inequalities. If we only care about innocence, we leave the political aspects of life unaddressed.

A focus on innocence—as in the focus on Alan Kurdi, the quintessential innocent victim—circumscribes who matters, and how. For Alan, focusing on his death as the ultimate shame leaves all others who died that day, including the rest of his family, unnamed, un-mourned, unaccounted for. A politics beyond innocence would create space to name, lament, or celebrate all those who are neither innocent nor guilty, hero nor victim—people who live ordinary and mundane lives; people who live difficult but joyful lives—all in a contaminated, impure, uncertain world. This is the space this book opens up.

CHAPTER THREE

The Science of Innocence

Absolving the Queer and the Criminal

In 1988, a big eight-by-twelve-foot cloth banner was draped over the Henry Street Settlement House on the Lower East Side in New York City, reading "All People with AIDS Are Innocent" (see figure 5). It was part of an art exhibition about AIDS, designed by the collective Gran Fury and inspired by the same ACT UP slogan, but the show was shut down because the banner was deemed unacceptable. Different explanations were given, some more innocuous than others—such as that the façade of buildings cannot take banners—but it was clear that the banner and what it conveyed were politically contentious. I was interested to see that this controversial insistence on innocence was recapitulated in the 2023 television series *Fellow Travelers*, tracing the lives of

FIGURE 5. "All people with AIDS are innocent" banner in front of Henry Street Settlement. Gran Fury, 1989. Manuscripts and Archives Division, New York Public Library.

two gay men from the era of McCarthyism to the crisis of AIDS; in the last episode, when Jerome, a young Black man, reveals that he is HIV+ and cries with shame, Marcus, an older friend, says to him: "You. Are. Innocent."

Innocence was the ground of debate about HIV/AIDS quite early on; indeed, this ACT UP slogan responds to the media usage of the term "innocent victims of AIDS," in reference to hemophiliacs, implying that they were not responsible for getting the disease. This framing cast those identifying as gay as guilty, immoral, and responsible for their own suffering. It enabled people to say, "Let them die." The banner tried to erase the blame, even if it did not entirely shift the terms of the debate. But in the 1990s, a discourse emerged that did shift the debate more forcefully: the argument was that people identifying as what we now label as "LGBTQ+" were "born this way."[1] They had no choice in who they were—their sexual preferences were biologically ingrained, or innate. Gay rights activists, communities, and supporters drew on new and emerging genomic science to make the argument, as well as brain sciences and sciences of sex difference. The stamp of scientific truth and immutability absolved gay people of responsibility—indeed, it rendered them innocent. They were victims of nature and its mysterious workings.

Around this same time, in the late 1980s and early 1990s, in the US, Ronald Reagan's War on Drugs and Bill Clinton's three-strike provision and his 1994 Crime Bill exponentially ratcheted up the population being incarcerated, targeting Black people, and "Black criminality" or Black guilt—indeed, the proportion of Black to white people in prison changed from 3:1 after 1976 to 6:1 in 1997 (Murakawa 2014; Reaven 2023). Drug use was framed as criminal, rather than an issue of health, addiction, or deteriorating social conditions. As many have argued, this was largely a backlash against the rise of Black Power and civil rights, which resulted in deepening and expanding the punitive state (Gilmore 1998). But in the 1990s, what has been called "the Innocence Revolution" began, with the use of DNA evidence to exonerate wrongfully accused death-row prisoners, and to challenge the fact that the criminal justice system worked fairly. The charge was led by the Innocence Project, founded in 1992 by Barry Scheck and Peter Neufeld at Cardozo School of Law in New York.

I started this chapter wondering if and how guilt can be transformed into innocence, curious as to whether innocence as an ontological status has any flexibility. I did not want to summarily dismiss the hope for rights that claims to innocence have offered many. But in following the two abovementioned cases, I realized that one's status—as innocent or not—seemingly never changes; we simply supposedly learn the inner and essential "truth" about someone. In tracing the transformation of guilt into innocence,

I discovered a set of epistemologies that are activated, which focus on knowing the nature or inner essence of individuals, with the goal of finding purity. In this sense, I trace the regime of knowledge that helps make innocence into an ontology—a way of being. I was fascinated to see that, perhaps counterintuitively, science plays a central role in this epistemology, and in building and maintaining a normative order that centers innocence, when it is surreptitiously combined with religious and liberal epistemologies and logics. This is an essentializing regime of knowledge, one that produces moralized (innocent) identities, sometimes individual and sometimes collective. But not only does this regime of knowledge help produce innocence, it often claims innocence itself—it purports to know the world in objective ways, decoupling agency, responsibility, and blame from both identity and behavior, and asserting a truth beyond any subjective claim. In the process, it works to exclude larger historical and structural factors that shape reality, from racism and homophobia to poverty and dispossession.

In following innocence as both ontology and system of knowledge, my goal is to better understand the central role innocence plays in maintaining the contemporary liberal political and social order, and how it produces a layer of Others who do not fit even as innocence promises to help adjudicate equality, inclusion, and justice. That is, even while a few may be absolved by claims to scientific or biological evidence, claims to innocence ultimately leave a very unequal set of systems intact. Indeed, the epistemology of innocence paves the road to the criminalization of many: Black people, poor people, and queer people, among others, insofar as it divides groups into a few "good gays" versus the many "bad gays"; and the exceptional and pure "innocents" versus the mass of true "criminals." Those deemed innocent can only claim that title if they are what Diana Meyers (2011) has called "pathetic victims"—those who have no agency and are unable to consent. This often assumes a certain form of cognitive impairment—passivity is a criterion of their innocence. Such victims cannot speak for themselves; "science" must do it for them, which reifies science as truth—this in turn opens the way to the dangers of biological essentialism, and ultimately, to the slippery slope of eugenics.

In this chapter I focus in on the US. I first discuss how some who identify as LGBTQ+ have worked against accusations of guilt and immorality, especially in relation to HIV/AIDS, by turning to biological explanations for being gay, and by transforming these into claims of innocence. After laying out the background to this story, I trace the regime of knowledge that has enabled and produced innocence, exploring the role of science and objectivity that work to take the question out of the realm of the moral into the natural; I then move to discuss the religious elements and the legal logics that work in consort with biological science to establish innocence. In the second case of "Black guilt," I look at the way the Innocence Revolution— and more specifically, the Innocence Project—has used DNA evidence and other forms of forensic science to exonerate those deemed guilty and condemned to death, and again, I trace how scientific epistemologies are used to produce, or rather, confirm, innocence; in this case, I look at how these are combined with liberal logics of racial innocence that focus on individual intent, rather than structural racism. While I read across these two cases to show the broad contours and reach of the epistemology that produces innocence, I want to be clear that innocence nevertheless works differently in relation to sexuality and race, helping invisibilize and reinforce structural racism, even as it offers a form of limited, normative hope to those who identify as LGBTQ+. Innocence always works in intersection with or in relation to other concepts and forms of power; as such, we see once again that it is best understood as part of a family of resemblances, wrought with contradictions.

I conclude the first section by discussing queer theory, and the second, by discussing abolitionism. Each of these posits a different view of how things could be, one that does not rely on an epistemology of innocence to absolve society.

Born-This-Way: Innocence by Immutability

The AIDS crisis was by no means the beginning of homophobia. The Diagnostic and Statistical Manual of Mental Disorders, or the DSM, medicalized and pathologized homosexuality as of 1952, classifying it as a form of sexual deviation; this was only removed in 1974. But AIDS certainly amplified this discrimination in an extreme way, condemning those who got the disease— initially identified in the US in the 1980s in gay men and intravenous drug users, a disproportionate number of whom were Black or Latine—as immoral, irresponsible, and blameworthy. AIDS was called "the gay plague," and it was treated with apathy by the Reagan administration. When it was responded to at all, it was mocked. The many, many painful and tragic deaths were not mourned nationally, because they were framed as justly deserved. In NYC there were only two graveyards that would bury people who died of AIDS—so great was the stigma. Because of the moralism defining the disease, at this time there was very little money put into fighting it or treating people—to be sure, this is what led to the formation of the Gay Men's Health Crisis and subsequently the famous ACT UP (AIDS Coalition to Unleash Power) in 1987, rousing people to anger, rage, and action;

they worked to change both perception and policy with a multipronged approach that included radical action such as die-ins.

After AIDS was identified in blood products and in different populations, including infants and those who identified as heterosexual, distinctions between those infected with AIDS appeared: there was suddenly a group designated "the innocent victims of AIDS," whose infection supposedly resulted from circumstances beyond their control. This was counterposed to those who engaged in "deviant" behavior and who were seen as morally responsible for their own demise. A thirteen-year-old hemophiliac named Ryan White exemplified this group of innocents; he was diagnosed with AIDS in 1984 after a blood transfusion. The media narrative was that he heroically fought the discrimination by people who tried to stop him from going to school and died in 1990 just before graduating from high school. Immediately after, the Ryan White CARE (Comprehensive AIDS Resources Emergency) Act was put in place to help those with AIDS, but its ideal recipients were people like him—not those who identified as gay. As both a child, and someone who got AIDS through a medical treatment, he embodied innocence; this was used to blame those who supposedly propagated the disease by their behavior—they were condemned as irresponsible and unworthy, and further denounced as guilty for the deaths of people like Ryan.

In the face of this deadly moralist discourse, it is not surprising that one of the major responses by people identifying as LGBTQ+ was to counter accusations of choice and responsibility with the impossibility of choice— indeed, with the certainty of immutability. It was also not surprising that this involved claims to innocence, since people were being called out as guilty and sinful. This happened by way of the search for a biological basis to gayness, and the search for a "gay gene." Biology—understood here as immutability, as essentialism—works with innocence as its moral counterpart, since it obviates the need for choice. It identifies an ontologically true interiority. This helped counter the increasing slippage and conflation between HIV/AIDS as contagious, and gayness itself as contagious—that gay people could recruit and contaminate others. As I will discuss, a series of concepts that describe the lack of agency and responsibility—from immutability, to the idea of "nature" and naturalness—have been mobilized in the overlapping realms of science, law, and religion, and woven into an epistemology of innocence that offers containment, and moral immunity. This epistemology plays on the slippages between concepts, and my goal is to understand how this works to produce moral judgments and secure innocence.

To be sure, questions about the etiology of gayness have a long history, with vigorous debates about whether same-sex desire is based in nature or nurture, and whether it is essential or constructed. Arguments made about characterological distinct "gay" types were countered by 1970s gay liberationists who repudiated this notion in favor of a Freudian view of human sexuality as "polymorphously perverse" (Bersani 1995). And yet, etiological quests for non-normative genders or sexualities are never neutral; too often, asking the question of why, or looking for a cause, leads into how to change people, or "cure" them (Saketopoulou and Pellegrini 2023). In this sense, Steven Epstein asks, "How do you protest a socially imposed categorization, except by organizing around the category?" (Epstein 1992, 254; see also Bersani 1995, 33). Similarly, in *The History of Sexuality*, Foucault writes of a "reverse discourse" in which "homosexuality began to speak on its own behalf, to demand that its legitimacy or naturality be acknowledged, using the same categories by which it was medically disqualified" (Foucault 1978). This is precisely what happened.

In the early 1990s, debates about nature and nurture transformed into a more rigid form, claiming an essence. *Science* published an article coauthored by Simon LeVay and Dean Hamer and a few others—what some have called "the gay gene manifesto" (Walters 2014). The former a neuroscientist and the latter a geneticist, and both openly gay, they argued that a gene on the X chromosome influences male sexual orientation. The conclusion—a reassuring one to them—was that to be gay was something natural, predetermined, *not* a choice. They fall on the spectrum of what Janet Halley calls "pro-gay essentialists," or those who argue for gay rights based on the idea that they are incapable of resisting their sexual orientation, and thus not responsible for it. As she suggests, this is an exoneration strategy (Halley 1994, 518).

There were several other studies in the 1990s that added to this evidence about homosexuality and gender identity, in what Nancy Ordover (2003) calls "the Great 1990s medicalization of Queerness": one on the size of the hypothalamus (LeVay 1991), others on endocrine systems and hormones, another on twin studies (Pillard and Bailey 1995), and so on. Arguments about gay genes are the strongest kind of essentialist argument possible—as Halley suggests, they are "essentialism-plus." Here, nature (as essence) provides the raw material and determinative starting and ending point for the practices and laws of the social. That is, gay characteristics are seen as not only biologically grounded, but fully determining of one's behavior. There is effectively no place for the social.

A great part of this was spurred on by the fact that the 1990s was also the decade of the Human Genome Project, which began in 1989 with the goal of sequencing and mapping the full human genome. This led to a search for a genetic basis in all kinds of behavior and personality types, including other sex differences (which has since been debunked).[2] While gayness was perhaps one among many in the search for genetic types, it had a particular moral reasoning behind it. As Suzanna Walters argues, while no scientist would claim a single determination (a gene, a hormone) for any other complex identity or set of behaviors, somehow this cluster of studies produced both a popular and a scientific perception that gayness (specifically male homosexuality) "is innate, immutable, predetermined in some finite and knowable way" (Walters 2014, 92). The translation of science into popular culture gave it a more brittle and binary frame, which assumed that the social categories themselves—gay and straight—were natural, timeless, and directly matched their biological correlates.

Born-this-way theories were appealing in various ways and to different constituencies, transforming exclusion into inclusion and guilt into innocence. For instance, it served to absolve the families—especially the mothers—of those who identify as LGBTQ+ for having borne "deviant" or pathological children. Earlier social and psychoanalytic theories of psychosexual development focused on deficient gender roles or pathogenic family life as the cause of homosexuality: bad mothering, absent fathers, failed Oedipal resolutions (Walters 2014; Sadjadi 2019). Parents were blamed for doing something wrong, and for having caused the gayness of their child (which was seen as a horrible thing). Born-this-way discourse offered relief, then, not just to those who identified as gay or queer, but to their parents; it suggests that whatever they did as a parent, it wasn't their fault. They bear no responsibility—they are innocent; their child was born this way and would always have been this way.

For all these reasons, as many scholars and activists argue, it is still hard to break with the now foundational and mainstream argument that if one is pro-LGBTQ+ rights, one has to believe that homosexual identity is (at least in part) innate, part of an essential nature or biology; that we have a core gender identity. As just one example, Lady Gaga's 2011 song "Born This Way" became an instant LGBTQ+ anthem, the motto of the generation, indicating that queerness was natural and immutable, not the result of something gone wrong. As Eve Sedgwick pointed out at the beginning of this turn to biology, this was motivated by a desire to insulate gay and lesbian identity from moral condemnation (Sedgwick 1990; Jakobsen and Pellegrini 2003). To be clear, a belief in being born-this-way is a view that is sincerely held even as it is politically strategic. Many queer people believe and narrate the true-ness of their own genders and desires, and this is honestly felt, even as these are part of larger cultural narratives (Saketopoulou and Pellegrini 2023). Various studies have shown that the more one believes that homosexuality is innate, the more accepting one is of gay rights; this belief in immutability has become "the mother's milk of gay rights discourse" (Walters

2014). This is based on a binary view of choice versus immutability, where choice has a negative valence, and is understood in a narrow liberal sense, as consumerist, and even fickle (Walters 2014). The danger of choice, of course, is that one can be subject to choosing otherwise, and compelled to conform to dominant norms. Choice does not counter the charge from the Religious Right that people who identify as queer are lapsed moral agents, who have willfully chosen to act contrary to God's law or the laws of nature (Jakobsen and Pellegrini 2003). In this binary decision, saying that "it is not my fault"—I am not guilty, I was born this way—is the position of liberation and moral respectability. Indeed, it is the position of innocence. Grounding homosexuality in "hard" scientific evidence suggests it can be moved into the amoral or supramoral realm of nature.

THE SCIENCE OF INNOCENCE AND THE INNOCENCE OF SCIENCE

With this history in mind, I turn to explore how innocence is produced and recognized by a set of knowledge regimes, piggybacking on and sometimes infusing the scientific logics of born-this-way discourses. After discussing this, I turn to the ways that scientific universality works hand in glove with religious discourses—sometimes they are indistinguishable, particularly in the case of the concept of the "natural." This gives born-this-way discourse a larger reach and a set of moral overtones. Insofar as the epistemology of innocence produces a lack of responsibility, the scientific, religious, and legal realms work in intertwined and overlapping ways to do this—and to allow for people (in this case, those identifying as LGBTQ+) to be absorbed (back) into the normative social order.

First, then, scientific epistemologies work in ways that locate their truths outside of time and space, in the realm of the universal and objective, untouched by morality—innocence as a concept draws on this same conceptual magic, transcending time and space, and it is fed and strengthened by scientific ways of knowing, even as innocence can give legitimacy to science and scientists. I will return to this latter point shortly.

Scientific knowledge works to enable and fortify claims to innocence by adjudicating entitlements. Science's appeal to the universal and objective is the most important criterion in claiming innocence—that is, the way it purports to take the problem out of the realm of the subjective and moral. Backed by the collection of evidence and the principle of falsifiability, science promises to give an idea of how the world *really* is—a faithful account of an objective world, independent of experience—and as such, it claims to stand outside political affiliations, identities, religious beliefs, moral judgment, and contexts. This gives scientific evidence a special claim on truth.

Objectivity is arguably the most significant element of this epistemology in relation to innocence. Historians of science Lorraine Daston and Peter Galison (2007) write about the concept of objectivity, and how it has only recently come to be considered an essential element of scientific thought, epistemology, and practice. That is, scientific knowledge was not always equated with objectivity, or with the erasure of the "knower." But insofar as it has become an unquestioned, hegemonic part of how we understand science, it is worth understanding how it enables and feeds what I am calling an epistemology of innocence.

Objectivity works to create the idea of impartiality, and disinterestedness. As such, science promises unfiltered access to the truth about the world (biological, physical, chemical, etc.), separating the knower from the knowledge. It offers a transcendent, universal truth that is available and applicable to all—regardless of where one sits in the world. Objective, scientific knowledge offers truth detached from desire, individual judgment, or will. It professes to be disembodied, unmediated. Scientific evidence is understood as detached and disinterested, so if there is science that suggests people are born gay, and that there is a biological substrate to homosexuality, this knowledge should be understood as unbiased. As Daston and Galison suggest, the development of objectivity in science always requires its double: subjectivity. The key is to separate subjectivity from one's way of knowing the world—or the relevant, contaminating aspects of subjectivity, which scientists are supposedly trained to do.[3] Objectivity promises emotional distance as well as lack of judgment. In this sense, it offers a truth that precedes and exceeds the social. While one individual or team may make a discovery, the object of discovery transcends that individual self. By way of its claims to objectivity, then, science is used to confirm innocence, and in this case, the innocence of those who identify as LGBTQ+—the knowledge it produces enables people to be absolved of responsibility.

While I have been arguing that scientific evidence helps secure claims to innocence, transforming amoral evidence into moral entitlements, innocence can also infuse these claims to scientific truth and authenticity; that is, in the claim to universality and disinterestedness, both knower and knowledge may also make a moral claim to be innocent, that is, outside of responsibility for the knowledge produced.

The current hegemonic idea of objectivity erases all marks of place and time: it is unmarked, unmoored. It assumes a certain disembodied reality: the producer of knowledge is mostly irrelevant, even if they have ethical attachments, as in the case of genetic research. In this sense, it is an easy slip for those who produce "objective" knowledge to also pretend to innocence about it; and yet knowledge always carries the traces of its location and production.

As Donna Haraway (1991) has written in her critique and reworking of dominant ideas of objectivity, this idea of science is a lot like God: omniscient, all powerful, a master, and monotheistic. In this sense, we can say that the claim to this kind of objectivity can itself be a claim to innocence, or lack of responsibility, accountability, or locatedness. As Haraway states, it depends on "the god-trick," where one is disembodied, and scientific vision is infinite. That is, scientific epistemologies can claim innocence for themselves, in a dialectical looping effect: they produce innocence, hence they are innocent. As such, it feeds into and shapes the epistemology of innocence, which is about both producing and assuming innocence.

To be sure, even as it remains dominant, this idea of science as objective and outside of history has been soundly critiqued; science studies scholars beginning with Donna Haraway and Bruno Latour (and Susan Harding, Troy Duster, Dorothy Roberts, Evelyn Hammonds, etc.) have long exposed how science can be imbricated in moves to power, not simply to truth. In the 1990s, post-structural and postmodern scholarship engaged in deconstructing science as a system of domination; they argued from a position that saw the world as historically contingent and socially constructed, and ultimately about rhetoric. But feminist science studies scholars like Haraway worked to reclaim a stake in science while heeding the warning call of these theorists. She did this by way of the idea of partial objectivity or situatedness; Haraway argued for a form of knowledge that is situated, responsible, accountable, and embodied—*non-innocent*—but that nevertheless gives us accounts of a real world that are more faithful to it than those offered by those on the Christian right, which deny realities like climate change. She and others like Sandra Harding (1986) argued for a "successor science" that offers a richer, more adequate, better account of a world, in order to live in it well and in critical reflexive relation to others. They were interested in both a radical historical contingency for all knowledge claims and subjects, and a commitment to faithful accounts of a "real" world that don't lose the materiality of things, from bodies to physical objects, because these also help in creating projects of material abundance and sharing, reducing forms of suffering, and enabling forms of freedom (Haraway 1991). In this sense, Dean and Hamer's important findings should nevertheless be read in relation to the political and historical contexts from which they emerge, as situated, contingent, and partial; and they should not be ashamed to acknowledge this context and the way in which it shaped their questions. This is part of the truth they produce.

What I am saying is that it is possible to have non-innocent and yet scientific and empirical ways of knowing the world; innocence relies on and props up certain dominant regimes of science, but there are ways to know the world responsibly. I will return to non-innocent forms of knowing shortly, by looking at queer theory.

"GOD MADE ME THIS WAY": INNOCENCE'S RELIGION

Let's turn to the second and less explicit aspect of the epistemologies that help us understand and produce innocence. While biology appears to be amoral or outside the realm of morality—precisely because of the concept of objectivity—in fact, biology gets mapped onto moral and religious distinctions and hierarchies, and sometimes, the two actually blend together. For instance, the scientific idea of genetic determination merges quite easily with "God made me this way"—this marries biological determinism with religious naturalism. Suzanna Walters (2014) argues that we should actually see born-this-way as creationist! In various progressive religious websites and other media, scientific evidence is combined with personal testimony to attest to the fact that homosexuality is "natural" and God-given; here, "natural" is conflated with "biological" and also with "immutability"—and if one believes that God has created nature, the transition is seamless. So much of what the movement for LGBTQ+ rights has fought against is the theologically grounded invocation that "sexual deviance" is "unnatural," so the concept of nature is a particularly fraught site. That is, in born-this-way discourses, it is hard to parse when nature is used as a materialist concept, and when it is a theological/Christian one: binaries between nature and culture are invoked, and nature and nurture, and the natural and unnatural—and these all get conflated. Indeed, there is a slippage between the idea of an "interior" self—the natural, fixed part or biological essence—and that of the soul; this is true even in the clinical literature, which in certain cases, as anthropologist and medical doctor Sahar Sadjadi has found in her research, uses brain and soul interchangeably (Sadjadi 2019). Insofar as one's pre-discursive interior is determined in advance, one is free to pick who determined it: God or biology. What is clear is that the blending of the two renders born-this-way a moral discourse as much as a scientific one, and it not only produces tolerance or understanding, it holds out the promise of innocence and absolution. This is a way of knowing that both pretends to innocence and produces innocence. This is particularly relevant when one is being labeled not only deviant, but criminal, as was the case with AIDS, where those identifying as gay or queer were seen as responsible not only for their own deaths, but for those of others, by "propagating" the disease.[4]

AGAINST CONTAGION: LIBERALISM'S INNOCENCE

Despite the feminist critiques of the dominant view of objectivity in science—and a lot of queer and feminist theory critiquing the medicalization of sexuality—many LGBTQ+ activists, liberal supporters, and others still claim a vision of science that is situated as innocent and disembodied in order to make their own claims to innocence. That is, innocence offers a position outside of both corruption and contagion; it offers fixity, certainty, purity, objectivity, omniscience, and most importantly, the lack of responsibility. To this end, in addition to being built out of scientific and religious epistemologies, innocence takes shape in relation to liberal and legal histories, including that of immutability.

Immutability arguments are not uncharted territory. More specifically, those who harness born-this-way discourses follow in the footsteps of antidiscrimination law, around which the civil rights struggle was built (Jakobsen and Pellegrini 2003). The idea is that "race" is a benign immutable difference, and it is illegal to discriminate against those who have not chosen to be a certain way and cannot change. Under the Equal Protection Clause, they constitute "a suspect class" (Halley 1994). To be sure, theories of immutability are continually evolving: that is, immutability used to be understood as an accident of birth, but others argue that the definition revolves around characteristics for which an individual is not responsible, from traits that cannot be changed to those never chosen. Immutability is not exclusively about biological traits; it can also refer to social categories assigned at birth. In this sense, an argument for immutability does not depend on a belief in race as a biological category, even as arguments about immutability for sexuality may rely on this. It can now even mean "a characteristic that is a core trait or condition that cannot or should not be required to abandon" (Clarke 2015, 4). As legal scholar Jessica Clarke (2015) argues, immutability is deeply connected to ideas of childhood innocence, and children as blamelessly subject to whatever they are given at birth.

In this sense, then, if homosexuality, like race, is an unchosen, immutable characteristic, one would need to be given similar protections. These arguments separate identity from practice—turning homosexuality into an essential identity. The turn to identity was pushed in part by the landmark case *Bowers v. Hardwick* (1986), which upheld the criminalization of same-sex sodomy based on the idea that it was a form of conduct, not an identity. So those who were fighting to decriminalize same-sex sex turned to identity-based protections. But identity claims have their own set of serious drawbacks for both race and sexuality; that is, claims to civil rights based on innate physical or biological characteristics are already extremely limited. In both cases (racism and homophobia), biology was the means of discrimination in the first place—via eugenics and racial science, and via the DSM, which characterized homosexuality as pathological. The turn to biology as a form of liberation may therefore seem to be a strange choice; but it is worth noting that it builds on the infrastructures and knowledge systems that are already in place, even as it attempts to reverse them. Nevertheless, it always threatens to reopen the door to these forms of discrimination.

Immutability arguments have traveled and been adopted as the route to acceptability in a range of areas; different sexual and gender identities now draw on this same reasoning, as the way to claim blameless recognition.[5] Julienne Obadia calls this the "liberal march of progress," where each marginalized identity seeks recognition on the terms that worked for those before (Obadia 2020, 290). Polyamory—a more recently claimed sexual identity—has followed this same route to respectability, with those who identify as poly now claiming that it is an innate and immutable orientation. Once again, arguments about immutability render sexual desires and choices innocent; in this case, an inability or lack of desire to be monogamous and "faithful" is understood not as a moral failing or as "cheating," but as simply part of an innate identity, where one has no choice. It renders this position respectable, and legitimate; indeed, it reinforces that polyamorists are worthwhile citizens, and that they can be included in the social order, without rattling, shaking, or bringing it down.

Born-this-way and immutability discourses follow the liberal strategy of progress by making standardized identity claims. But they are also fundamentally liberal positions and claims insofar as the goal is tolerance, and acceptance of those who identify as LGBTQ+ as respectable people. The born-this-way position implies that no one would consciously *choose* to be this way—and this indicates that it is a problem, a challenge to be explained, rather than a way of being that is desired, valued, or respected. As Bersani writes, "how we got this way" would not be asked "if it were not assumed that we ended up the wrong way" (Bersani 1995, 57). That is, the goal is not to shake the foundations of heterosexual normalcy, but simply to be accepted into the social order by way of the category of suitable difference. Suitability, to be clear, is fundamentally about innocence; differently put, these claims of tolerance are founded on assertions of innocence. These are innocuous forms of difference. This is part of how liberalism adjudicates inclusion and exclusion, normalcy and nonconformity; liberalism is streaked through with moralism, and difference is often adjudicated by way of claims to difference that are seen as innocent. In this way, liberalism is also shaped by epistemologies of innocence.

Paradoxically, while liberals have hung their hats on a form of biological essentialism in relation to sexuality, conservatives and the Christian right often follow a more social constructivist perspective.[6] That is, the Christian right has never fully let go of the idea that being LGBTQ+ is a choice; to be sure, they see it as an immoral choice that can be changed, with the correct commitment and faith. But they do not distinguish or demarcate identity from behavior or practice, invoking a sexuality that is curiously less fixed and medicalized than those who believe in narrow, born-this-way theories. Certainly, their ideas of social constructivism are significantly less nuanced than secular progressives and queer theorists (or "pro-gay constructivists"), who have an expansive and complex understanding of identity, becoming, and desire. Perhaps most significantly, these anti-gay constructivist theories have invoked and implied an idea of contagion—that being near someone who is gay can make one gay. It can spread. Unlike race, to which one cannot be converted, they believe that queer people can recruit others into their sexual orientation. As Bersani says (1995), homophobia is a response to an internal possibility, where racism is a response to an external threat. In fact, it is a mix of contagion and corruption that the Christian right fear—the added moral valence to corruption once again implies guilt. They draw on a mix of biological, theological, and social theories—but they nevertheless understand context as exceedingly powerful.

The Christian right and many of those who are against LGBTQ+ rights believe in a natural social order based on a binary sexual distinction between men and women; and they are terrified that the wrong social context and the wrong types of education can alter this in ways that will "ruin civilization" (Robcis 2015). This is the grounding fear behind the global backlash against what has been termed "the theory of gender"; this is the belief that if one is taught that gender is culturally and historically contingent, and if one learns about the relationship between gender and power, and the fact that women and those identifying as LGBTQ+ do not have equal rights—this will actually *produce* a gender-fluid world, erasing sexual differentiation and complementarity. Already, many blame the "theory of gender" for the legalization of gay marriage and same-sex adoption. As historian Camille Robcis recounts, in this world—what in French has come to be known as the "cathosphère" (Robcis 2015) to denote its predominantly right-wing, Catholic makeup—sex is biological. In other words, male and female are "natural," complementary biological categories, and we need to stick with the laws of nature if we are not to fall into a civilizational abyss. This increasingly global Religious Right believes deeply in the power of the social, even as they also believe in nature or the natural—they just want biological propensities to win, as they see it as the natural, and hence, moral, way.

Acknowledging the newest, fascist expressions of fear of contagion and corruption, and how these have metastasized into a fight against those who identify as queer or trans and against gender equality, feminism, and queer theory, we can see why pure and rigid theories of biological fixity are compelling, why they reassure by containing and stabilizing potentially contagious substances; indeed, here, the innocence of biological fixity is invoked against the idea of corruption of others, especially children. On valuing biological essentialism, curiously, the right and the liberals agree. Yet what are the effects of simply working within a binary framework of nature and nurture, choice and biology? Why is the innocence of biology necessarily the answer to claims of the guiltiness of choice—how about shifting the terms of the debate altogether?

THE FALLOUT OF INNOCENCE

The epistemologies that produce innocence, which work to stabilize people and identities into immutable, universal, and natural forms in order to take away responsibility and blame from other ways of being, have had a number of counterintuitive effects. Fighting discrimination on the basis of immutability has never worked; it has not worked in the case of race, or gender. Such discrimination continues, and while antidiscrimination laws may soften its expression, they have not touched the deeply held beliefs and the solid legal infrastructure that uphold the heteronormative world; this same set of discriminatory structures is easily evoked and reinstituted, as we saw with the 2022 "Don't Say Gay" law in Florida, which rendered discussions of LGBTQ+ issues and identities illegal in the classroom. People would do well to remember that slavery and segregation were based on the idea of immutable, natural difference! Similarly, by drawing on discourses of medicalization that have been used to pathologize and stigmatize homosexuality for decades, creating categories of deviance, disease, and aberration, born-this-way keeps alive the idea of biological inferiority.

If in the previous section I was laying out how the regimes of knowledge that produce innocence also structure the general ways people come to know the world, I turn now to the effects of these epistemologies at work in born-this-way discourse. I will discuss three examples of what the search for innocence has produced as part of its regime of knowledge. First, innocence works to perpetuate stereotypes of what it means to be queer, in turn producing an external, excluded Other. More specifically, I have already mentioned how born-this-way discourse creates immutable identities, rather than acts; it separates identity from behavior, in order to stabilize and contain queerness. This has several consequences. If identity is what is protected and immutable, it must be consistent and recognizable; the very act of looking for something predetermines the fields in which it will be found. In this sense, dominant ideas of what it means to be queer get instituted as an essential, transhistorical nature—what it looks like, what behaviors it entails, and so on. These scripts become the norm, and they produce their own abnormal. And sexual behavior gets imprisoned in a rigidly gendered sexuality, where the main thing that matters is genitalia, that is, same-sex sex, even though behavior is always embedded in non-sexual, cultural, and social forms (Halley 1994; Bersani 1995). We need only think of the stereotypes of gay men as inherently more feminine, lesbians as masculine, and so on, while other expressions and combinations of sexuality and gender are disqualified. The moralized language of innocence embedded in born-this-way discourses works on and with these stereotypes. If one does not follow the norms, one's behavior is framed in moral and often religious terms: one is guilty of choosing a sinful life. This divides people into the "good (innocent) gays" and the "bad (guilty) gays," creating only one acceptable way to be in the world—one way to innocence, one way to acceptance. Innocence has an ontological status; either one is innocent, or one is not—it functions as an essential identity, even as I'm tracking the epistemology that helps produce this ontology. But this always produces an external Other, an outside that is excluded.

This has serious consequences in many areas of life. Asylum offers a case in point. People fleeing homophobic violence and persecution can now apply for asylum, but this does not include everyone persecuted for their gender or sexual orientation. To be sure, the asylum regime itself is inherently exclusionary, as it works by making distinctions between deserving and undeserving, innocent and guilty, and so on, as we saw in chapter 1. But insofar as the refugee regime exists, the question is on what basis judges and organizations make the cuts: in this case, it covers the LGBTQ+ person, cleaned up and rendered innocent. To be gay in this sense is to be born this way, but this "biological" condition is only recognized in certain scripted, social forms: only masculine women or feminized men qualify, and only those who can perform their authentic, inner, or natural selves—those who have "come out." When people do not perform these stereotypes as expected, asylum proceedings in Europe and in Canada have judged that people are not "gay enough." In Austria, immigration officials denied an applicant on the grounds that "neither your walk, your behavior, nor your clothing indicate even in the slightest that you could be homosexual."[7] Needless to say, recognizing the persecution of legitimized LGBTQ+ asylum seekers in their "innocent" form also keeps intact the innocence of those receiving them—the nation-state accepting refugees can assert its righteous moral status, in a form of pink-washing, all the while keeping in place the racist structures that exclude the majority of immigrants and refugees.

Second, as a way of knowing, innocence opens the door to new forms of eugenics. Socio-biological arguments have a long history of being used to discriminate against those deemed inferior by "nature," including those identifying as LGBTQ+. This has been used to demonize and to sterilize people. With the ability to map and manipulate DNA, hereditarian arguments are even more dangerous. The gay liberation movements of the 1960s and 1970s fought against this idea, to de-pathologize and de-medicalize homosexuality and take it out of the DSM. When morality gets mapped onto biology and disease, it is not far-fetched to imagine eugenics policies that see "bad gays" as a separate biological problem—as having distinct and separate biologies—leaving them to be eliminated (however this happens—by selective abortion, genetic modification, violence, etc.), with the explanation that this will enable the innocent, good gays to survive. Anytime biology is coupled with innocence and guilt, it opens the way to an argument about the need or desire to alter people's biology for the good of society.

Third, epistemologies of innocence produce those who identify as queer as being without agency, as victims of higher forces. To return to the etymology, innocence means to be without intention, will, or knowledge, but also, "to be without desire." To claim innocence, then, is to deny that desire has anything to do with sexual preference; an identity as someone "innocent" must be divorced from action, desire, or will. The concept of sexual innocence extends this notion: it means to be innocent of sexual desire, inexperienced and ignorant in that realm. Indeed, it seems contradictory to claim sexual innocence as a foundation of any sexual identity. Yet the innocence claimed by born-this-way discourse only works if agency is removed; one's sexuality is determined before birth, before language, before history. Biology is understood as a pre-discursive force. Desire is largely irrelevant, as it is produced by biology. What is left, then, is what philosopher Diana Meyers (2011) calls the "pathetic victim": one who is innocent of any wrongdoing relevant to one's treatment; helpless in the face of the larger forces, in this case, biology or nature; and subject to deep suffering that one is not responsible for (i.e., wanting to be with someone of the same sex, despite it being considered morally wrong, socially unacceptable, and/or illegal). This kind of victim is pure, and blamelessly passive. Most importantly, this type of victim cannot consent. The passivity confers the innocence. In other words, if they are understood as actively choosing, they can be held responsible for their own predicament. Yet how can anyone be totally passive? Meyers argues that there are a few ways: through cognitive impairment, by being too young to understand, or by being subject to force, fraud, or coercion. The case of being born-this-way could be seen as a case of being forced (by one's biology), or otherwise impaired (unable to reason one's way through)—one is simply unable to choose. The pathetic victim is pure—desire cannot corrupt their innocence. But in this sense, they are also diminished in their humanity, insofar as they are incapable of reason, autonomous choice, or action—as previously noted, innocence places one at the limit of a liberal humanity, both denigrated (as incapable of being a thinking, engaged, active, or informed subject) and exalted (insofar as one is pure, and above the fray of corruption that comes with political life). Pathetic victims are not the kinds of people who are even capable of exercising rights or demanding justice. Innocence is at odds with any form of sexual motivation.

QUEERING INNOCENCE

It is difficult to argue against the epistemology of innocence that underlies born-this-way discourses, and yet it is also difficult not to, when one sees how it confines one's being in the world, and how it restricts forms of pleasure, embodiment, and relationality by understanding them to be effectively programmed. Andrea Long Chu (2018), a trans writer, states, "It must be underscored how unpopular it is on the left today to countenance the notion that transition expresses not the truth of an identity but the force of a desire. This would require understanding transness as a matter not of who one *is*, but of what one *wants*." Chu and other queer theorists do not believe in purity in any sense—pure desire, pure choice, pure biological determinism—but that these come together in ways that require a complex and historically contingent understanding of, and engagement in, the world. They see gender and sexuality as unfolding, dynamic processes that are not static or predetermined for anyone, but instead, grounded in complex psychic realities. The problem with writing out these processes, including desire, is that anyone who acts on it risks stigmatization, even criminalization. The late art historian and AIDS activist Douglas Crimp (2003) wrote about living with the perception that gay men had a sexual compulsion and a murderous irresponsibility around AIDS, and described the moralistic attacks on gay men's desires, behaviors, and public sexual spaces. He explained that the queer people who dare to critique gay marriage—one of the institutions that has solidified the claims to (sexual) innocence and belonging—are condemned as having brought AIDS on themselves. He quotes Larry Kramer making this argument in 1997, after people learned about the causes of AIDS: "We brought AIDS upon ourselves by a way of living that welcomes it . . . . Nature always extracts a price for promiscuity."[8] On one side is immoral desire and promiscuity; on the other is gay marriage, and self-contained, controlled behavior. In this context, Crimp asks, why do people still have unprotected sex? He suggests that even though the majority of gay men practice safe sex most of the time, everyone slips, "to express feelings of trust and intimacy, the desire to live in the moment, to overcome shame, to break the rules. Everyone feels these emotions, simply because we are human. To suggest that gay men should not feel them, or should put them aside for the rest of our lives, is to deny us our humanity" (Crimp 2003, 198). To be innocent all the time is to forgo being alive in all its complexity and impurity.

Queer theorists and activists offer an alternative: a form of anti-normative positioning that values the indeterminacy and changeability of ways of being in the world, rather than stable identities and ontological positions of gender or sexuality. But to be clear, they do not argue that desire is infinitely malleable or chosen. We should recognize that deconstructing identity does not undo the habit of desire or psychic reality—erasing identity altogether (as do some constructivists) also risks annihilating difference. According to Saketopoulou and Pellegrini (2023), gender formations are the phenomenological manifestations of psychic realities, but these are always provisional and mobile, because we are always in the process of becoming. All sex and gender identities and formations are historically contingent, informed by what they call "mythosymbolic" patterns. These collective patterns help each of us narrate ourselves—agency is shaped by historical and social realities in conjunction with psychic lives. As early queer theorists like Leo Bersani and Tim Dean have argued, modalities of desire are at the core of our very imagination of the social and political; they shape how people come together. Much queer theory joins sexuality and the political in an inextricable embrace; it does not try to tame or erase sexual desire, in order to fit a (hetero) normative social order. It recognizes a long continuum of loving and being together, not grounded on categories of innocence and guilt. Bersani argued for a queer specificity rather than identity—he called for an exploration of the links between specific sexualities, psychic mobility, and potentially radical politics (1995, 56). This position is neither essentialist nor constructivist; it takes seriously the psychic and social histories that structure ways of being, without turning to biological determinism. That is, as he says, even if we were straight or gay at birth, we would still have to learn to desire particular people, and not to desire others—the economy of desire is a cultural achievement, not a foregone biological conclusion. The search for innocence among LGBTQ+ communities forecloses not only desire, but possibility and change. Moving beyond innocence offers the chance to create more varied, open, inclusive, and imaginative worlds.

The Innocence Revolution: DNA Evidence and the Science of "Black Guilt"

I turn now to a second example of how innocence is produced by certain ways of knowing the world that work to absolve some people, while keeping a system of inequality and discrimination largely intact. If in the previous case, those identified as LGBTQ+ forged a collective moral identity grounded on the ontological status of being "born-this-way," rendering them innocent, we will see that this possibility is not available to people of color, especially Black people. With claims to innocence, regimes of sex and racialization overlap, but also pull in different ways. There is no collective absolution for Black people in this regime of innocence. Only a few specific individuals can and do work to transform accusations of guilt into innocence, but more importantly, they require experts and mediators to do the work for them. They are not considered reliable witnesses themselves. This demonstrates that some people and groups can better harness the epistemologies that produce innocence, as they are ultimately grounded in whiteness. In what follows, I give some background on the carceral system in the US, and the problem of "Black guilt" that the Innocence Project was established to address. Then I turn to thinking about the way the epistemologies that produce innocence work in this case.

In the US courts, the presumption of innocence was established as an essential right in 1895 with *Coffin v. United States*. In doing so, the Court referred to both Deuteronomy and Roman law, and claimed that the presumption of innocence is found in every code of law that has humanity and religion as foundation (*Coffin v. United States*, 156 U.S. 432 (1895); Reaven 2023, 412–13). In subsequent references to this founding case, it is repeatedly claimed that the presumption of innocence is at the base of any free society. In the US, there is a long tradition of full confidence in the criminal justice system, with the belief that wrongful conviction is nearly impossible. The common wisdom was that, while occasional error is inevitable in any human system, such errors in criminal cases are rare, aberrational, and not worthy of serious concern. As Justice O'Connor put it in her 1993 concurring opinion in *Herrera v. Collins*, "Our society has a high degree of confidence in its criminal trials, in no small part because the Constitution offers unparalleled protections against convicting the innocent" (Findley and Golden 2014, 4).

Despite this, in the US, Black people are habitually presumed guilty, rather than innocent: as many Black Studies scholars have demonstrated, Blackness and criminality are regularly conflated (Alexander 2010; Murakawa 2014; Wang 2018). As Ruth Wilson Gilmore has stated, this system has created some people who are "permanently not innocent, no matter what they do" (Gilmore 2022). In this section, just as with those who identify as LGBTQ+ who were designated guilty, I inquire into how people have fought to counter this ontology of Blackness with an epistemology of innocence—which involves understanding the world through certain scientific logics, undergirded, again, by religious and liberal logics. That is, while there is now an increasingly widespread, radical movement for the abolition of prisons and other carceral institutions like detention centers, and more specifically, the abolition of the conditions that produce them as the answer, one of the more significant earlier ways the brutalizing system of mass incarceration in the US was challenged was by way of a liberal, reformist "innocence revolution," which fights against wrongful convictions. But the process requires understanding the wrongfully convicted person as "truly" innocent, that is, pure or untainted. In this sense, the challenge to a collective ontology of guilt has been replaced by individual cases of innocence, ultimately keeping intact a system that is grounded on a priori assumptions of Black guilt.

Before proceeding, I want to clarify the difference in the meanings of innocence. I have so far foregrounded the ethico-moral concept of innocence—as experiential or epistemic purity—and largely approached it in the secular, liberal context. But the concept of innocence at play in the courts is based on its juridical version, to be free from specific wrong or guilt.[9] As already mentioned in the introduction, in contemporary legal terms, innocence is about acquittal—a decision to free someone from their criminal charge means that the judge or jury had a reasonable doubt as to the defendant's guilt. It may be based on evidence that exonerates the defendant, or not enough evidence to prove guilt. The goal is not to have absolute certainty. In theory, the legal concept leaves room for uncertainty; it does not presume absolute truth. This is not the case with innocence as an ethico-moral concept, which is much less conciliatory, since it constitutes identities in relation to purity. And in this case, science adds another epistemological dimension to this: when it is brought to bear to prove innocence, it too brings a different method and relationship to probability than the law. For science, "beyond a reasonable doubt," which is the benchmark for legal conviction in criminal cases, is not enough to validate a scientific claim—there needs to be certainty.

In what follows, I show that, in part due to the turn to science to prove innocence, the legal and moral definitions come to be conflated; those working for innocence in the prison system actually end up searching for moral purity, rather than reasonable doubt. We caught glimpses of this in the case of LGBTQ+ people who were deemed not only morally culpable for propagating HIV/AIDS, but criminally responsible. Innocent acts are often only recognized when attached to innocent ontologies. The consequences are such that a few exceptional individuals get exonerated, and the rest are seen as even more deserving of their punishment and imprisonment.

The conflation of Blackness and criminality has a long history. I draw on the many scholars and activists, particularly women of color (often Marxist) feminists like Ruth Wilson Gilmore and Angela Davis,[10] and organizations such as Critical Resistance that have already powerfully demonstrated how this conflation is informed by racial capitalism. They have rendered visible the process of systemic criminalization. Following their lead, my goal is to draw attention to the way that innocence has been brought into the story, and how it functions. As they show, the carceral state's link to slavery and its afterlives is overwhelming, even if it isn't entirely determining.[11] Enslaved people did not have civil rights, and they were rarely able to claim victim status in criminal cases—they were objects of criminal law, not the subjects of it. The civil death produced by slavery now extends into criminal law (Reaven 2023). The afterlives of slavery have been built into infrastructures that in turn work to deny the presumption of innocence to Black people and many other people of color—this denial was embedded in the Black Codes, which were put in place after the abolition of slavery and restricted Black people's right to own property, conduct business, buy and lease land, and move freely through public spaces; in vagrancy laws that criminalized unemployment; and in Jim Crow laws, which legalized racial segregation right up until 1968 and the civil rights movement. These were all based on the idea that Black people were lesser—that they were not full persons under the law. If they tried to assert equality, they were criminalized.

The 1960s and 1970s civil rights movements challenged this deeply entrenched, institutionalized racism, overturning many of these laws. It is no accident that soon afterward, in the late 1970s and 1980s, threatened by the gains of the civil rights movement and other forms of Black radical politics, Nixon and Reagan created the War on Drugs as a form of backlash, framing drug abuse as a criminal issue rather than one of health, social neglect, and state withdrawal. The War on Drugs associated drug use with Black communities, by focusing on crack. This turn to criminalization accompanied various forms of organized abandonment, from economic degradation of the urban peripheries to the divestment in Black communities, and the devolution of responsibility to local state and non-state institutions to fragment political struggles (Gilmore 2017). Punishment became the default solution to this broad array of social problems, and ending poverty was collapsed into fighting crime (Hinton 2017). In the 1990s, the Clinton administration continued this aggressive law-and-order rhetoric, expanding and deepening the punitive state, albeit coupling it with a discourse of empathy for some, while keeping a discourse of "super-predators" for others. This worked to separate out a few exceptional people from the mass of the guilty, suggesting that there were some innocents caught in this carceral web. As mentioned previously, the proportion of Black people in prison grew exponentially, and in 2004, 60 percent of young Black men without a high school degree had spent some time behind bars (Murakawa and Beckett 2010).

In this context of the continued criminalization of Blackness and the growing carceral state, the Innocence Project was initiated, as part of what has been called the innocence revolution; others have called it a new civil rights movement, as it professes to recognize the deep racism built into policing and the prison system. Nevertheless, it is important to recognize that it has always been reformist, rather than about radical change; by not addressing the underlying causes of the racial and economic order and its systemic manifestations in the law, it keeps the main systems of inequality intact. This liberal movement called into question the belief that all people receive equal justice—that all are granted the same presumption of innocence. More specifically, the idea of an "innocence revolution" describes the moment when, starting in the late 1980s, lawyers and judges, and increasingly, the American public, began to question the perceived infallibility of the criminal justice system. Drawing on new forensic DNA technology that became available in the mid-1980s—part of the same scientific and technological advances of the Genome Project that informed born-this-way discourses—lawyers began to find evidence of mistakes in death penalty cases, leading to exonerations. This relied on what they understood as new, unprecedented scientific certainty, the result of these new technologies. In 1989, David Vasquez and Gary Dotson became the first Americans convicted of serious crimes to be exonerated by post-conviction DNA testing. The governor of Virginia granted Vasquez a pardon at the joint request of the prosecution and defense when DNA testing on crime scene evidence linked the rape and murder to another man who had committed two other murders.[12]

By the early 1990s, DNA evidence had led to three exonerations of people on death row; exonerations happened primarily in cases of rape and murder, since rape cases are most likely to have the necessary biological or DNA evidence. By 2002, there had been twenty-five exonerations, and since then, exonerations have not subsided—according to the National Registry for Exonerations, as of 2023, there had been 3,565 since 1989.[13] This led to what some have called "innocence consciousness": suddenly there were stories of wrongly convicted innocent people on TV, in dramas like *CSI/ Law and Order* and *The Good Wife,* and in newspapers (Zalman 2011; Findley and Golden 2014).[14] Post-conviction litigators began to review evidence for innocence in a wider number of cases. In 1992, Barry Scheck and Peter Neufeld started the first Innocence Project at the Benjamin N. Cardozo School of Law in New York City, using the new DNA technology to prove innocence, and in so doing, they laid the institutional foundation for the Innocence Movement. They write about this in their book, coauthored with Jim Dwyer, *Actual Innocence* (2000), calling for changes in the American criminal justice system, and for the creation of similar projects across the US. Since that time, Innocence Projects have spread to twenty-five states, and they have expanded their network to other common-law countries like Canada, the UK, and Australia. Indeed, part of their appeal is that they have bipartisan support—everyone loves to identify with the innocent—it feels *good*. Unfortunately, as we will see, this does not work to create equality.

FORENSIC INNOCENCE

As with the born-this-way discourses described in the previous section, the appeal to the universal and objective is seen as the most effective, and really the *only* way to prove "true" innocence—indeed, to undo ontologies of guilt—by moving away from value judgments, identities, political affiliations, and belief systems. Once again, we see the epistemology of innocence at work here, relying on scientific knowledge; in this case, it is forensic science, in addition to biological science. Nevertheless, the claims to truth and objectivity are the consistent thread, and they are what make the difference when arguing for innocence. As Hlavka and Mulla (2021) write in their book on the role of science in sexual assault adjudication, forensic evidence is regarded as independent, dispassionate, and objective; and as such, biological evidence has taken on new significance. Indeed, one of the reasons for the turn to all kinds of science, including forensic science, is a distrust of human testimony; the object or biology (depending on the kind of forensics) is believed to be a more reliable witness. As expert witness, the scientist gets assigned an almost mythic status, as objective, unbiased truthteller (Hlavka and Mulla 2021, 180). This shift must be understood as part of a set of racialized histories, where certain voices are not trusted. As Eyal Weizman (2011) writes, forensic science can turn into a form of fetishism, where an inordinate amount of power and agency is attributed to objects, DNA, or technologies.

According to the deputy executive director of the Innocence Project, Meryl Schwartz, the project was put into place to counter what they understood to be a creeping reversal of the presumption of innocence—that is, to counter a turn to the racialized assumption that certain people (i.e., Black people) were a priori guilty. They wanted to show that innocence still matters.[15] They argue that they are ridding the criminal justice system of unfounded practices and replacing them with science-based evidence.[16] They began with the advent of DNA technology, which offered them a tool with which to push back against racist analyses; they saw forensic evidence as a way to make a case more objective. As Stanford legal scholar Lawrence Marshall—and former legal director of the Center on Wrongful Convictions at Northwestern University—has written, the innocence revolution was "born of science and fact, as opposed to choices among a competing set of controversial values" (Marshall 2004, 574). Once again, we see the idea of science providing a way to transcend social, political, and moral contexts to get us to the amoral truth—this is presumed to be the only route by which to actually know innocence. The Innocence Project's legal team makes a point of staying up to date on the latest scientific technologies, establishing a Science and Research Department. They hold firmly to this as the way to "truth" and see wrongful guilt cases as the result of a lack of objectivity. In a special 2019 issue of the Royal Statistical Society and American Statistical Society's journal *Significance*, which the Innocence Project helped coordinate, one of the articles discusses the question of objectivity in relation to innocence. The author, Karen Kafadar (2019), suggests that the key problem before the innocence revolution was a lack of objectivity in procedures. While she argues that there was no problem with the scientific technologies themselves, there were no objective standards, giving too much leeway to the examiner. Once again, as we saw with the role of science in born-this-way discourses, science, by way of objectivity, promises unfiltered access to the truth, supposedly detached from individual racism or bias.

The case of Steven Mark Chaney, whom the Innocence Project helped exonerate in 2015, serves as an example. As they recount in their materials, Steven Mark Chaney was convicted in 1987 in Texas for a grisly double murder based on bite marks on the victim's body and sentenced to life in prison. Two forensic dentists supposedly matched Chaney's teeth to the bite marks. However, in 2015, drawing on new forensic analysis, the Innocence Project challenged this evidence. In the appeal, the Texas court found that "the body of scientific knowledge underlying the field of bitemark comparisons evolved in a way that discredits almost all the probabilistic bitemark evidence at trial," and went on to find that the new "bitemark evidence, which once appeared proof positive of . . . Chaney's guilt, no longer proves anything."[17] Their investigation resulted in a moratorium on the use of bite mark evidence in future criminal prosecutions in Texas; they argued that it is a technique that cannot be scientifically validated and that it is inherently unreliable. Investigators cannot determine when an injury is caused by a human bite, nor what the source of the injury is. As Chris Fabricant, director of strategic litigation for the Innocence Project, stated, "We are encouraged that the law is beginning to catch up with scientific reality. The scientific community is unanimous in concluding that bite mark evidence has no place in our courtrooms and has all too often been used to destroy the lives of innocent people, convicting them for crimes they had nothing to do with. Hopefully, this decision will be a turning point in purging unscientific and unreliable forensics, which has no place in any criminal trials, from our legal system."[18]

After twenty-eight years in prison, Chaney was released, and in 2018 he was declared "actually" innocent (i.e., not just legally innocent—see below). The Innocence Project says their work set a precedent against the use of unscientific evidence in the courtroom. In this sense, they suggest that it works to produce system reform by fighting for more sound procedures for everyone, from access to DNA testing, to police procedure reform in relation to eyewitness testimony; and they have also pushed mandatory videorecording of interrogations. After his release, as they also recount, Chaney spent the remaining years of his life until he died in 2021 as a "devoted prison missionary" ministering to those who were still incarcerated, composing and singing gospel music to them. He was a devoted husband, full of love, not bitterness.[19] In other words, this portrait of Chaney reinforces the idea that he was always someone good—his essence was innocent; his innocence was not simply legal, but about who he was as a person. The epistemology of innocence relies on the confusion and conflation of legal and moral logics.

To be clear, there are several versions of juridical innocence at play here. These include actual or factual innocence, and legal innocence. As we saw, Steven Mark Chaney was declared not just legally innocent, but *actually* innocent. Actual or factual innocence means that the defendant did not commit the crime they are accused of, even if found guilty at trial—one might say they are "truly" innocent. Legal innocence is where one starts: with the presumption of innocence. For legal innocence, as stated previously, one only needs to be acquitted based on reasonable doubt. In the Innocence Project, these definitions get mixed up—legal innocence slides into moralized versions of innocence, by way of actual or factual innocence. Once again, this is enabled by a reliance on scientific methods, which require a different standard of evidence. The key point is that in the US, the Innocence Project now works only with actual innocence, to show that some people do get wrongly accused. The belief in science and its infallibility enables the idea that we can access *actual* innocence, and indeed, that this is the ultimate standard, even though it exceeds legal standards. By insisting on actual innocence, legal innocence risks losing its value, with the result that many more people are incarcerated in the process (I will return to this).

The turn to science by the Innocence Project reinforces the idea that we should not and cannot trust people's testimonies; those accused must be spoken for, by an "objective" source, an expert who knows better and can be trusted as neutral. Perhaps paradoxically, innocence imposes an epistemology of experts and expertise; but here, the scientist replaces the lawyer as the most legitimate expert. Whatever the case, people cannot speak for themselves.

I want to be clear that I believe in the importance of scientific evidence; but I follow the feminist science studies scholars I discussed earlier in calling for scientific knowledge that offers faithful accounts of the real world, but that is simultaneously situated and responsible. If people can prove their innocence in this way, all the better. But as Donna Haraway and others have pointed out, the concept of objectivity sustains the idea that we can have impartiality, and a clear line of access to the truth about the world, separating the examiner from the evidence, the knower from the known. Those with the Innocence Project believe that before the founding of the Project, the evidence could be interfered with by subjective, potentially racist, people. But with new objective standards in place, they believe that they have access to the unmediated truth. True innocence can be accessed. They suggest that by way of science, all forms of abuse and injustice can be exposed. But the corollary is that if it isn't found out and phrased in scientific terms, people are not innocent, and they should be in jail. This erases the fundamentally important *processes* of criminalization that render some people more likely to be policed, arrested, and ultimately, locked up.

RELIGIOUS INNOCENCE IN THE US CONSTITUTION

While we have seen how innocence is identified and facilitated by way of medical and forensic science, just as in the case of born-this-way discourses, this is aided and infused by the US's dominant Christian tradition, where innocence and guilt are part of a deeply embedded moral order. In particular, religion and law, as grounded in the American Constitution, are not so easily separable, and the role of innocence in one colors that of the other. The US has a complicated relationship to the separation of church and state; as legal scholar Philip Hamburger (2002) has argued, the First Amendment did not enact this separation, even though it officially provides that Congress make no law respecting an establishment of religion or prohibiting its free exercise. This separation was fought for later by Protestants who joined a motley coalition including anti-Christian secularists, to stop the influence of Catholics, but not ultimately to take religion out entirely. The founders were not defending individual liberty against religion, so much as they were defending Protestantism against Catholicism. Indeed, the US founders wanted to protect religion from government more than the other way around; the US promotes religiosity, even as it tries not to promote one specific religion over another (Feldman 2005).

We see the explicit encroachment of evangelical and other Christian norms on the legal order by way of the Supreme Court's overturning of *Roe v. Wade*,[20] and the challenges to gay rights; the Supreme Court all but explicitly overturned the "Lemon test," a 1971 precedent that protects the First Amendment by prohibiting the establishment of religion.[21] In the US House Committee on Education and the Workforce hearings about the Palestine solidarity protests on university campuses in spring 2024, Georgia Republican Congressman Rick Allen asked the president of Columbia University about a passage in Genesis 12:3, and the covenant with Abraham that blesses Israel, and whether she wanted Columbia "to be cursed by God."[22] There could be no more explicit conflation of legal, political, and religious orders.

Insofar as religion is increasingly explicitly a part of the legal order, the sacred place that innocence holds in the moral and religious order is transposed into the legal realm and upheld in both moral and legal terms. In this sense, to disrupt the centrality of innocence is to also threaten a particular type of political and social chaos and disorder, in the minds of many (Reaven 2023). Differently stated, the certainty offered by the science of innocence is reinforced by the righteousness of this moral order, and the central place innocence holds in it.

RACIAL INNOCENCE IN LIBERAL LAW

As with born-this-way discourses, the innocence revolution is sustained by a form of liberal logic and reasoning and the belief in reform—that we just need to get the process right, to establish true right from wrong, and then justice will be done. Only the right people will go to prison. The goal in establishing better scientific standards in the examination process is to "identify the true perpetrator" (Kafadar 2019, 18) and, ultimately, to "raise everyone's confidence in the criminal justice system" (Kafadar 2019, 20).

On the one hand, the innocence revolution, and its leading proponent, the Innocence Project, have succeeded in calling the death penalty into question in the US, by showing how often innocent victims are falsely accused. But on the other hand, the innocence revolution is still guided by a belief that the problem is one of evidence being improperly evaluated; they believe that the issue does not lie with the criminal justice system more broadly, or with racialized stereotypes of people, which help determine their innocence and guilt. Those involved with the Innocence Project believe that discovering and protecting actual innocence is the ultimate goal.

Perhaps it is unsurprising, then, that the innocence revolution happened at the same time as the turn to a form of liberal, racial penology, which understands racism as a problem of individuals, and individual intentions, rather than one that structures our very society, creating and enabling carceral geographies.[23] That is, the innocence revolution draws on liberal epistemologies to make it work; innocence is sustained, valued, and protected by liberal logics. In relation to the criminal justice system, Murakawa and Beckett (2010) call this phenomenon "the penology of racial innocence." They use this phrase to describe what they see as a paradox: on the one hand, a belief that racism is waning—that, post–civil rights, the US has entered a color-blind society, and that racism only remains in the bad intentions of individuals. On the other hand, it describes the opposite trend: that of an expansion of the criminal justice system, and indeed, penal control and surveillance more broadly—including immigration imprisonment and detention. There are various reasons for this enlargement, including the turn to the War on Drugs and broken windows policies, both of which allowed enormous police discretion and a widening carceral net. They describe how in this context, antidiscrimination law changed, demanding proof of intent to discriminate, narrowly defined, with a very high bar.

This paradox ensures that racism is underestimated; that larger contexts of racial power are rendered invisible. Not only does this cast institutions themselves as racially innocent, it frames the juridical problem of innocence—that is, wrongful guilt convictions—as one that can be rectified at the individual level, with the appropriate objective, scientific procedures. The demographics of exonerations show that Black people are only 13.6 percent of the American population, but they are the majority of defendants wrongfully convicted of crimes and later exonerated. Indeed, according to the National Registry of Exonerations, more than half the people exonerated between 1989 and 2022 are Black. Black people are seven times more likely to be wrongly convicted than white people.[24] The belief is that racism is addressed by these exonerations; and yet instead, this individualized logic renders invisible the systemic racism that assumes Black guilt, as do the very processes of criminalization, from organized abandonment to the legal infrastructures that assume and are grounded on it. Just as with LGBTQ+ people, the search for innocence is about reform, not about shaking up or exposing the system. It assumes that the problem with the carceral system is one of individual, potentially racist mistakes that can be rectified with scientific investigations. In this sense, the innocence revolution is primarily about getting the evidence right, addressing instances of bias in specific individual cases, and when necessary, addressing discrete, individual instances of racism that led to the wrongful accusation. The epistemology of innocence harnessed by the innocence revolution casts the blanket conflation of Blackness and guilt as the problem of a few individuals. In other words, it responds to the system-wide problem of structural racism, where one group of people is condemned as ontologically criminal/guilty, with an individual-level response. The innocence of a few replaces the guilt of the many. This epistemology holds that overall, while we may need reform, the larger system should stay intact.

This liberal turn away from systemic critique happened even in the Black community, where, as Jackie Wang (2018) recounts, following Loïc Wacquant (2007), there was a dramatic shift in the official line of the NAACP and the Urban League starting in 1986, when they switched from identifying imprisonment as a central issue and a structural and political problem to one of individual responsibility (Wang 2018). Black convicts suddenly became "them" instead of "us" in official NAACP discourse, to distinguish between innocent and guilty Black people. As both authors suggest, this was also shaped by class politics, and the development of a Black middle class who wanted to distinguish themselves from the lower classes by showing that they had no sympathy for criminals. A liberal focus on individuals and technicalities enabled the reframing of the problem of mass incarceration as one that needs to find the truly innocent and save them, not to dismantle the system. Indeed, the very concept of innocence enables and justifies this focus on the individual level, at the expense of the collective and structural. The epistemology of innocence is deeply intertwined with liberalism, and with ways of knowing the world that start and end with individuals.

FURTHER FALLOUT OF INNOCENCE

As part of the innocence revolution, science professes to offer certainty. And yet, after a few decades of drawing on science-based evidence, what do we see? In the case of sexual assault, Hlavka and Mulla (2021) argue that forensic science repeatedly fails to resolve questions of guilt and innocence, having little impact on sexual assault trial outcomes. Instead, they suggest that it works to fix racialized populations in place, imprisoning Black defendants and generating permanent court records. The focus on science ends up being exclusionary, rather than about comprehensive justice. People have come to similar conclusions when evaluating the Innocence Project.

While the Innocence Project has fought to institute DNA testing statutes in all states, enabling wrongfully convicted prisoners to demonstrate innocence and secure freedom, it turns out that DNA evidence is only available for a tiny fraction of cases, rendering these cases exceptional. Furthermore, the main source of exonerations is not attributable to DNA testing—the great majority of exonerations come from false accusations (legal scholar Joseph Margulies [2018] suggests that as of 2018, only 459 exonerations have come through DNA, whereas 1,731 have come from non-DNA sources). Yet, these statutes that allow one's status to be reviewed are limited to DNA evidence and make no provision for prisoners to examine other types of evidence that might have led to wrongful conviction. That is, an epistemology of innocence grounded in forensic science and DNA analysis immediately eliminates most of those who could be legally innocent. Margulies (2018) lists the various other hurdles that make it almost impossible to challenge a guilty verdict, such as the fact that the prisoner must make a preliminary showing of innocence before they can get hold of DNA evidence—that is, they must effectively prove innocence before they have access to the key evidence. And in other places, the statutes limit challenges to one or two years after conviction, which is extremely brief.

While the turn to DNA technology is offered as the answer to breaches of justice in the criminal system, and the way to challenge racist practices and blanket understandings of Black people as guilty, this way of knowing and thinking already sets up most people to fail. Scholars have shown how there is no need to explicitly name race and class for them to play a role in the courtroom—this is true, from who gets access to courts and understandings of court processes, to the way the court is invested in appropriate gender roles and "ideal" (heteronormative) households when they evaluate guilt. In the latter case, racist stereotypes about Black families are seen as valid, particularly in the cases of sexual violence (Hlavka and Mulla 2021).

But it does further damage. Insofar as the Innocent Project only takes on cases that involve DNA—a belief in the "irrefutable proof" of science[25]—they only take on cases of people who are truly or factually innocent. And in looking for actual or true innocence, they end up threatening the principle of the presumption of innocence for all. That is, they have begun to hold people up to this exceptional standard. They look for a form of purity (*real* innocence) that is grounded not just on legal, but moral distinctions. That is, even if Innocence Project advocates are working in the courtroom, with legal concepts, a desire for moral purity compels their work, turning the concept of innocence that they use into an ethico-moral one. They are looking for people whose character is unimpeachable; this has moved beyond actions to identities, and to innocence as a moral identity—and even further, as an ontology.

In an article "In Praise of the Guilty Project"—and critiquing "innocentrism"—Abbe Smith writes about a flyer put up by one of the chapters of the Innocence Project, seeking clients, but stating in big font, "We do not help guilty inmates lessen their sentences or get off on technicalities." This language purports to distinguish the deserving from the undeserving, the real from the malingerers or the fraudulent; and such moral distinctions get repeated in remarks like that of one of the founders, Barry Scheck, who stated that "he had not represented a guilty person in twenty years" (Smith 2010, 321). Because of the focus on DNA evidence as unmediated access to truth, the Innocence Project comes armed, as Smith states, "with both justice and certainty, a lethal combination" (Smith 2010, 322). Here, we see moral distinctions not only between the innocent and the guilty, but also between the lawyers, particularly those who claim their own version of innocence by way of helping only those they deem factually innocent, demeaning the rest in the process. In going for true innocence—for the clients "who were in the wrong place at the wrong time and are unfortunate victims of imperfections within the American criminal justice system," as stated by the same Innocence Project flyer—there is a claim to virtuousness, to self-righteousness.

There is no room for political complexity in those defended by the Innocence Project, or in the underlying epistemology of innocence; no place for the not-quite-innocent, who, with the presumption of innocence, still deserve to be fairly treated. Perhaps most importantly, the processes of criminalization are rendered entirely invisible; that is, how certain neighborhoods and people are policed more than others, how certain schools have no funding, and how history has mapped privilege and opportunity onto other places and bodies. We end up dealing with ontologies, like Black guilt, which are presumed timeless, embedded in people's DNA. Even as born-this-way discourses render innocence possible for certain queer people, the Innocence Project does nothing to challenge such understandings for people of color; rather, it focuses on people who are untainted and separate them out from the rest—that is, those who have not committed a crime, full stop—not those who might have been unfairly sentenced, or sentenced for something different from what they did, or who have extenuating circumstances that might explain why they did something deemed illegal. It does not focus on local-level crimes, and those held for violating parole or minor drug crimes, which bloats the prison population. This emphasis on the pure reinforces the idea of good and bad criminals, just like the distinctions made between good and bad immigrants; good and bad gays; or the deserving and undeserving poor. This allows for the further mistreatment of those designated "bad." In looking for truth, rather than proof, this type of innocence slips from legal to ethico-moral, and once again, moves to create distinctions between people rather than instituting equality for all.

I am not trying to defend the law as the best way to achieve equality and social justice, because I do not think it is—the law is grounded in liberal logics, which places its full weight on the protection of individuals and liberties, without touching structural inequalities. Indeed, as abolitionists have argued, the law is complicit with the state in the abandonment of rights for poor people and people of color. But it is worth noting that the Innocence Project does not even respect the underlying principles of the law. It searches for and decides who is innocent, and then represents them as the most deserving, rather than representing all clients, and allowing the legal process to determine innocence or guilt. Proliferating Innocence Projects and training new law students to work in these clinics undercuts everyone's rights, shifting the limited resources available to defend those without means to those who are seen as factually innocent, and training young lawyers to fight for this kind of "pure" justice. It institutes not just the search for innocence, but an epistemology of innocence in the law that ensures that a few get saved at the expense of the many. Only a few will have access to the presumptions of innocence. Furthermore, as Smith writes, this undercuts the issue of wrongful convictions as well, insofar as one can be wrongfully convicted without being factually innocent: if the person is guilty and there is demonstrable unfairness, it's still a wrongful conviction (Smith 2010). But these mistakes are ignored in the search for the "actually" innocent.

The epistemology of innocence is simply not flexible enough to address the injustices of the ever-expanding carceral system, where certain people are born into carceral geographies and forms of political and economic abandonment. The slippage in the concept of innocence (from legal to moral) precludes struggles for a different kind of justice—for more systemic equality. Rather than framing the problem as inequality created by racial capitalism, the innocence revolution defines the problem as one of locking up the wrong people. As Reaven suggests, "the most potent utility of innocence is the way it sharpens the blameworthiness of the guilty by pitting them against an 'innocent ideal'" (Reaven 2023, 409).

As with the many examples of innocence we have discussed thus far, there is a focus on individuals, not the collective nature of the injury. Indeed, as discussed in the introduction, "victimhood" in this context primarily describes victims of *crime*, not victims of police violence or other kinds of structural violence (Smith 2010). Paradoxically, one needs to be recognized as innocent before being considered a real victim. And as we have seen, innocence is nearly impossible for people of color, but especially for Black people, where ideas of Blackness and guilt remain locked in a death embrace. While a collective identity could be forged in the case of LGBTQ+ struggles as being "born this way," that possibility is ruled out here; the entrenchment of innocence as white in the US overrides all other logics, and every other case to the contrary must be exceptional. The Innocence Movement has only reinforced this association, by suggesting that only a few exceptional Black individuals in the carceral complex are innocent and deserving of better lives. The rest belong in cages.

ABOLISHING INNOCENCE

So, how else might we tackle the conflation of Blackness and guilt, and the problem of ever-expanding carceral geographies? Abolitionism offers a map that takes us out of the language of innocence. As Ruth Wilson Gilmore suggests, the problem that organizes the carceral geographies of the prison-industrial complex is not innocence or guilt, but human sacrifice for others' profit (Gilmore 2022). To look to innocence, as she states, is to fail or surrender politically, because the goal should not be to find the right kinds of punishment, or the right people to punish; it should be how to prevent or diminish harm. Rather than managing social problems with technologies of punishment, whether these are forms of policing, prisons, or migrant detention centers, the goal of abolition is to imagine a better alternative world based on mutual interdependencies and relationality, centering adequate housing, mental and physical healthcare, flexible childcare and jobs, and mobility. It is to focus on collective care, or what Deva Woodly (2020b) calls "structural care"—abolitionists want to distribute care, not violence (Threadcraft in Woodly et al., 2021).

Abolitionism, as a continuation of the long history of Black radical insurgency, holds that brutality in the carceral system is not an exception to law and order; it is a core component of it. The carceral system is in place to protect the racial capitalist order, and in this sense, policing is used to address social and economic problems. Insofar as the Innocence Movement never challenges racial capitalism, it upholds hierarchies based on race, class, and gender, designating some people and populations as a priori guilty. Abolitionism is about doing away with this system of power—defunding the police, the prisons, and the migrant detention centers—but only as it simultaneously builds up positive life-affirming institutions: it shifts from institutions and practices that entrenched slavery to those that create the conditions of possibility for Black freedom (Chua 2020; Rodríguez 2019). Abolitionism takes on the question of nation-state borders and migration, too, insofar as the same carceral logics and infrastructures within nation-states are engaged to criminalize those who cross borders, upholding global practices of racial capitalism that sacrifice some for the racialized benefits and privilege of others. In this sense, abolition must include infrastructures for mobility, as well as for housing, education, and health. I will return to this question in chapter 5.

In this spirit of forging better futures for all, Critical Resistance—arguably the most well-known abolitionist organization in the US—includes three strategic frames: dismantling, changing, and building. It centers pragmatic programs even as it expands a utopic imagination (Dilts 2019)—it envisions what Angela Davis calls "a new conceptual terrain" (Davis 2003), building toward a future, a new horizon. This is necessarily an ongoing process, an enduring struggle to reimagine and make ourselves into new subjects while still in a racial capitalist system. Abolitionism is, as Anne McNevin writes, a world-building project, even as it refuses to lay out a detailed alternative world-building plan in advance: it insists on the constant provisionality of its visions, engaging in practical experiments and pivoting if these do not produce greater flourishing (McNevin, forthcoming).

How does abolitionism challenge the epistemology that produces and instantiates innocence? There are a few essential ways in which it undoes and reworks this epistemology. First, innocence relies on the hierarchical framework of victim and savior; an innocent person needs someone to save them. As we have seen, innocence is established with the help of scientific technologies and the help of experts. With abolitionism, the people who are experiencing discrimination—indeed, these are often communities that have inherited centuries-long legacies of oppression, but they may also be migrants or other people of color—are the same people who are both fighting for revolution and doing so by caring for themselves and others. Innocence is about being without the means, knowledge, or desire to act, but abolitionists take control of their future. Second, abolitionism is about a long-term politics of care that changes subjectivities, communities, and infrastructures; it is a radical undoing and remaking of the world. Innocence Projects are not about change; they set out to prove an existing ontology. That is, their goal is to provide evidence of what always was. Third, while innocence plays on sentiments of compassion or pity, abolitionist forms of care center and amplify "Black joy" (Woodly 2020a). Woodly states that this is based on a form of "unapologetic Blackness" that makes room for everyone—it does not divide people into categories of worthy or unworthy of care, reputable or disreputable, deserving or undeserving, and refuses to shame anyone for their needs or desires. While abolitionists do not profess to have all the answers—abolitionism is messy, unfinished, and it inherits harm and conflict—as Chua argues, neither does racial capitalism. And despite this, most people make decisions to continue on with this dominant system every day, to push it forward (Chua 2020). Why not choose instead to counter this social order, grounded on greed and punishment, and focus on collective and structural care?

Conclusions

Innocence is part of a dominant way of knowing the world—weaved into and out of science, religion, and liberalism—and it helps reproduce this world, with all its hierarchies. The epistemology that produces innocence works by absolving people and the systems of which they are a part of responsibility for inequality by offering a process of inclusion to a few who conform to the dominant social order, while neutralizing the outcasts and outliers and any challenge they pose. Recognition and full citizenship are granted to those who perform in the terms of acceptable (innocent) difference: they marry, just to the same sex; they have kids, just in a different way. They own private property and aspire to the same goals of security and safety. But thinking across the two cases I have just described, it becomes apparent that these homonormative goals are always tempered by racial affiliations. Innocence is not accessible in the same ways to people of color; as we have seen, Black people cannot lay claim to innocence as a group, as can white LGBTQ+ communities, but only as exceptional individuals. In this way, innocence is a regime of knowledge that consistently works to stratify both individuals and populations.

By relying on essential types and playing the same game of biological determinism as the religious and extreme right, the epistemology of innocence—as enacted by born-this-way discourses and claims to "actual" innocence—risks trapping us in authoritarian political modes, which eschew both radical difference and equality. Indeed, these same forms of medicalization and science risk reinforcing racial typologies and hierarchies, which open the gates to eugenics. Reading across these two movements shows how innocence, when produced by an interwoven set of epistemologies based on science, religion, and liberalism, works as the handmaiden to discrimination and to growing forms of illiberalism or fascism.

So, why do so many insist on innocence as a political and moral claim, as a desired outcome? Equality and respect can be demanded and created in other terms. What if the ACT UP slogan were not "All People with AIDS are innocent" but "No one is innocent"? I am not referring to the Christian refrain that we are all sinners. If we look at these two movements more carefully, we can see that the opposite of innocence is not guilt; it is contamination, desire, radical difference, and impurity. These concepts provide a richer place from which to think about how to live in, and change, this world.

CHAPTER FOUR

Innocence as Planetary Politics

Animals, the Fetus, and Mother Nature

In May 2016, a three-year-old boy fell into a gorilla's enclosure in the Cincinnati Zoo. Harambe, the seventeen-year-old silverback western lowland gorilla, looked like he was picking up the child to protect him but got confused and agitated by all the noise and screaming around. The zoo's response team, fearing for the child's life, shot and killed the gorilla. But the killing provoked a global uproar, with many angry that the zoo had killed the gorilla rather than trying to protect him or save the child by other means. People were also furious at the child's parents, and in a series of posts and a petition signed by 300,000 people calling for "Justice for Harambe," it was suggested that his mother be held accountable for neglect of the child, and for the killing of Harambe, an endangered animal. Some wrote that the gorilla was protecting the child more than the parents were. The video of the event was turned into a meme, as people mourned the gorilla, framed as an innocent victim of the cruelty of zoo culture, parental neglect, and gun violence.

How is it that a 450-pound gorilla—a magnificent, smart, and deadly animal—was so quickly framed as an innocent victim, in need of protection? The focus on the suffering and rescue of (certain) animals is increasingly present in the media, and indeed, the storyline is familiar. The victims being rescued recall pitiful women, innocent children. From the global industry to rescue homeless dogs in China (Paumgarten 2021), to the humanitarian infrastructures and NGOs put in place to rescue animals after disasters like the 2010 earthquake in Haiti, or Hurricane Sandy in New York in 2012 (Ticktin 2014a, 2017b), certain (usually charismatic) animals have taken center stage in figuring innocence and have mobilized a significant amount of political energy in the process. Insofar as the politics I have been discussing throughout this book depends on the figure of the innocent victim as the highest moral good—in an attempt to steer clear of explicit political solutions or goals—in this chapter, I suggest that the politics of innocence, like that of capitalism, works through a logic of expansion, in which new territories of innocence must be constantly discovered and incorporated. To be sure, this expansion is accompanied by the abandonment or sacrifice of other subjects and areas that no longer fit its parameters, and occasionally the active expulsion of these Others, as criminal or guilty. I think of it as a version of the racial-spatial "fix" for the imminent contradictions of capital that Ruth Wilson Gilmore theorized, building on David Harvey. Harvey argues that capital requires geographic expansion to deal with crises of overaccumulation, or a spatial fix; Gilmore revised this in light of theories of racial capitalism to say that capital always builds on previous power relations and deepens the forms of differentiation that capital produces. In this sense, race is the way that capitalism enshrines inequality. But this fix is always a mirage. As a key part of racial capitalism, innocence also works to help differentiate, racially and otherwise.

The ability to expand and shift its objects is what gives innocence its methodological power, which in turn elongates its reach in both time and space. The concept of innocence is fickle, promiscuous—easily and contagiously attaching to new territories. This facilitates its imperial logic. The need for movement and expansion is explained by the fact that the innocent sufferer can never be isolated for long enough to remain uncorrupted by history or context. We can never "catch" it; innocence is always located in the past or the future, never in the present—it is driven by logics of anticipation and nostalgia. In this sense, politics based on innocence is constantly being displaced to the limit of innocence, a border that must be drawn and redrawn.

My argument is that innocence comes to play on a planetary scale, and that it does so by reshaping the boundaries of who and what matters, challenging and reworking the category of the human and creating new taxonomies and hierarchies. It responds to an apocalyptic discourse—a crisis of climate change as much as one of humanity, and its ability to reproduce itself. To make this case, I trace innocence as a methodology of power that intersects with and modifies the contours and meaning of "humanity." That is, innocence helps define who is considered part of the category, insofar as humanity is a category that designates forms of life worth valuing and protecting. I use the term "planetary" to indicate that innocence is being pushed into terrain beyond the biological human, toward nonhumans and the more-than-human natural world. Innocence functions to expand the terrain of politics by both reconfiguring space, that is, beyond political configurations like nation-states; and reconfiguring time, pushing beyond human lifetimes into the very conception of life, and to different, more enduring geological temporalities.

In this chapter, I attend to borderland areas or zones where the concept of humanity gets questioned, challenged, and reworked by way of innocence, as the criteria by which some forms of life are incorporated into the category, and others, expelled. Harambe offers a good starting example of how these taxonomies intersect and get remade, valuing some lives over others: that is, the anger about the killing of Harambe cannot be separated from the fact that the child who fell into the zoo enclosure was Black. The event was immediately racialized; the innocence of the gorilla was enabled by the parents being condemned as criminal and neglectful. Media reports pointed to the decades-old criminal convictions of the child's father, who was not even present; this framed the gorilla's life as worth more than that of the Black child or family. In addition to these dog whistles and racist tropes, there were direct online comparisons between Black people and gorillas. Black communities contrasted the outpouring of grief for Harambe to the lack of attention to the deaths of ordinary Black people, and certainly, to the murders of so many Black people by the police—this occurred at the beginning of the Movement for Black Lives.

Here, humanity is not simply defined in relation to (and as the antithesis of) the animal, but in relation to innocence—innocence provides the power of humanization. It plays at the intersection of race and species difference, to make the life of Harambe grievable, while dismissing Black lives as less worthy. To be clear, I am not saying that Harambe should not be mourned; my goal is to counter such racial-species logics that pit some lives against others, and to stop playing into binary valuations of life based on proximity to a denigrated "nature" or an exalted "culture." Rather, I point to the way that the politics of concepts such as humanity and innocence enables forms of violence and domination that are deeply troubling. As various scholars have argued, we should not have to resubordinate the animal in order to defend Blackness, or vice versa (Kim 2015; Boisseron 2018); Blackness should be not pitted against animality. Rather, we need to attend to the systems that create these binaries in the first place.

To be sure, the distinctions and relations between humans and nonhumans have been tackled in various recent literatures, perhaps most notably by way of what some call the "nonhuman turn"; this set of approaches— from posthumanism and animal studies to the new materialisms and actor network theory (ANT)—has worked to decenter humans and anthropocentrism, often downplaying distinctions between human and nonhuman and demonstrating the agency of nonhumans. On the one hand, I am sympathetic to the underlying presumption in these theories of the ontological relationality between beings; I feel the term "more-than-human" captures the idea that the boundaries between human and nonhuman are specious at best, insofar as *how* we are human is determined by our relationships to our environments and larger ecologies, from the DNA level up. For instance, chemical and environmental toxicities and forms of everyday racism both shape differential access to life. This approach enables us to see that Black people and animals are interconnected by real, material struggles against slavery (Boisseron 2018). On the other hand, starting from this ontological approach of co-constitution, I nevertheless hold on to the category of the human as an important relation of power, and potentially, of political liberation, as theorists like Sylvia Wynter have suggested (see chapter 5).

After a brief introduction to the malleability of the conceptual category of humanity, I trace how humanity is being reworked at multiple scales, from the body, to the nation-state, to the planet. I look first at nation-states, to think about who and what is allowed to cross borders; innocence helps determine who has mobility, and who does not, but as I demonstrate, this goes beyond determining which people are allowed to cross and which ones are rendered immobile; animals and ideas of "nature" get brought into this story, expanding the role of innocence in determining the value of life. As philosopher Achille Mbembe writes, increasingly life itself is merged with mobility—those whose lives are valued have the right to move; the rest are not only rendered immobile (or incarcerated), but their very lives and livelihoods are discounted and disposed of, as would be non-life (Mbembe 2019). Innocence helps map physical landscapes—it is a spatial technology as much as an ethico-moral one. Second, I discuss how claims to innocence push the boundaries of what counts as life, by looking at the debates over the fetus. If the debates about nation-states demonstrate how innocence helps map the category of humanity onto certain geographies, spatializing it in a way that adjudicates mobility, debates about the fetus take us into the temporality of the human, with innocence working to push it back to the moment of conception. Third, I briefly scale up to think about Mother Nature, and how debates about climate change once again rely on the gendered, innocent subject that needs protection. I trace how innocence works once again as a methodology of power by way of the expansion and contraction of who qualifies as innocent. In the landscape of racial capitalism, I think of this as a form of sacrifice: Whose lives are being sacrificed as "nonhuman" or "less than human" for others to live as human? In a brief concluding discussion, I point to a different kind of politics, not one that works as an expansionist or imperialist project, but rather, one grounded on the acknowledgment of mutuality and co-imbrication.

Humanity's Inconsistent Boundaries

A few key points from the conceptual history of humanity explain how innocence helps reconfigure the category. The malleability and porosity of "humanity" is not new, even if the current configurations push it in new directions. Indeed, as theorists such as Sylvia Wynter have suggested, the prevailing liberal, secular category of humanity is just one variation of what humanity could be: it is a monohumanist ontology, dominating all ways of being human. But even within this Enlightenment category, there is much instability. As historian Thomas Laqueur (2009) argued, in the late eighteenth century, the human began to be conceived not as physiological fact, but as ethical subject. Humanity referred to this shared sentiment of sympathy or benevolence—which did not necessarily mean shared species or biological fact. On the one hand, the lack of rigorous definition of the human allows for an expansion of the types of life it includes, scrambling what we might have thought of as species or biological taxonomies by joining humanity with its cognate, "humane"; on the other hand, it can work on a case-by-case basis, providing a poor or inconsistent basis for ethics, arbitrarily including some and excluding others. Indeed, the sentimental mode of "humanity" and being humane that eventually turned into abolitionism was, as historian Lynn Festa writes, "notoriously indiscriminate in its choice of objects, embracing not only human beings but lapdogs, dying birds and (as one eighteenth century critic grumbled), 'efts, toads, bats, every thing that hath life'" (Festa 2010, 5).

Humanity is constructed by way of a series of interrelated and co-produced taxonomies of difference, each helping constitute its external "border"; these include race and species, as well as gender, sex, religion, and so on, and their affective connotations. What constitutes the "human" is not something natural or biologically fixed, but rather, it is the work of a constantly changing project of taxonomy, something that comes into being in relation to ethical and affective judgments. I understand innocence as part of this set of taxonomies; if one can lay claim to innocence, or be captured in its frame, one may have a better chance at life, even if innocence also places one in hierarchical relation to those who have reason, agency, and knowledge. The concept of innocence does not offer a consistent or coherent logic because it has multiple meanings and histories; it depends on how it intersects with humanity and these other taxonomies. It plays out in contradictory ways. However, I maintain that it works to determine what is considered valuable life.

We can see how humanity's borders are a constant work in progress by looking at how humanity has been defined in relation to species, race, and nature. The historian Joanna Bourke (2011) writes about a woman known as the Earnest Englishwoman, who in 1872 asked to let women "become animal" in order to reap the benefits they were denied because they were not part of "mankind." In other words, women were excluded from the category of humanity, while certain animals were included; here, gender acts as the border. But animality and humanity have been co-constituted in different ways, as well; for instance, animal cruelty organizations aided in the project of creating a compassionate sensibility in humans, and as such, in producing the very category of humanity as an ethical subject who cares for others (Esmeir 2012). Species classifications are epistemologies that produce ontological distinctions, rather than the reverse—it is our way of ordering that creates discontinuous, unequal categories of being, some with rights and value, some without, erasing the continuities or overlaps. As Claire Kim writes, "the idea of the animal has been a vital prop of the project of defining the human" (2015, 31); the exclusionary work of humanity is done by way of a metric of animality. That is, a common strategy to dehumanize is to liken people to certain animals or insects. Animality in turn cannot be separated from race and racial classification, which orders bodies according to how animal they are (Kim 2015). Different groups of humans are classified hierarchically as closer to or farther from "nature," and in this sense, animalistic metaphors have been integral to racist representations (Hage 2017). To be sure, not all animals are equal; some humanize, while others serve to dehumanize.

Nature as a concept is similar (but not identical) to animality, and it too has a long history of being used to draw the boundaries of the human. In Western Enlightenment thought, nature has been seen as the realm of the given, the backdrop, while human life is qualified as active, allowing for artifice and for culture. But as I will discuss, nature—especially in the form of Mother Nature—is also used as a foil, as the opposite of human corruption, as a space of purity that must be protected. In these various ways, humanity and nature are co-constituted, and as I will discuss, innocence comes to play in the intersection with these as part of a conceptual cluster that includes purity.

Nature holds a particular place in the theological history of the concept of innocence. Humanity's expulsion from innocence in the "state of nature" is the beginning of our social existence, our state as political animals—this is the beginning of humanity as both a religious and a secular category. Perhaps unsurprisingly, then, those associated with innocence tend to be at humanity's edges; they mark its border, in the sense that they are not corrupt (as is a normative humanity)—they are not fully socialized creatures, and often get figured as incapable of being thinking, active, or informed subjects. As such, innocence acts as the boundary for liberal ideas of personhood, where this constituent outside is simultaneously romanticized and disparaged. In this sense, playing with the borders of innocence also means playing with the borders of humanity: this is its power, and its danger.

Nonhumans at the Border: Innocence
at the Boundaries of National Space

The nearly 2,000-mile border zone between the US and Mexico traverses some of the most beautiful, biologically diverse, and complicated landscapes in the US, and much of it is protected in the form of national parks, wildlife refuges, bird-watching venues, and federally protected public lands. Indeed, there are at least eleven US and three Mexican designated conservation areas along the border.[1] In January 2016, I went to one of these protected areas at the US-Mexico border wall with my colleagues from the Multiple Mobilities Research Cluster;[2] we started in Brownsville, Texas. We went to an area that was well known as a bird-watching venue: a refuge called the Hidalgo Pumphouse, bisected by the border wall. We were accompanied by an activist named Scott Nicols who at the time was working with the Sierra Club. He was talking to us about the intersecting politics of immigration and environmentalism. As we got up close to the wall, we saw something in the tall grass. We went over to look and saw a person—body—face down. Scott asked carefully, "Are you okay? Can you hear me?" After what seemed like an eternity, the person lifted her head, and in a fear-stricken voice said in Spanish, "Please don't tell anyone that we are here!" Her companion, who was much better hidden, raised his head to nod from another spot farther down. They were hiding in plain sight, in the middle of a nature preserve full of tourists; we calculated that they must have just recently scaled the wall and were trying to hide in the grass until sundown, when they could disappear. We offered them water, but Scott quickly ushered us away, so as not to draw attention to them. We moved to a spot farther away where we still could see them and tried to focus on what Scott was saying. Within ten minutes, one of the birders—there in theory to appreciate the life of birds and the beauty of the landscape—spotted them. He made a beeline to Border Patrol and reported them. Within minutes, they were handcuffed and led away.

I have been trying to make sense of this act. Whatever interpretive frame I may put on it, they all end with migrants as a threat in this bird sanctuary. Border Control (CBP) was called to remove them as such. What is not clear to me is what kind of threat they were perceived to be: Were they seen as a danger to American citizens, or to the birds? Or perhaps both?

It is not accidental that this geographic border zone is also a conceptual borderland for the determination of whose lives matter—and who counts as part of humanity. Indeed, liberal notions of humanity have a spatial grammar—who is counted as human also helps determine, and is determined by, where one lives and how one moves through space. As Hannah Arendt (1951) stated so presciently, the loss of a nation-state is effectively the same as being expelled from this concept of humanity. Humanity is composed of citizens of nation-states, insofar as one needs the sovereign nation-state to give and protect one's "human rights"; and Arendt argued that those who fall outside the nation-state are considered beast-like—that is, less than human. Nation-states are both political and spatial containers, and one needs to be a part of both to fully accede to the category of humanity. This bird-watching refuge at the border of the nation-state renders explicit the ways in which these taxonomies of difference intersect in spatial terms: it is a liminal zone both spatially and politically, in which humanity and animality get assigned and reassigned in relation to the nation-state.

Transnational migration is one of the most contentious political questions of our times—the problem or scapegoat that reveals other key inequalities, the "crisis" that threatens to reveal and challenge our ways of being—so it is not surprising that the politics of humanity is increasingly playing out at nation-state borders. Innocence is used to reconfigure these borders by adjudicating who can and cannot move. Innocence plays at multiple levels, in relation to multiple "Others." I am not only speaking of how migrants or people-on-the-move fight to be designated innocent and hence deserving, which is now effectively a prerequisite for the status of refugee (Ticktin 2020). I am interested in the expansion of this field to include more-than-humans. Certain nonhumans are increasingly spoken of or framed by the conceptual grammar of innocence, and hence come to be treated with humanity. This in turn creates the conditions for others to be designated non-innocent, guilty, or criminal. In particular, nonhumans are being brought into the discussion of nation-state borders and framed as innocent victims or bystanders of irresponsible migrants. To be sure, there is a long history of migrants being pitted against the environment and condemned by conservationists as sullying the land, a point to which I will return. But I want to discuss a new site of contestation where nonhumans come into play: border walls. Increasingly, walls stand in as the ideal form of a global politics of closed borders; according to some estimates, there are currently seventy border walls or fences worldwide, compared to fifteen in 1990. These are built by liberal and illiberal states alike, and they are often enhanced by other smart border technologies—from biometrics to drones and other infrared technology, which all work to detect movement in order to then catch, detain, or deport border crossers (Aizeki et al. 2021). The location of border walls as markers of the nation maps very clearly onto places where there is significant socioeconomic inequality—indeed, the biggest predictor of who constructs the walls and where they do so is the wealth gap between the nation-state constructing the barrier and the place and population defined as a threat (Aizeki et al. 2021, 39). In other words, border walls—as one manifestation of the nation—help keep out the "have-nots," casting them not only as undeserving, but as criminal.

ANIMAL INNOCENCE

The Israeli Separation Barrier—now regularly called the apartheid wall—offers one example of the way innocence works to reshape the politics of humanity, valuing the mobility of certain nonhumans over Palestinian humans. Initiated in 2002 by Israel at the height of the second intifada, the barrier comprises electric fencing, iron, barbed wire, and a lot of concrete snaking in multiple directions; it is imposing and mostly impassable. And yet the barrier includes small holes for animals such as hedgehogs, ibex, and gazelles, thanks to the efforts of Israeli ecologists, who insisted that "animal families should not be separated." Animals are framed as innocent victims of a human political conflict. A legal case was made to Israel's High Court, to overturn a plan from the Ministry of Defense to extend the barrier in the southern West Bank, where the ibex move between the vegetation of the winter and the water source of the oases in the summer. The Israeli ecologist Ron Frumkin said the barrier could wipe out the ibex altogether.[3] Environmentalists fought for the passage of small wildlife—which is no doubt important, the goal is not to diminish their lives—but they did so without mentioning the fact that freedom of movement was being denied to hundreds of thousands of Palestinian people at the same time; in this sense, their arguments weaponize an implicit understanding of the innocence of animals, as contrasted to Palestinians.

To be sure, it is possible that this was a strategic move from which to subsequently challenge the legitimacy of the border wall for all. Strategic or not, the binary logic of innocence underlies the argument, and it has exclusionary consequences, regardless of the intentions. A different argument could have been made about the far-reaching violence of the border wall, which hurts everything around it: from people to animals and surrounding ecologies. Instead, a species/racial logic is used to sort those at the borders by valuing the lives of small and innocent animals in a way that simultaneously erases Palestinians. Palestinian mobility is only considered insofar as they are to blame for the wall (due to their supposed terrorism against the state of Israel) and as such, they are also seen as the source of the problems for these animals and the environment. In this sense, the innocence of animals is tacitly pitted against the criminality of Palestinians who must be fenced in (contained) and out (expelled, and increasingly, murdered). To be sure, hedgehogs, gazelles, and ibex are anthropomorphized incarnations of sweet harmlessness, and it is not surprising that these were the animal lives foregrounded in both the court case and the media. Not all nonhumans are understood as potentially innocent; as with people, some are already seen as guilty, and used to dehumanize, from rats and insects to snakes.

This claim to morally inflected concern for animals also serves to render Israelis innocent. That is, the concept of innocence is doing different kinds of work, enabling humane treatment for some animals, expelling some humans from their land, and absolving still other humans from blame for any of it. The term "pinkwashing" was coined in relation to Israel's strategic use of gay-friendliness to both excuse and distract from their treatment of Palestinians; that is, attention is put on Israel's liberal tolerance and acceptance of queer and trans people, in contrast to the illiberal (or "uncivilized") banning of queer people and practices. Similarly, we might use a variation of the term "greenwashing," to describe Israeli practices. While greenwashing often signifies deceptive claims to environmental practices in order to gain commercial advantages, we can bend it a bit here to describe their treatment of animals and the environment to gain moral advantage—that is, using humane treatment to distract again from the violence of the Israeli occupation of Palestine, of which the wall is just one aspect.

Israel has a history of foregrounding animal lives and saving innocent animals as part of a politics that condemns Palestinians as abusive. For instance, they have denounced the treatment of animals in Palestinian zoos; in this sense, Israel is portrayed as a benevolent state that rescues innocent victims from gratuitous violence. Yulia Gilich calls this "settler innocence," which she argues allows Israel to deny responsibility for the dispossession and military occupation of Palestine, instead presenting themselves as the only "democracy in the Middle East" (Gilich 2020). As she states, the aesthetics of Gaza's zoos reflect the material conditions of Gaza's humans: they are starved and traumatized. But rather than understanding zoo animals in the frame of the violence that touches all life in Gaza, through the lens of innocence, animals are used against Palestinians to designate them as cruel and depraved.

Israel is not the only country to design holes in its border walls for animal crossings, even if it was likely the first; indeed, I found that across the Global North there is increasing concern for innocent animals hurt by the proliferation of border walls, embedding a form of care in these violent infrastructures that redirects our understanding of their politics. For instance, this strategy made its way to the US-Mexico border wall, where environmentalists and conservationists lobbied for passageways or holes in the walls (see figure 6). They succeeded by negotiating for 8" × 11" openings in the fence—the size of a piece of paper, or a prepared measure to fit with previous bureaucratic measures[4]—to allow endangered animals such as ocelot and jaguarundis (both small felines) to cross. They achieved this as a compromise, shaped by the constraints of the law, and in particular, by the Real ID Act that was passed in 2005, exempting the Department of Homeland Security (DHS) from all federal state and tribal and municipal laws, including all environmental protections, which had initially prohibited the building of the wall in various places. While many American environmentalists supported this strategy in the hope it might open the way to other concessions, others argued that it simply legitimized the wall, making it slightly more humane for animals while tacitly accepting its inhumane practices against people.

Ceuta and Melilla—the Spanish enclaves that mark the border between Morocco and Spain, Africa and Europe—also sport impressive border walls. The enclaves have the most militarized borders within the European Union, with four layers of fencing (one on the Moroccan side, three on Spain's),

FIGURE 6. Animal hole, US-Mexico border wall, at
Brownsville, Texas. Photo by Miriam Ticktin.

some sections of which are thirty-three feet tall; the barriers are comple-
mented by a variety of technologies aimed at stymieing the movement of
people through, under, or over them. Since the first fences were built in
the 1990s, hundreds have died from being shot or beaten, and from injuries
sustained while trying to cross the barrier. There, too, the Spanish state
has made accommodations for animals to pass. However, in this case, the
holes are much bigger, according to the Guardia Civil in Ceuta, with whom
I conducted an interview.[5] When I asked if they had received complaints
about animals getting hurt by the wall or caught in the holes, they explained
that no, but rather, they had discovered children caught in the barbed wire,
trying to cross through the holes for animals. Here, by virtue of a mix of the
fence design and a politics of innocence that regulates whose lives matter,
certain children attempt to become animal; and in contrast, certain animals
have the right to "humane" treatment. Again, we see how categories of being and kind get reworked at the nation-state border, with innocence as
their guide, ultimately maintaining a level of violence for all.

ENVIRONMENTAL INNOCENCE

This competition for deservingness between people-on-the-move and nonhuman Others extends to the nonhuman landscapes they cross, and once
again, innocence helps create the morally relevant distinctions about who
matters. Most notably, these valuations of life have played out through movements for immigrant rights and environmentalism and/or conservationism;
the latter have often been framed around protecting a pure and innocent
"nature" from the harm done by immigrants. Conservationists have had
a long and often contested relationship to the politics of migration transnationally, and while more progressive environmental justice movements
work in solidarity with immigrant rights organizations, in the US, there is a
long history and important strain of what Park and Pellow (2013) call "nativist environmentalism" that links efforts to save the earth and protect Mother
Nature to efforts to control certain groups of people; these are subtended
by a logic of racial exclusivity. As Park and Pellow suggest, this becomes a
convenient anti-immigrant strategy, without mentioning the words *race* or
immigration. There is a history of expelling local people from what became
wilderness preserves, in the name of the purity of nature, and against its
contamination by people—initially by Native Americans, and later, by immigrants. As with Israel, this is part of a settler colonial logic that extends
into the treatment of migrants. Initially, Native Americans were designated
incompetent stewards of the land; more recently, immigrants are held responsible for overpopulation—they are likened to animals breeding, and

accused of having too many children—and hence exploitation of resources and the environment. Another common refrain of nativist environmentalists is that immigrants do not respect the land, leaving their trash as they cross over the border, and that they damage natural and fragile habitats along their journeys. They are thus cast as a threat to the purity of nature.

The term "Fortress Conservation" has been used more recently to name the ways in which conservation as a practice is inseparable from colonialism, racism, and their attendant forms of violence. The argument is that conservation itself needs to be decolonized. The dominant model claims and encloses land, to protect it in the face of the damages of racial capitalism; but this may also be a way to engage in further extractivism. Ashley Dawson (2024) gives the example of the enclosure of India's forests, the first broad-based environmental law of the nineteenth century, in the name of scientific management. This dispossessed forest-dwelling people and criminalized their traditional customary practices, and the same thing happened and is still happening across the globe—in the US, in South America, in Africa. Such conservation practices enclose previously common lands and community-stewarded natural resources, making it one of the biggest enemies of Indigenous people. Dawson argues that it is a spatio-temporal fix for the built-in contradictions of capitalism, and yet it also actively produces extinction, or what he calls accumulation by extinction, playing on David Harvey's notion of accumulation by dispossession.

As scholars have documented, in the early twentieth-century American and German contexts, environmental and conservation movements joined racialized notions of national purity with Romantic ideals of natural purity. That is, a search for purity in "nature" cannot be separated from a notion of racial cleansing. Indeed, the concept of purity is historically linked with hygiene, and cleanliness; and through ideologies of racial purity, whiteness became part of this conceptual cluster, as clean, light, and right (Berthold 2010), and as associated with civilization. There are similar conceptual and political echoes in the Indian context, as Naisargi Davé (2023) argues; the ostensible innocence of the natural world that leads to vegan purism is not just coincidental to fascism, but inherent to it; it figures certain people as having the potential for evil. Many of the most prominent leaders of the environmental movement in the US in the early twentieth century were affiliated with or sympathizers of the eugenics movement, understanding people of color as naturally inferior. This conflation of national and natural purity has endured; it was apparent as recently as the 1990s with an attempted takeover of the Sierra Club by nativists. The ideology of overpopulation has joined and justified these struggles (Park and Pellow 2013; Hultgren 2015).

Purity and innocence are closely related concepts; in the first of its two key meanings or etymological roots, purity is defined as "freedom from admixture," or freedom from corruption or contamination. But the second meaning is morally inflected, and innocence is listed as a synonym, which includes "freedom from moral contamination," "stainless condition or character," and "chastity" (*OED*). In this way, protecting the purity of nature slips quite easily into understanding nature in moral terms, as innocent; nature can be "captured" in this sense, to protect it. The relationship between purity, innocence, and nature is underscored by the theological history that haunts the collective consciousness of the secular, liberal West, insofar as the Garden of Eden is precisely the space of nature uncontaminated by the wiliness and sinfulness of humans; innocence is located in that pre-political, natural environment. And once again, nature in this sense is both venerated and depreciated, as outside culture. The nature-culture binary enables a civilizational hierarchy, where those who are less civilized are seen as closer to nature. And yet when the "less civilized" are not "in place," they also contaminate nature. The innocence of nature is emphasized by gendered and sexualized grammars used, such as "virgin land," or "Mother Earth." It must be enclosed in refuges or parks or sanctuaries—indeed, in this way nature is implicated in the projects of border and boundary making.

Purity and innocence are conceptually blended in these discourses, shaping space and decisions over whose lives matter: people-on-the-move are excluded by conservationists in order to protect pure, innocent nature. The case of the former location of "the Jungle"—the makeshift camp on the outskirts of Calais, France—makes this binary between immigrants and nature explicit. As we learned in chapter 2, and as I will elaborate on further in chapter 5, people-on-the-move claimed the area later called the Jungle starting in 2015 as a place they could live for however long it took them to cross over to the UK, by way of trains or ships or trucks; they made a home of it, created communities. The French state cleared it of people in October 2016, initially by replacing the migrant tents and informal housing with a far smaller number of shipping containers, precisely in the name of cleanliness. As Prime Minister Manuel Valls stated, they had to get people out of the informal settlements of the Jungle, into these containers, "because we, in France, cannot allow people to live in such wretched conditions" (September 2015). The people who did not fit into the shipping containers were displaced or deported, and eventually the camp was closed.

In its place the French state built a nature reserve called *Fort Vert* (Green Fort); the goal was to "return this territory back to nature," as Minister of the Interior Bruno Le Roux stated.[6] The French state claimed that this project of "renaturing" was beneficial for the environment, restoring habitats and protecting endangered species, from migrating birds to the fen orchid. Fort Vert is presented as cleaning up the damage that people-on-the-move had wrought, as restoring order and purity. However, the contamination of the landscape preceded people-on-the-move; this area, called *La Lande*, was in fact closer to a toxic wasteland, contaminated by the proximity of two chemical factories, as well as asbestos from a demolished holiday camp, and illegal dumping of toxic waste (Rullman 2020). State authorities actually pushed migrants into this area when the town of Calais became full of migrant encampments, initially using the holiday camp as a day center for humanitarian aid. The migrants lived in this zone of increased chemical hazard, and those who were present over a longer term regularly got sick from it (Dhesi et al. 2018). It is revealing that in the process of purification, "invasive" plants were removed as well, and likened to waste; as I have written elsewhere (Ticktin 2017b), similar understandings of invasive Others of different orders—whether plant, people, pathogens, or ideas—enable analogous treatment of all those designated "invasive." The removal of both the people and plants from this zone reinforces the idea that some beings and forms of life naturally belong to a place, and others do not, and must be exterminated.

While Fort Vert is presented as returning this land to its former "natural" state, it also involved constructing sandbanks, lakes, and ditches, all to prevent new encampments. That is, in this case, "nature" has been weaponized as a security measure against people-on-the-move, rendered hostile to them, even as the landscape is designed to welcome "native" birds and flowers; it is not accidental that the UK Border Force is a partner in the landscape design (Rullman 2020; Van Isacker 2020). Natural landscapes have been similarly weaponized in the US (De Leon 2015; Sundberg 2011), where people-on-the-move are funneled into the desert's hostile terrain, and the European context, where those coming from Africa and elsewhere have been directed into the Mediterranean, by blocking crossings.[7] The UK's policy was explicit: it was designed to create "a really hostile environment for illegal immigrants." Nature is cast as simultaneously innocent and threatening.

Through the lens of the protection of pure natural landscapes and innocent animals at the border, we see the borders of humanity—and whose lives matter—being reworked. Characterizations of innocence and purity allow exceptional small, loveable animals to be brought in closer to the category of humanity, while people-on-the-move get expelled from it, as a contaminating force. Instead, people-on-the-move are associated with different parts of the natural world, with the "low animals" capable of infection. As Claire Kim notes, animals are racialized as well; certain animals are whitened, and treated like individual, innocent victims, while others are configured as dangerous, cruel (i.e., pit bulls), menacing collectives or hordes. Such racializations come into being in relation to owners, in a form of racial, anthropomorphizing contagion. In media and public discourse in Europe and North America, people-on-the-move are regularly likened to vermin or insects, described, for instance, as swarming, scuttling, or scurrying (Anderson 2017); and insofar as they are associated with entities such as viruses, the borders have been closed to them as invasive or contagious. Indeed, insofar as this logic of environmentalism is transnational, so is the politics of innocence.

THE AESTHETICS OF NONHUMAN INNOCENCE

While I have suggested that innocence works as part of a set of interrelated taxonomies of difference—exaggerating certain kinds of difference, while minimizing others—not everyone can qualify as innocent (and hence, as part of the category humanity); the expansion of this form of politics is nevertheless selective, erasing structural violence and injustice in order to focus on a few individuals. A collective moral desire to protect these innocent individuals, for whatever reason (to feel good about oneself; as a way to be a moral person today; as a form of apolitical action; and so forth), and the political economies that help produce and sustain this desire, is what enables the colonization of landscapes and the production of new innocent subjects. In what I have shown so far, not only does the larger politics of border walls and the political economy of global migration fall out of the frame, but so too does the larger context of institutions and practices like factory farming and agribusiness, which affect billions of both people and animals, leaving just a tiny few to be saved. The larger circulation of capital and labor is rendered invisible, whether it has to do with humans or nonhumans, excluding any consideration of how to address its workings or effects. In these forms of extractivism, life is transformed into commodity, both human and nonhuman, and the rest is laid aside or abandoned, as waste; as Marisa Solomon so poignantly writes, extraction requires the production of toxic landscapes, and this process includes racializing certain people as waste, as animal—what she calls the ecological afterlives of slavery (Solomon 2022).

Which forms of life can access the conceptual frame of innocence, then? How does this politics of expansion work? I return to the question of the aesthetics of innocence, as discussed in chapter 2. This includes what Jamie Lorimer (2007) has called "non-human charisma" and aesthetics like cuddliness and cuteness, which trigger strong emotional responses. We can think of companion animals, or charismatic species like chimps, dolphins, and pandas. As noted in chapter 2, Sianne Ngai (2005) describes the aesthetics of cuteness, and how it emphasizes powerlessness and defenselessness. As ethologists have long noted, cuteness is associated with juvenile features in humans as well as animals, and it is accompanied by a desire to protect (Lorenz 1971). Innocence, like cuteness, is a minor aesthetic concept (unlike the more prestigious ones like the beautiful, sublime, and ugly), and its very diminutiveness is critical to its appeal. Indeed, innocence, like cuteness, seems to name an aesthetic encounter based on an inflated difference in power; it works in relation to a socially disempowered Other—the lack of animal "speech" only adds to this effect. The characteristics of those who fit include docility, often meekness, and an ability to obey.

This aesthetics of innocence finds its place in humanitarian photography, as we saw in chapter 2, whose goal is to elicit sympathy and compassion for those who suffer; it does so most effectively by featuring innocent victims. But humanitarian photography is not limited to people: the ideal ethical subject of humanitarianism is simply one who does not deserve to suffer. In this sense, it is a critical space for the evocation and elaboration of the category of humanity—indeed, aesthetic techniques help make and remake humanity's boundaries. This happens, I suggest, by way of the aesthetics of innocence. For instance, at the time of the so-called "refugee crisis" or

FIGURE 7. Great horned owl caught in fence. Image shown in an article on the Slovenian online news site *Svet* about the new border wall with Croatia, condemning the suffering of animals that fences cause. Photo courtesy of Blanford Nature Center.

the long summer of migration in 2015, newspapers reported protests at the new border wall between Croatia and Slovenia—Croatians were upset that animals were getting caught in the barbed wire. In one newspaper, graphic images of maimed owls and deer caught in the fence were accompanied by text stating "These are the horrific images of suffering animals."[8] One of the images that accompanied the text featured an individual owl, caught in and hanging from a barbed wire fence (see figure 7).

There are a few aspects of this photo that work to produce innocence: first, the way the suffering is shown as undeserved—an owl that inadvertently got caught in the cruel politics of people. The owl has no responsibility for the fence. Second, the photograph centers forms of suffering or injury that are recognizable to humans, such as bodily mutilation. We see its eyes, looking listless with pain; we see its torn flesh. This mimics the suffering of people, encouraging a fantasy of rescue; it invokes a familiar, humanitarian response, which also configures the rescuer as innocent, with no responsibility for the suffering. Third, and relatedly, the focus on the individual is critical; animal suffering is made visible in individual human frames. The owl is alone, not in a flock or parliament. This evokes the individual personhood associated with innocence, and with rights. Here, the individual owl is the victim, and the cause is the barbed wire fence, not the larger politics of enclosure—from prisons to detention centers and border walls—that harms untold others, humans, nonhumans, other beings and things, in different ways, on different scales, and in different capacities. The messiness of uneven and only partly commensurable forms of structural violence cannot enter the frame of innocence. The individual injured owl becomes the problem to resolve—not the politics that has led to this, like nationalism or racism. And while people may be worried about other owls getting hurt, the problem is framed as the suffering of individual beings, who must be saved.

Returning to the case of Israel, Israelis' treatment of animals as exceptionally humane is regularly figured and photographed in newspapers: for instance, an article in the *Jerusalem Post* recounts a story about an Israeli Border Patrol officer who rescued an injured female owl while patrolling the West Bank security barrier near Jenin. The officer said that "protecting the environment and animals is an integral part of our job" and "as soon as I saw the suffering owl I took off my protective vest, and picked the bird up to evacuate it for treatment."[9] The photo (see photo by way of the link in the footnote) frames the rescue of the owl against the backdrop of the barbed wire of the border fence, opening the question of what the owl was harmed by (was it something on the dangerous other side of the fence?), and showing this side of the fence as a safe, humane zone. The soldier is carrying the owl in a vest that resembles a baby carrier, once again playing into an aesthetics of innocence grounded on the distinction between children and adults, where children are configured as innocent by way of their roundness, their dimpled hands, and so on. Its wide eyes evoke innocence, in the sense of naïveté. But interestingly, the owl as a figure of wisdom also plays on the idea of the child as all-knowing—that is, a traditional view of the child as unknowing seer of truth. Once again, this is a classic humanitarian image, figuring the Israeli soldier as heroic savior, or moral leader.

The article states that the owl was taken to the Israeli Wildlife and Rehabilitation Center outside Tel Aviv, where it received tests and treatment for a serious cut to its wing. The juxtaposition of the care for the owl on one side of the border wall, with the violence enacted against the Palestinians imprisoned by it, demonstrates how innocence plays in reworking taxonomies of life, and of humanity; care for the owl works to render Palestinian suffering morally insignificant, despite the fact that they share the same space and landscape. Once again, rather than entering into a binary frame where the lives of owls or other animals are pitted against those of Palestinians—and where people must side with either one or the other—my goal is to highlight the system that creates a situation in which care for the owl comes at the expense of care for the Palestinians, where the owl must be seen as innocent, so the Palestinian can be cast as guilty, and their treatment justified. I want to refuse this frame altogether. This is part of a racialized system that hurts all involved: the fact that the owl is the largest nocturnal predator in Israel—not an innocent victim—is erased by this narrative, robbing it of its particular form of life. This aesthetics of innocence works to strengthen Israeli settler colonialism and other forms of nationalism, which enclose some people and things in order to let others dominate.

Fetal Life: Innocence at the Boundaries of Time

In borderland geographies, the aesthetics of innocence further help determine which forms of life are valued. But the category of humanity is not only determined spatially; it has a critical temporal dimension. When does human life begin? What counts as human life? In this section, I explore how innocence is harnessed in deciding these questions. As we saw in chapter 3, innocence figures prominently in both scientific and religious epistemologies, which are the primary discourses used to configure this debate. Indeed, innocence functions in overlapping ways in both science and religion to push the beginning of "life" back farther and farther—to extend or expand what counts as a lifetime.

To reiterate one of this book's key points, innocence is unattainable; it is a form of mythical, nostalgic desire for purity and simplicity—one that is constantly out of reach. As already noted, while children may be seen as exemplary innocent subjects, child soldiers also exist, corrupting this idea. History and context always find their way back into the imagined subjects of innocence, sullying or discrediting them. I have been arguing that people go in search of innocence elsewhere when children or other subjects are not suitably innocent, not suitably naïve, vulnerable, and pure, in order to satisfy a desire to protect, purify, and dominate. In this sense, I suggest that contemporary political life involves the search for and production of new innocent subjects. Politics works by extending the frontiers of innocence; and the fetus represents one of its more potent temporal limits.

The concept of personhood has been used to mark and acknowledge the fetus as a part of humanity, as a being with rights; and debates about when fetal personhood begins have been passionate and often violent. The Supreme Court of Alabama issued one of the most controversial rulings around this topic in February 2024, stating that frozen embryos, extracted in the process of IVF, are children or people, and that disposing of them can be considered wrongful death of a minor. To be sure, the concept of personhood helps determine the boundaries of humanity, but not all persons are humans. Since the nineteenth century, corporations have been considered legal persons. More recently, we have seen that rivers and other so-called "natural" entities have been granted legal personhood, which gives them rights and protections that approach those of human persons. While personhood is certainly one prominent avenue into the debates about fetal life, I am interested less in personhood as a concept (and the huge legal and scholarly field around it) than in how innocence comes to play in valuing certain forms of life, and in assessing which lives matter. In other words, I am not as concerned with law as I am with the shape of an affective and ethico-moral field.

A fetus inhabits a liminal space: neither fully human, nor nonhuman. It is a cluster of cells—life, but of a particular sort. While it cannot speak or exist autonomously, it can exert agency in relation to other persons—namely, the pregnant person carrying it. It is felt in interaction with this other being, but it is not viable on its own, until approximately twenty-four weeks. Indeed, as scientists and others have suggested, we might think of it more in relation to a parasite, living through the body of the other. I want to explore how the concept of innocence helps make the fetus into an exemplary human life, even as I ask what kind of life it is made into.

The idea of fetal personhood has been created in large part by way of an aesthetics of innocence, one similar to the humanitarian aesthetics already discussed. This includes photography as well as digital images. As I have already argued, innocence is not simply represented, but *produced* by images. Visuals build consensus especially when they are ubiquitous. But scientific imagery plays an important role too, or more broadly, what Latour calls "inscriptions," which encode scientific knowledge in charts, graphs, models, and so on. Indeed, images of the fetus are rendered innocent in part by a techno-medical mode, which purports to represent an objective reality, not one that is politically, socially, or morally situated. As I will explain in more detail below, scientific images that frame the fetus as a baby are viewed as objective, despite the fact that this is very much a contested terrain. Indeed, as historian Barbara Duden writes, the fetuses we live with today "were first conceived not in the womb, but in visualizing technologies" (1999, 16). This idea of objectivity is accomplished by various visual technologies—such as photography, electron microscopes, and ultrasound technologies—which can convert religious or mythical logics into the language of positivism. As we saw in chapter 3, as part of this process the moral is rendered invisible as it assumes the objective mantle of the medical. While ultrasound technologies are considered to be part of a scientific regime of knowledge, in fact, photography can function to create claims to objectivity as well: as Petchesky (1987) suggests in an article on the power of visual culture in the politics of reproduction, the origins of photography can be traced to late nineteenth-century Europe's cult of science, and inextricably related to positivism, which isolates data and separates it from its historical or social contexts and relationships. Photography appears to capture reality without art or artifice. But, as Roland Barthes reminds us, in fact, the image is heavily coded, grounded in a context of historical and cultural meanings (Barthes 1977; Petchesky 1987).

Before the fetus was invented as a "techno-scientific fact" (Duden 1999), pregnancy was a somatic experience that could mean the state of being with child, or the state of an untoward, fleshy growth, classified as Other (these growths were understood as mooncalves, monsters, or moles). While there were drawings of the unborn in the seventeenth and eighteenth centuries, these showed the child one hoped for, the child-to-be—a three-month-old babe resting on a placental cushion. As Duden writes, this is the result of "optical prejudice"—they saw the future they wanted to see. And in fact, when anatomists referred to something that looked like what we would call a fetus today, this was interpreted as "a big-headed monster, a mooncalf, a misshapen thing" (Duden 1999, 20).

In these current times, optical prejudice is as active as ever. The fetal image that once appeared to people as monstrous, as repulsive, has now been manipulated to appear like a sleeping human—and this has become the conventional way of representing fetal development (Newman 1996). I say "manipulated," because this image was created by extreme enlargement and cropping to show only the head and hands of the fetus. This made it seem not only lifelike, but like a fully formed baby. This imagery was pioneered in a 1965 *Life* magazine article, with photography by Lennart Nilsson. The images were described as the "first portrait" of a living embryo. As literary scholar Karen Newman points out, the very word "portrait" makes a claim for fetal life and personhood, since it depicts a picture of a person, especially their face. Interestingly, even though the magazine issue's goal was to protect fetal life, the images were taken from aborted fetuses— whether spontaneous or surgical. These are simulated images of life, or as some might have it, images of life after death. Through abortion, Nilsson got access to moments of fetal development that would not have been visible otherwise. He used techniques like suspending the embryo in a clear fluid to make it visible and to render it an object of photography, along with backlighting and photographic enlargement. Indeed, by way of aesthetic artifice, the new visual technologies endowed the fetus with a public persona, and with the status of person.

When pictured as a baby, the fetus is immediately placed in the framework of human life, with all the attendant rights; it is figured as autonomous. But the visuals also strategically deploy the aesthetics of innocence—the fetus is framed as passively sleeping, and hence entirely helpless and exposed, in need of care and protection. The appearance of being asleep evokes a lack of agency. To reiterate, the concept of innocence entails lack: lack of desire, lack of ability, lack of experience; these are also its visual markers. Indeed, because of the emphasis on lack, innocence is most vividly figured on the ends of the temporal spectrum of life: in this case, not only death, but now, increasingly, the so-called beginnings of life. Innocence is located at the very limits of life. As I suggested in chapter 1, the iconic image of the three-year-old Syrian migrant Alan Kurdi, whose drowned body washed up on a beach in 2015, exemplifies innocence in its state of absolute nothingness. This emptiness is the blank slate on which adults can project whatever fantasies they like. If Kurdi represents proximate or recent death, the fetus represents proximate or imminent life; both embody innocence, as utterly pure. Both are free from life's corrupting forces. Images of the fetus echo the tropes of innocence, which include the cherubic look of the almost otherworldly, especially when seen as floating on its own. The aesthetics of childhood innocence deployed here emphasize the aspects of the fetus/child that distinguish it from adults (Higonnet 1998): the exaggerated big head and small body, tiny bare toes, and a genderless quality. These establish fetal life as part of childhood, with a distinct ontology, or way of being:

but they also confirm it as a *human* life. Once again, certain earlier representations of pregnancy—as early as the seventeenth century—also represented what was later called a fetus, as autonomous, as part of the larger Enlightenment project of establishing independent, possessive, liberal individuals (Newman 1996); but these images took the form of homunculi, or fully formed, tiny adults. It is the aesthetics of childhood that produces the fetus as innocent.

In early examples of this new visual regime, fetal personhood was accentuated through other forms of visual manipulation, again emphasizing innocence. For instance, as Newman recounts, in 1985, in the magazine *Christianity Today*, an image of the director of *Americans Against Abortion* was figured, cradling a fetus, beside a full-page advertisement on behalf of starving children in Ethiopia. The ad was designed to mirror the fetus—a child with a bloated stomach, its head exaggeratedly large compared to its frail, skinny arms, pictured as vulnerable and in need of protection. This is humanitarian imagery at its finest. Innocence was and still is the hallmark of such racist campaigns, which center paternalist understandings of Africans as children, in need of help. The visual layout in the magazine links the two figures—starving child, and fetus—by lining them up side-by-side; by virtue of this visual sleight of hand, the fetus becomes a needy human child (Newman 1996, 24).

WOMAN VERSUS FETUS

Separating the fetus from the pregnant woman or nonbinary person is arguably the most important photographic trick to produce fetal personhood; and this relies once more on the aesthetics of innocence. The fetus is presented as solitary, as a separate being, and this in turn leaves it vulnerable to the world. In ultrasound technology, the fetus is presented as floating in space (Petchesky 1987)—an intrepid explorer, without connection to Mother Earth. The woman or nonbinary person is absent or peripheral—we do not see their body at all. They are redefined as the uterine environment for the development of fetal growth (Duden 1999). Furthermore, everything that sustains and makes *them* who they are, including all their connections to other beings, is erased in this production of a new individual person. The absent mother/parent opens the way for others to assert their role as protectors of this innocent being. In this way, the pregnant person is simply considered alongside other, potentially better guardians. When the pregnant person and fetus are framed as two equal and autonomous persons, viewers can be asked to consider their lives independently, as if the existence of the fetus did not depend entirely on that of the pregnant person. As we have seen, in fact, innocence can be deployed to make the fetus seem not only like a person, but a more valuable or worthy person than the woman or person carrying it.

Indeed, the various visualizing and scientific technologies often work to create and amplify this idea of competition between the fetus and the person carrying it. For instance, while framed as a medical procedure, ultrasound can also function as a form of surveillance. It was invented for submarine warfare, as a form of sonar detection, and then transferred into obstetrics in the 1960s; the transducer sends waves through the amniotic fluid so they bounce off fetal structures, producing a moving image in an area where one would not otherwise have access. It is used to do anatomical workups, to measure things like fetal sex organs or fetal weight. It can show complications, like ectopic pregnancies, or birth defects like a cleft palate, and sometimes, it can identify congenital problems, but these diagnoses are not accurate, especially in the first trimester, and must be confirmed by other tests. Rather, ultrasound functions in two other ways: first, as a checkup for the fetus as patient, as if it were already in the world; and second, as a form of surveillance of the womb. It provides a view into the pregnant person; to give those outside a way to "see inside." As much work on the "gaze" has shown, techniques of visualization are difficult to separate from forms of domination and control—visualizing can enable objectification. Early feminist theorists like Laura Mulvey and Luce Irigaray have argued that such looking/objectification is a specifically masculine way of knowing. That is, the clinician can use the ultrasound to bypass the mother/parent and their own sensory evidence of the fetus and replace it with "objective" scientific evidence. This enhances their ability and legitimacy to "know better" and to take control; innocence is produced and works in this intersection, as the quality of the fetus that requires protection from the world, and thus justifies surveillance.

Once again, innocence works here to reshape the boundaries of who and what matters, by enabling new taxonomies and hierarchies. We see this kind of rhetoric in debates about abortion, where the innocence of the fetus is pitted against the criminality of the pregnant woman, in a form of fetal separatism that tries to legally separate pregnant women from the fertilized eggs, embryos, and fetuses inside them.[10] One of the most extreme cases of this is the 2024 Alabama Supreme Court ruling, which judged frozen embryos to be children. As with other cases where innocence comes into play, using innocence as a primary descriptor of one person invariably results in proximate others being framed as guilty. Again, this is increasingly the case with pregnant women who are not seen as fully advancing the "rights" of their fetuses. When the fetus is considered an innocent person, the pregnant person is always under suspicion, if not already guilty. Even before the right to an abortion in the US—formerly protected by *Roe v. Wade*—was overturned by the *Dobbs v. Jackson* decision in June 2022, "endangering the life of the fetal person" included anything from having a home birth, which some may consider a risk, to accidentally falling down a flight of stairs, delaying a C-section, or using a controlled substance. Women were arrested for these very "offenses."[11]

With the overturning of *Roe v. Wade*, forty-one US states have abortion bans in effect, with limited exceptions: thirteen have a total ban, and twenty-eight have bans based on gestational duration.[12] Many of them have civil and criminal penalties associated with these bans. Most target the medical providers of abortion, threatening them with felony convictions and penalties of up to ten years in prison, with no exception for rape or incest, but some also criminalize pregnant women for travel for abortion out of state. In September 2021, in the lead-up to the overturning of *Roe v. Wade*, Texas passed Senate Bill (or SB) 8, which at the time was the most restrictive abortion law in the US, banning abortion after doctors detect a fetal heartbeat, about six weeks into pregnancy. But it could not criminalize abortion itself, because *Roe v. Wade* was still in effect; instead, the law put power into the hands of private citizens, urging them to sue doctors who performed abortions and to bring lawsuits against anyone who aided in the process of getting an abortion, such as driving someone to a clinic. The law was grounded on the belief that citizens must act to protect the innocent fetus from the person carrying it, who is rendered suspicious, and willing to harm it. Indeed, it is the separation of the fetus from the person carrying it—and the adversarial dynamics that are enacted in its place, with the fetus in need of protection—that made this law even thinkable in the first place. Another extreme case of figuring the pregnant person as a threat to their own fetus was the proposed 2022 Louisiana bill, HB 813, which wanted to subject any person who has an abortion to murder charges (criminal homicide). Ultimately the bill was tabled, with objections from the governor and many others, but all the Republican committee members supported this bill.

The language of innocence is ubiquitous in these anti-abortion laws, including in the language that subtended the legal challenge by Mississippi's "Gestational Age Act," which banned abortion after fifteen weeks, and which in December 2021 went to the Supreme Court to judge its constitutionality, and resulted in the overturning of *Roe v. Wade*. As Paul Gosar, representing Arizona's Fourth District, stated, "50 years ago, when the Supreme Court decided Roe v. Wade, doctors falsely claimed that innocent, unborn babies were not viable until after 28 weeks"; but he asserted that "at 15 weeks, a preborn baby is fully formed and can taste, feel pain, yawn and suck their thumb."[13] Similarly, Rand Paul, Republican Senator for Kentucky, stated in relation to *Roe v. Wade*, "It is unconscionable that government would facilitate the taking of innocent life."[14] And in the October 2024 vice presidential debate between Republican candidate JD Vance and Democrat Tim Walz, JD Vance responded to a question about abortion, and his earlier statements that he wants to ban abortion without exception. He stated that as a Republican, he "wants to proudly protect innocent life in this country."[15] There is no mention of the life of the woman or pregnant person and how it might be impacted; the innocent fetus trumps all.

Unsurprisingly, the politics of race is a significant factor in determining which "fetal persons" require more protection, and which pregnant persons are considered guilty. As we have seen throughout this book, innocence is largely racialized as white, in a broad sense of racialization and whiteness that changes across transnational contexts. Initial ideas about childhood innocence in the US are inseparable from whiteness, with innocence constructed against understandings of Black children as non-innocent, juvenile laborers (Bernstein 2011)—and as we have seen thus far, claims to innocence help maintain systems of white supremacy and dominance, absolving white people of collective responsibility (see chapter 1). In this case, Black women are immediately seen as less competent potential mothers of their innocent fetuses; and the "War on Drugs" in the US that was kicked off in the 1980s in response to the civil rights movements of the 1960s and 1970s has left them most vulnerable to claims of criminality and to being considered unfit mothers, drawing on racist stereotypes of "crack babies" (Mason 2000). As Dána-Ain Davis writes, "obstetric racism" is a consistent feature of Black women's lives, where pregnant Black women are treated poorly, leading to higher rates of maternal mortality and forms of reproductive injustice. As she argues, these are part of the afterlives of slavery (Davis 2019).

In these racialized landscapes, the need to protect the fetus from the pregnant person is assumed from the start; these fetuses are seen as subject to contamination by virtue of being carried by Black parents. Indeed, it is unclear whether even in conception, embryos or fetuses of Black women are considered innocent. In this sense, it is important to note that pushing back the temporality of personhood to the moment of conception enables a form of politics that both expands and contracts the borders of humanity, often expelling pregnant people as part of a deep form of sexism and misogyny, but it is equally important to note that racism persists at the moment of conception, in conjunction with the sexism. Black women and girls are expelled, but fetuses of Black people are also often seen as tainted from the start. In this sense, it is not surprising that projects to sterilize Black women and women of color are ongoing.[16]

GIRLS VERSUS WOMEN

Fetal life as human life plays out on the terrain of innocence, and insofar as it does, it requires individuals to compete for status as the most pure or the most vulnerable in order to get rights at all. This formulation works to pit girls' lives against women's lives, and against their own pregnant bodies, rendering them more at risk of losing their constitutional rights. In this sense, I suggest that expanding humanity by way of innocence is harmful to all, starting most concretely with those who can get pregnant: this is not abstract or theoretical. There are very real, often dire consequences, which are worth recounting, even if briefly.

In an essay about abortion rights litigation in Latin America, Lisa M. Kelly (2014) tells us about the centrality of narratives of innocence, and how these immediately circumscribe who gets rights. Starting from the 1990s, she covers five successful claims in the Inter-American Human Rights System, each of which involved denial of a lawful abortion at a public hospital. These all involved young girls, who were raped or sexually abused and became pregnant as a result. To be sure, the lawyers chose cases that they felt would be high-profile internationally and could win both at law and in the court of public opinion; the tried-and-true strategy of human rights organizations is naming and shaming. With this in mind, the lawyers chose those who could best foreground the exceptional elements of cruelty and inhumanity in current abortion laws, creating the possibility for shaming: innocent sufferers.

Anti-abortion advocates and similarly inclined civil society groups are active in these Latin American countries. And anti-abortionists frame their struggle in terms of innocence: they pit a universal fetal innocence against the guilt or lack of moral fiber of the person requesting an abortion. The key point is that the lawyers arguing for abortion rights did not challenge this frame. Instead, they chose to take on the cases of those whom they could also configure as innocent, and who could therefore compete with the status of the fetus: they chose the figure of the childlike rape victim to personify innocence. In this sense, they limited their cases to girls, with no sexual experience, and who did not consent to sex. For instance, there was the case of *Paulina de Carmen Ramírez Jacinto v. Mexico*. Paulina was a thirteen-year-old who became pregnant as a result of rape, and was unable to get an abortion because medical staff dissuaded her mother, citing the dangers of abortion. In the Inter-American Commission, Paulina's team argued for compensation, and that by failing to provide adequate procedures through which she could access lawful abortion, the Mexican state had violated its obligations under human rights treaties and declarations (Kelly 2014).

Kelly demonstrates how the language of childishness ("la niña") is used in each of these cases, to distinguish girls from teenagers, since the latter are more likely to be seen as sexually active. Once again, we see innocence being used to draw the line between humankinds: girls deserve abortions, teenagers do not. We saw this distinction being made in the US as well, after the *Dobbs* decision that overturned *Roe v. Wade*: one of the most me-diatized cases immediately after the Supreme Court's decision was that of a ten-year-old Ohio girl who had been raped but could not get an abortion in her state after the Supreme Court decision took effect. She went to Indiana to get abortion medication, and the doctor reported this to demonstrate the horrific effects of the law.

That is, while these human rights lawyers may be fighting against the idea of fetal innocence as that which can trump all, in response, they propose a different set of hierarchies and exclusions. Their arguments for abortion rights involved demonstrating the mental and physical health consequences of having girlhood innocence violated—their grievous suffering—and as girls, their particular vulnerability. Not only does this reinforce stereotypes of girls as somehow lesser, requiring protection, it marginalizes the rights of other women.

Insofar as human rights movements agitate for political change, one can say all these cases were successful. However, they all draw on rape excep-tions, which only provide safe access to abortion for a very few. They rely on women's non-consent to sex—their sexual innocence; this means that women who do consent to—or desire—nonprocreative sex do not have reproductive rights and must either resort to informal means of termina-tion or take on unwanted pregnancies. It also disqualifies women who are economically vulnerable and financially unable to raise a child. In general, arguments based on innocence cast the majority of those who want abor-tions outside the realm of justice, framing only the exceptional as deserving. Furthermore, *sexual* innocence is smuggled into these struggles, making moral distinctions about who deserves rights or justice; women who have consented to sex are seen as morally compromised. Overall, when fetal per-sonhood is asserted, expanding the category of humanity, it requires the language of innocence; and this in turn stratifies lives in new ways, creating new forms of inequality and exclusion.

Mother Earth: The Innocence of the Planet
Versus More-Than-Human Futures

We have seen that innocence is increasingly used to describe nonhumans and more-than-humans, bringing them into the sphere of humanity as eth-ical subject, and playing a role in whose lives are given value, and whose lives are sacrificed. If it has worked at a micro scale—that of an embryonic cluster of cells—it should not be surprising to see that innocence also works to categorize the whole planet—Mother Earth. As the most privileged of the earth finally take stock of their role in climate change, and how in the "Anthropocene" or "Capitalocene" or "Chthulucene" people and capitalism together have become planetary forces (Chakrabarty 2021; Haraway 2016), humanity is being rethought at a different scale, that is, in relation to the earth. When understood as the victim of humanity's greed and folly, the earth, figured as Mother Nature, has often been configured as the ultimate space of innocence. As noted earlier, humanity and nature—and nature and culture—have been co-configured as binary opposites in so much of modern thought that framing humans as guilty for climate change immediately suggests that "Mother Nature" should be understood as the victim. This in turns opens the world for those who want to be saviors.

While I have focused much of this book on the contested notion of the child as the ultimate figure of innocence, in this case, Mother Earth—as the supreme, all-giving, all-caring, nurturing, and normatively gendered mother in need of saving—has indeed become a key figure of global environmentalism. But as we have seen, to cast mothers as innocent requires some work; imbued with sexual knowledge, mothers are not easily or obviously (sexually) innocent or in need of protection. So how does this work?

To be sure, the personified form of Mother Nature is not new; nor is it simple or pure. It is a form derived at least in part from the Indigenous Andean deity, Pachamama, which is embedded in a very different set of ontologies and relationalities. Pachamama is described by Indigenous thinkers and scholars as the earth's generative powers (Macas 2010; Pacari 2009; cf. Tola 2018)—it is the condition of possibility for life itself. While it was identified with fertility in the pre-colonial period, later, throughout the period of colonization, it began to be defined through the qualities of purity and virtue that characterized the Virgin Mary (Tola 2018). That is, unlike Mother Earth, Pachamama was not chaste, virginal, or pure; she/it was not considered sexually innocent, but rather, she evoked lust, lasciviousness, and moral chaos. She was not benevolent or all-giving. And Pachamama was not consistently feminine; some parts were feminine, while others, such as mountains or stones, were described as male. As with much of Andean ontology, she was not fixed or permanent, but shifting in relation to other elements. With colonization and the enforced assimilation into Christianity, Pachamama and other such figures were rendered a version of Mother Earth, and turned into a universal divinity, or a single goddess that subsumed all other deities (Dean 2010; Tola 2018). They were pushed into Western modernity's rigid binary between nature and culture, where nature constitutes the passive, feminized, and racialized background for human progress—indeed, where nature is rendered at once innocent and impotent.

Mother Earth, when centered by environmental organizations, is often about an all-giving female body, and about reproduction and care; but also, about purity, docility, and subordination. Shaped by Christian notions of the Virgin Mary, the call to protect Mother Nature also draws on the idea of sexual innocence. Mother Earth is violently penetrated by drills, in an unbridled desire for oil, her mountaintops are blown off as part of extractive mining, she is forced open in the process of fracking—all of these draw on images of sexual violence, from which she must be protected.

The personification of Mother Earth as innocent has been emphasized and amplified in various ways by the Swedish activist Greta Thunberg, even though the message she carries has been articulated by Indigenous people for centuries; and even as they have been treated with rage and suppression. Indigenous scholars and activists have been clear about the inseparability of people from the land, from rivers, and from mountains, and that extractivism (of oil, minerals, etc.) will lead the destruction of the earth;[17] the 2016 Standing Rock protests against the Dakota Access pipeline are simply one recent case in a very long, brutal history. The question is why Thunberg is being heard, and not others: the answer, I suggest, is in large part about the way she mobilizes innocence. Insofar as nature is already personified, Thunberg represents this version of Mother Earth; as a blond, white girl when she started her activism—smaller than many her age, and still very girl-like—Thunberg embodies the innocence of the earth, which she is in turn trying to save. To be clear, saving the earth is also saving herself, and her own future and the future of her generation. She is often described as "speaking truth to power," which is another feature of childhood innocence—as already mentioned, children are seen as figures of wisdom, even as they stand outside time.[18] Thunberg further embodies innocence through what she calls her "secret power": her autism. Indeed, one might argue that her neurodivergence qualifies her even further to speak truth to power. That is, insofar as innocence acts as the boundary for liberal ideas of personhood, it marks the constituent outside, including by exclusion those who are pure; those with differences and disabilities often embody this border. Thunberg's autism situates her as innocent of political and strategic concerns; innocent of the more mundane or instrumental forms of knowledge, even as she embodies the knowledge of the planet's imminent death. In this sense, Thunberg's power in mobilizing against climate change is unparalleled, unlike Indigenous people and many others in solidarity, because they use a different set of moral and affective registers; to a dominant, liberal mainstream, Thunberg is compelling, insofar as she embodies innocence.

Conclusion: Contaminated Possibilities

Not only does personification of Mother Nature perpetuate the binary of nature and culture, and frame people as separate from and outside of nature, rather than imbricated with and constituted by it, it reinforces gendered stereotypes and patriarchal ideas that rely on a gender binary, and figure all feminine things, including the earth, as passive, designed primarily to reproduce and to care for things. Perhaps most importantly, this personification of Mother Earth as innocent directs our political responses: it produces a politics of rescue, and a politics of purity—the goal is to save Mother Earth, to protect her through projects of conservation and purification, rather than by living in and with other beings, and by understanding beings and entities of all kinds as part of the world. This is the same politics that puts UK and EU money and energy into protecting Fort Vert (outside Calais) from people-on-the-move and that justifies their detention and deportation. But care for the earth cannot require the sacrifice of certain populations; tackling climate change cannot be subtended by racism and disenfranchisement.

Science and Technology Studies (STS) feminists, queer theorists, and scholars of Black ecologies have led the way to understandings of the body as embedded in and part of larger ecologies, as inseparable from them. These theories challenge the idea of independent liberal selves. As Julie Livingston (2020) writes, "The body is an act of exchange and a site of vulnerability in a complex and more-than-human world." It is, as she so aptly notes, a tentacular relationship, where the air we breathe and exhale eventually gets inhaled by someone else, somewhere else; where the water that goes through our bodies to keep us alive may next nourish a farmer's field. Or, as Mel Chen notes (2021), where the smoky air, from the climate-change-enhanced wildfires of California, gets inhaled by an unmasked, infected pedestrian, creating a doubly potent inhalant for the next passerby. But to be clear, these interconnections are deeply imbricated in relations of power. As scholars in the field of Black geographies and ecologies have shown, racism conditions people's relationship to environments: there is no way to further environmentalism without taking racism seriously, from the location of waste disposal to that of chemical or nuclear industries.[19] For instance, Solomon understands enslavement, displacement, and dispossession as environmental harms, and rethinks waste infrastructure in terms of the histories of plantation monocultural economies, which exhausted the soils of the Southern US, rendering them ideal spaces for toxic industries. These ecological afterlives of slavery—the soil and the air—have entered into the bodies of Black and Native American populations, among others, creating forms of illness and vulnerability that lead to premature death (Solomon 2022).

We are interconnected, co-constituted. Through the 2020 COVID-19 pandemic, our connections were rendered visible in a way that is impossible to ignore; if people do not succumb to fear, this experience can help challenge the violence of hierarchical species classifications, and of the category humanity, even as it draws attention to how these taxonomies are put in place and maintained.

Innocence is a way to categorize individuals, or individualizing entities; I acknowledge it is also used for forms of collective personhood like nation-states, such as American innocence or German guilt. But understanding the world as a series of entanglements shifts our moral grammars, where interrelationality becomes the grounding ontological condition. In such a world, it becomes impossible to use the language of innocence, because interrelationality necessarily demands responsibility. For instance, one may never have intended to transmit COVID-19, and one may have done everything possible to avoid it—mask wearing, vaccinations, isolating at home—and yet one may have transmitted it to a loved one, or a friend. Certain conditions and ways of life exacerbate the transmission of viruses, regardless of intent, rendering everyone in some way complicit, or at least implicated.

Recognizing that we live in a connected world is the only way to survive today: we are in a life-and-death embrace with each other that no one can wriggle out of. This is not a romantic statement, that equalizes all forms of being or pretends that all forms of interrelationality or interspecies relationality are comfortable; for instance, everyone must live with viruses, microbes, mosquitoes, ticks, and other pests. We will have to learn to protect ourselves from (certain) viruses even as we acknowledge that a big portion of our DNA is made up of viral DNA—viruses are part of us, around us, we cannot live without them, *and* they can kill us. The key is to acknowledge that the risks are differently distributed among different populations. There is no purity here, no easy victims or perpetrators. Accepting an interconnected world is also not a dystopic statement; if we do recognize this, many more might not only survive, but eventually flourish.

CHAPTER FIVE

Beyond Innocence

Toward a Commoning World

At an event I attended in 2018, at the height of the newly invigorated Sanctuary movement in the US, an artist-activist engaged in the movement stood up to say that she thought of the project of sanctuary as spurring the imagination, and "training for the not-yet."[1] This focus on political imagination was confirmed to me later by many people-on-the-move and activists, on both sides of the Atlantic. Opening the way for a world beyond nation-states, where the rich and the poor are not segregated by borders, necessarily involves a set of imaginative acts. So does thinking of a world beyond private property, and beyond racial capitalism. Innocence acts as handmaiden to these regimes, and yet, the political work it does remains invisible, cloaked as moral good. Innocence works to reproduce and enhance forms of inequality, to further claims to power, and to create exclusions. What other moral and political grammars might we be attuned to and cultivate, to open the way to more egalitarian worlds? How can we begin to see and think and be otherwise? Imagination and creative experimentation could not be more necessary in this authoritarian world.

Feminist scholars have called attention to the problem of innocence in politics for some time now. Ruth Wilson Gilmore has taken on the problem of innocence in the prison-industrial complex: while both liberals and conservatives express their commitment to saving "innocent" people when wrongly accused, they nevertheless believe that others deserve to be in cages. Gilmore shows that this desire to distinguish degrees of innocence ultimately results in some people becoming permanently not innocent, no matter what they say or do. To insist on innocence is to surrender politically because innocence skirts the real problem: how to diminish and remedy harm, rather than finding better forms of punishment (Gilmore 2022). She moves beyond innocence, to focus on abolition, which is a form of non-innocent politics that refuses to divide, hierarchize, or sacrifice anyone.

Similarly, Donna Haraway (1991) has insisted that there is no innocent standpoint, no space of purity or moral transcendence. Politics is difficult, messy. In her more recent work on nonhumans (Haraway 2008), for instance, she suggests that it is a mistake to pretend that we can live outside killing—all ecologies are mortal beings—we kill for food, for clothing, for medical care. To pretend that one can do so is to pretend to innocence—to refuse to take responsibility for the things we do kill. For her, then, the question is how to live responsibly with the necessity and labor of killing, without thinking of mortal beings as disposable. This is an ethically attuned form of non-innocent politics: it is a form of care that assumes responsibility for violence.

Here, I draw on tools—feminist, materialist, anti-racist, decolonial, and speculative—to help dislodge the grids of our current reality, structured by innocence and guilt, victims and perpetrators; but I do this without the promise of delivering easy answers. Rather, I identify experiments that try to move beyond innocence, to amplify what creeps out around the edges of a more hegemonic racial capitalist, (il)liberal politics. Feminist theorizing has always been about identifying the way the world is, and simultaneously opening the way to new worlds—helping bring them into being.[2] Opening the way for a world beyond innocence necessarily involves a set of imaginative acts.

Innocence plays a critical role in reproducing the world of (il)liberal individualism. What would it take to produce a common world, not one partitioned between morally deserving and undeserving? What kinds of political subjects might both be created by, and in turn generate this world? In what follows, I discuss several places and moments where I see the political grammars of innocence being reworked; where new spaces of political enunciation are being opened and sensibilities shifted. I have chosen to discuss two sets of experiments because, first, they illustrate the emergence of collective subjects, challenging the liberal individual at the heart of the politics of innocence; and second, they reveal emerging forms of differently partitioned (often horizontal) sociality, once again challenging the hierarchies established and maintained by the concept of innocence. Finally, these experiments eschew purity, and grapple with the very real forms of violence caused by racial capitalism, without trying to lock it (or anyone) away. In other words, I track experiments—some big, some small—in different ways of *being* (as collectives versus individuals) and *being together* (sometimes configured as horizontal versus hierarchical, but we can think of them as different social geometries). I find it helpful to think of these experiments in the frame of *commoning*, even as they are also contributing to new configurations and understandings of this emergent political form, as I will discuss below. In many ways, I use the idea as a placeholder for an emergent form of political imagination. I propose these experiments as potential ways in which to think and be otherwise, but they are not the only alternatives, nor do I want to suggest they necessarily succeed: they are simply imaginative preludes, which draw on many things to prefigure futures, including recovered pasts.

To alter political grammars—indeed, to create a new "common sense"—requires work on several levels, at different registers, changing the fabric of the sensible while also remaking place. As we have seen, innocence is shaped as much by its visual forms and representations as it is by social categories and geographies. To take this seriously requires that we be attentive to the aesthetic and its imbrication with and manifestation in the realm of the political. To really uproot or rewrite a politics of innocence, intervention must happen in both registers: that is, to shift consciousness as well as practice, we need to counter hegemonic practices, engaging in what Gramsci referred to as revolutionary art—art that reveals the social contradictions at the heart of this political formation.

To this end, in the first part of this chapter, I discuss visual experiments in two sets of aesthetic projects and decolonial films, one set in Syria, the other in France. But I take seriously the intertwined relationship between aesthetics and politics. As philosopher Jacques Rancière suggests, the goal of the political is to shift the grammar of the sensible, and what is rendered visible and invisible (Rancière 2010). Only in this way will we be able to forge new forms of collective expression, new forms of being and becoming, beyond innocence. The goal of aesthetic interventions is not to offer a new model of behavior, but to re-partition time and space, to enable a different sense-making of the world; the ambition is to question the natural order, creating what Rancière calls "dissensus," or a disruption in the fabric of sensory experience.

In these films, then, I track disruptions in the realm of the sensible. On the one hand, I am interested in the undoing and remaking of representations of women and children—two classic tropes of innocence. On the other hand, I am interested in the ways these visual experiments create space for new ways of coming together: What is the moment of incipient change, when a potential collective political subject appears, yet before it has a coherent voice? I am interested in the appearance of new forms of popular assembly and political association—new forms of being together. I explore the appearance of collective subjects, from the mob and multitude to non-Eurocentric ideas of humanity.

The distinction between appearance and visibility is important here. As political theorist Jason Frank (2021) suggests, drawing on both Hannah Arendt and Jacques Rancière, visibility—what we see or note—is shaped by our current ideas of common sense; the political mode of *appearance* is the rupture of the consensus by the vital surplus—those who are not legible, who do not count, and who are invisible until that moment. In this sense, appearance is the moment of true political possibility—the condition for the emergence of new collectivities and political subjects. It's a disruption of the realm of the sensible. To be clear, this does not need to be a major revolutionary event; such shifts can be part of the everyday.

In the second part, I look at what is happening on the ground, although in both cases, I am interested in new forms of collective enunciation. I look to "no-borders" or border abolitionist movements for experiments beyond innocence, because they are already pushing beyond many of our foundational liberal political terms and concepts, experimenting with new horizontal forms of sharing, collectivity, and sociality that challenge the hierarchies of moral deservingness built into liberal regimes, foremost among which is perhaps the regime of citizenship (see chapters 1 and 4). Artists are key in sanctuary/no-borders movements, just as activists are forging new forms of political consciousness through film. In both, I trace and help imagine modes of appearance that challenge the consensus based on innocence.

∵

Let me explain why I use commoning as a frame for these experiments in non-innocent becomings. As I mentioned in the introduction, commoning has come to mean many things and is practiced by many different people, but it is often referred to as a struggle against enclosures, against the privatization of spaces of freedom, against exclusion, and, perhaps most importantly, against private property. It can also mean the sharing of wealth and resources on the basis of collective decision-making; sometimes it is spoken of as grounded in social relations built on reciprocity, respect, mutuality, and responsibility (Hardt and Negri 2009; Dardot and Laval 2019; Federici 2019). I use "commoning" rather than "the commons" to highlight that this is always a process, always in motion, not a fixed or defined set of spaces, people, objects, or resources. The idea of "the common" is also helpful insofar as it describes the political principle that animates and guides the activity of commoning (Dardot and Laval 2019, 7).

In this and most other ways, I depart from the older literature on the commons by scholars like Garrett Hardin, who, in 1968, wrote about the tragedy of the commons, and Elinor Ostrom (1990, 2000), who successfully countered his theory. Both stay within the frame of capitalist economics, with a focus on common "natural" resources, even as Ostrom shows how communal resources can be collectively managed without sacrificing economic gain. For them, "the commons" are external things or objects with an essence that prohibits people from appropriating them, such as air and water. And yet, such entities are currently being commodified.

Instead, I highlight different genealogies. In many ways, commoning overlaps with autonomist traditions, from the Zapatistas and the informal settlements that fueled the Arab uprisings, to the Spanish encampments and the Occupy movement. It overlaps with squatters movements. But it is not identical to these. Similarly, feminist scholar-activists like Silvia Federici (2019) emphasize the feminist nature of the common in terms of the communing of reproductive activities—meaning the day-to-day activities that are producing people's lives. Examples include the collective kitchen, urban gardens, and squats. Perhaps most importantly, Federici states that the common is not just a site of reproduction and redistribution; it is also a site of struggle. It builds the grounds of resistance, refusing to separate the time of political organization from that of reproduction.

With the examples I provide, I also challenge the association of whiteness with commoning: from its history with the Diggers in seventeenth-century England, to those who have made it a liberal pursuit, to the white anarchists of Occupy Wall Street. More recently, Black and Latine scholars have reassured those who worry that the goal of equivalence in a (future) world of commoning would erase or ignore existing differences in power. They have been thinking about commoning as a form of reparations—a new set of connections to the land that go against capitalist enclosures (Touray 2021; Roane 2018). As Robin Kelley notes, these scholars are rediscovering and emphasizing instances of commoning in the seventeenth and eighteenth centuries among semi-enslaved communities, who managed their own plots of land and joined with Indigenous communities to pose a threat to capital (Kelley 2024; Roane 2018). José Muñoz calls commoning a process of thinking and imagining otherwise in the face of shared wounding (Muñoz 2020). Feminist abolitionist politics arguably offers the strongest example of this for me, insisting on the interconnection between carework and political organizing, where, for example, as with the Chicago group Mamas, mothers of those who are incarcerated model collective ways of being by taking responsibility for each other's children, and extend their care to friends, neighbors, and cellmates (Naber et al. 2020), demanding justice for all—carework and revolutionary political organizing are conjoined. This is a variation on the work that Ruth Wilson Gilmore wrote about in *Golden Gulag* (2007), where "Mothers Reclaiming Our Children" (Mothers ROC) transformed their caregiving and reproductive labor into activism to reclaim all children in the criminal justice system, regardless of race, age, residence, or alleged crime. In this sense, for me, in addition to being anticapitalist, the placeholder I call commoning is necessarily feminist, anti-racist, and decolonial.

Two aspects of commoning are most relevant to me here. First, theories and praxes of commoning point to the emergence of a collective subject. Who or what is the subject, and how does it come into being? In what capacity, and with what affective ties? I take on these questions in thinking through these various experiments. Second, if innocence is a tool used to reproduce hierarchies at many levels, what are the political space, nature, and scale of commoning? How do people live together: How are violence and conflict managed, and where is the place for difference? I draw on and amplify attempts to create autonomous zones that supersede nation-state borders with capacious structures and infrastructures of political care.

I see these examples as experiments in new ways of being and being together, but in thinking with them, I also try to imagine where they might go—that is, I am interested in pushing our political imaginations. While some have proposed commoning as a future (or utopic) project, I insist that commoning already exists all around us, if we look carefully—as the excess of racial capitalism, these are the spaces and formations that we cannot quite see; but they are already prefiguring new ways of being, and my goal, then, is to help them into forms of political appearance.

In that sense, this is both an empirical and speculative exercise, insofar as speculative thinking is a blur, as designer Benjamin Bratton (2015, 14) writes, "between the real but-as-yet-unnamed and the imagined but-as-yet-not-real." Indeed, what I offer is as much of an amplification and a call for new political formations as it is a description of emerging collectivities or commonings. I have tried to be attentive to present experiments, to see the way they imagine and work to produce the future in the gaps, in the "loopholes" (Syedullah 2014); and indeed, my hope is to imagine with them, to speculate and proliferate the practices and ideas, in order to help produce a different future.

Visual Experiments in Non-Innocence

Innocence is produced in part by visual regimes that center victims and perpetrators: this involves accentuating the naïveté and vulnerability of the victims, and often the Otherness of the perpetrators, making them seem monstrous, inhuman. As we have seen, humanitarian organizations often draw on such visual frameworks, featuring young, wide-eyed children as victims,[3] and this in turn prompts action to "save" them. But these visual regimes that work to save the most innocent-looking also shape our perception of whose life matters, and whose does not. As I have tried to show, to save the innocent necessarily means creating a line that distinguishes between them and another group who are rendered guilty, criminal, or otherwise morally unworthy. In what follows, I am interested both in the ways these aesthetic projects rework these stereotypes and in new forms of appearance: the opening for new collective subjects.

ABOUNADDARA AND THE RIGHT TO THE IMAGE

The work of Abounaddara, an anonymous Syrian film collective, is interesting to think with and against as a form of non-innocent politics, as it directly opposes the discourses and imagery of humanitarianism, and the subjects it calls forth. They posted a film online about daily life in Syria every Friday between the start of the revolution in 2011 and 2017. If the language of humanitarianism, while seemingly well intentioned, nevertheless traffics in the discourse of abjection, this anonymous Syrian film collective offers one of the most powerful examples I have found of work that undoes a Western desire to witness victimhood, and to feel pity, while claiming innocence themselves. Abounaddara works to restructure the debates that configure people as either invasive threat or pathetic victim. Indeed, they work to reframe the real; in so doing, they enrich our political and affective grammars, stretching them well beyond the logics of innocence.

I see Abounaddara working in the tradition of what has been called "decolonial film," which is not necessarily representational, but facilitates spaces and enunciation as ruptures into the field of the sensible, visible, and audible. Perhaps just as importantly, decolonial film is not contained by the discrete space of cinematic production; it creates an expanded field of media practice, direct action, and political organizing—it seeks collaboration and solidarity between struggles and is committed to making and screening films in the communities that develop around them, and in contexts such as the street, village, or museum (MTL Collective 2020). As others have shown, watching films together can indeed help shape political consciousness (Razsa and Guillén 2017).

Abounaddara has been engaged in changing images of Syrians and of the war, overthrowing the frameworks that represent Syrians as either victims or terrorists. But more importantly, they have developed a strategy to produce a different political landscape. Their strategy calls for "the right to a dignified image." As the collective's one named representative, Charif Kiwan, states, the Abounaddara films "deal with the indignity of war without representing indignity." To explain what he means by this, he points to the fact that we rarely, if ever, see bloodied or dead Americans or Europeans in the media, despite their perpetual military engagements and occupations. The US military tightly controls images of dead American soldiers, but the mainstream media follows suit. Media elsewhere in the Global North is not so different; for instance, French television stations refused to show images of the victims of the Paris terror attacks in 2015. Pointing to such differential treatment, Kiwan asks, why were images of Syrian corpses all over the media? Why the graphic images of violence and tragedy? He states, "Once you watch those photos all the time, then you are not surprised . . . you consider those people not very important, because they are dying all the time. So you finish by telling yourself, these people are not like me, not human like me."[4] This conclusion about a racialized hierarchy of humanity is repeatedly supported by mainstream American media. Abounaddara objects to having to trade in the indignities of debased corpses in order to leverage compassion.

Since the 1990s, when reporters began to be systematically embedded with fighting forces in war zones, war has become a battle of images. Sometimes the possibility of representation precedes and in fact makes the event—this was the case with images in Somalia with Operation Restore Hope in the early 1990s, where photojournalists on site, ready to photograph, effectively initiated action: the event happened for the sake of the picture (Keenan, in Strauss et al. 2011). As Abounaddara suggests, the media not only represent, but *produce* a different battlefront; war needs to be waged in these corollary terms as well. Indeed, Karen Strassler calls such political work "image-events"; she refers to the political processes set in motion when an image or set of images erupt onto or intervene in a social field, becoming a focal point of discursive and affective engagement across diverse publics (Strassler 2020, 9–10). Increasingly, images have become the terrain of political struggle, shaping and manipulating publics. She suggests, in fact, that in a world where political recognition is imbricated with publicity and visibility, all political events are also image-events. In this sense, political action is inseparable from action on the visual front, understanding that images are never static, but performative—they are constantly unfolding in specific contexts.

I am interested in when the visual medium enables a new form of political appearance, and when it simply reinforces the existing consensus or status quo. The question for Abounaddara is how to create new image-events that allow dignity to appear, to be perceived. To be clear, Abounaddara understands dignity in relation to systems of exploitation; indignity is produced by representing people as ends to market gains or profits: "we must strive to represent the other as an end in herself or himself and not as a means" (Abounaddara 2017). I will return to their concept of dignity in relation to the concept of humanity, but for now, I want to note that the concept was central in the uprisings in Tahrir Square and in many of the Arab uprisings in 2010–2011. Abounaddara's ideas of dignity echo these calls, requiring seizing the means of production in order to be able to represent people with respect; for them, dignity is understood as a concept that underpins both freedom and justice.

One way that Abounaddara produces dignified images is by reworking the common figurations of innocence: women and children. That is, to them, a dignified image is precisely one that allows for complexity and respect in everyday life—images of innocence preclude moral nuance. Abounaddara's films are short—just a few minutes each—and often quite intimate. They are nevertheless set in the context of war. Abounaddara does not try to forget or erase what they call the "nightmare" of war, but to show people living their lives within it, beside it, or despite it. One film, *The Lady of Syria* (2015), opens with a woman looking into the distance from a hilltop, stating, "See . . . it fell over there . . . in the next village . . . not on houses." We cannot see what she's looking at, but we can imagine it's the aftermath of an explosion or drone strike. But then she walks along, descending into the basement of a building, where, through the dim light, we gradually see that women are engaged in a beauty lesson, learning how to style a bride's hair. There is no electricity, but the teacher says, in a playfully ironic tone, "War or no war, we are following fashion!" Such scenes challenge Western perceptions of Muslim women as long-suffering, innocent victims who require saving—perceptions that scholars like Lila Abu-Lughod have long critiqued (2013). Some watch attentively, others chat; the teacher reminds them that tomorrow they have a nursing lesson.

In another film, called *Vanguards* (2011), we see little children lined up, in uniform, shouting war slogans and other propaganda, repeating after a voice that guides them. They shout, "Revolution!" and "Bearers of immortal messages!" and "Always ready!" and "Freedom! Freedom! Freedom!" and raise their arms in salute. Once again, this film departs from and challenges key humanitarian tropes, which feed into the grammars of innocence. Unlike the now-iconic image of Alan Kurdi, discussed in chapter 2—the three-year-old Syrian boy whose body washed up on the beach in September 2015—these children are politically active and engaged. Kurdi's innocence is represented by his inert, vulnerable, passive body—a small body overcome by the larger, dangerous forces in the world. These children are active, loud, insistent. Similarly, as we also saw in chapter 2, the images have no likeness to the video that went viral in August 2016: five-year-old Omran Daqneesh was shown dazed, covered in blood and dust, sitting in an ambulance in the aftermath of an airstrike in Aleppo. Again, in the video and related photographs, Daqneesh appears confused, unknowing, alone, and vulnerable, while the children in *Vanguards* are portrayed as part of a larger political and historical context in which they participate as full actors. While many say that photographs such as those of Kurdi and Daqneesh are what finally jogged Europe into action (to help migrants, to stop supporting the war in Syria), as we have seen, images of innocence—and the moral imperative they engender—far too often end up harming those they intend to help, by producing the very idea of worthiness, and in the process, also producing its opposite: the unworthy. Such images work to separate deserving from undeserving, often penalizing or criminalizing those who are perceived to be in the latter category. In this sense, to shift images, as the collective of Abounaddara argues, is a matter of life and death; images produce physical harm. We see this over and over again in the case of the ongoing genocide in Gaza, where images are a central battleground.

Using innocence as a key ethico-moral lens shifts all those who do not qualify as innocent into the category of guilty. Abounaddara's visual work breaks this binary, filling out the frame that currently restricts the possibilities to *either* identifying with the victim *or* bracketing the subject as a distant and barbaric Other. To return to the film *Vanguards*, the children actively participate in learning propaganda. Surely the children lack full contextual understanding, but they are nevertheless engaged in all the complexities of childhood, figuring out who they are, when to lead, whom to follow, when to obey, how to resist, when to speak back, and when to run away. Some shout, some look gleeful, others look bored. None of them is passive or pure.

Abounaddara's films are beautiful and often poetic; they offer an intimate glimpse into people's lives. They manage to capture the global scale of war in these intimate frames without showing explicit violence. As such, they challenge the visual and affective vocabularies of innocence, and the related attempts to generate care and concern by way of images of horror, or affective responses such as pity or compassion. They also open the way to questions about responsibility and implicatedness—how is their audience part of this story? As Charif Kiwan stated when he hesitantly accepted an award for Abounaddara from the Vera List Center for Art and Politics in October 2015, Abounaddara hopes that people in the US will join their struggle. By this, he did not mean joining the conflict in Syria—he asked for people to stay out of that—but instead the struggle against the "banality of evil" created by the humanitarian apparatus within mainstream global media, which undermines what Abounaddara holds most dear: dignity. Rather, the goal is to suture together a common world, not one partitioned between haves and have-nots, victims and saviors.

NON-INNOCENCE IN THE FRENCH *BANLIEUE*

Abounaddara talks explicitly about challenging humanitarian imagery and action in their work. I shift now to another film where a similar challenge to the stereotypes of children is attempted. I chose the 2019 French film *Les Misérables*, by filmmaker Ladj Ly, as it has received a lot of attention and offers an example of the blending of fictional and non-fictional worlds. As I will explain, I place it in the category of decolonial film as well. The film's title is a reference to the Victor Hugo 1862 novel of the same name, written and set in the same community of Montfermeil where Hugo's novel is partially set and where Ladj Ly grew up. It is based on a real occurrence of police violence that took place in the city in 2008, which Ladj Ly filmed, although the film is cast as drama. Montfermeil is in Seine-Saint-Denis, the region in which the massive 2005 popular uprisings—more commonly known as "riots"—took place, when policemen racially profiled and chased two young boys to their death. They were electrocuted after fleeing to an electricity substation. The ensuing revolt and unrest in the *banlieue* in response to the plague of police violence spread across the country and led the government to call a state of emergency.

The film follows on more recent forms of police violence in France, including the murder of Adama Traoré in 2016 by the police in the *banlieue* of Beaumont-sur-Oise, after they came looking for his brother and demanded ID from him, which he did not have. His death in police custody sparked massive protests in Paris, Lyon, and Toulouse in the style of #BLM, and focused on the similarly brutal and disproportionate violence that Black and Arab communities face at the hands of the French police. A report in May 2020 clearing the police officers of wrongdoing once again triggered protests across the country, and demonstrated the impunity of the police and the French state. The film remains timely, as police violence and impunity continue: as mentioned in the introduction, the murder of seventeen-year-old Nahel Merzouk by French police in June 2023 for a supposed violation of a traffic stop prompted the largest nationwide protests France has seen in years, with thousands of arrests and statewide curfews. Nahel had no weapon; he had done nothing wrong. He was punished for being a young man of Algerian and Moroccan descent, living in the segregated areas of the *banlieue*.

In some ways, *Les Misérables* takes its place among "*banlieue* films," a genre begun with *La Haine* in 1995, about the urban peripheries in France, mostly spaces of abandonment, racialized poverty, and violent policing. *Banlieue* films have depicted the marginalization, joblessness, and hopelessness of those who live there—so-called "immigrants," but often from three and four generations back. In France, where "race" and racism are not recognized by the state, this terminology keeps them as perpetual foreigners. The language of migration stands in for discourses of race and racism, describing racialized Others in ways that are rendered acceptable. These communities have been spatially, socially, and economically segregated from the rest of French society, fomenting disillusionment and unrest.

Depictions of *banlieues* have occasionally been called "misérabiliste"— the attitude that the poor are victims of their situations and lack the tools to change their lot. While "misérabilisme" aptly identifies the structures—as opposed to specific individuals—as the problem, it nevertheless focuses on misery and suffering, and risks reproducing these spaces as culturally stigmatized. While it does point to racist discrimination and disenfranchisement, I want to suggest that *Les Misérables* largely avoids the trap of "misérabilisme," offering instead a more nuanced account. The film depicts the harsh conditions of the *banlieue*, but it nevertheless challenges stereotypes of pure victims and perpetrators, especially among children. There are no innocent children here, but nor are they unsalvageable criminals. The film refuses such easy binaries. The film follows the gaze of the police, but they are not let off the hook for the violence they commit. This strategy works to both draw in audiences sympathetic to the police, and simultaneously hold them accountable. The policemen in the film share many of the circumstances of the *banlieue* children, such as having grown up in that same *cité*. It is this tension—and the lack of innocence all around, in a situation that is heartbreaking—that makes the film so noteworthy.

The fictional film tells the story of a day in the life of Montfermeil after a new police officer (Stéphane) gets hired into the Street Crime Unit, working to find his place in a three-person team in which the white officer is a bully (Chris), and the Black officer (Gwada), who himself grew up in Montfermeil, follows along without challenging Chris. This film centers a conflict between the kids of the area and these three police officers. As we saw in chapter 2, there is a tendency to use the descriptors of "youth" or "teenagers" for children who are not easily innocent, to keep and protect a time of untroubled purity (Malkki 2010). In the film reviews of *Les Misérables*, the language alternates between these categories. The main characters are somewhere between ten and twelve years old, and still very much children; but they are mostly from families of North African and Sub-Saharan African descent, and therefore immediately subject to the racial regimes that deny them a time of innocence. While they are mischievous and frustrated, their tricks and vandalism are still shaped by the fact that they are children. For instance, the police receive a report of a kidnapping, but it turns out that the kidnapping is not of a human, but a lion cub; Issa, the most prominent figure in the group of kids, has taken "Johnny" from a circus. This is clearly the work of children; we see the playful aspect—they are fascinated by the circus animals, but they are also naïve about the dangers of wild animals. When they do eventually catch Issa, the circus owners put him in the ring with a full-grown lion to teach him a lesson, and he wets his pants in fear. He is a child, playing at adulthood.

The trouble really begins when, while chasing down the kids, the Black police officer, Gwada—temporarily blinded by his own use of tear gas—shoots Issa in the face with a flash ball, and seriously injures him; the police officers worry that "le petit" (the little one) might not live. They know what they have done is wrong. They subsequently realize the footage of the violence was unwittingly captured by a small drone flying overhead: a toy that belongs to another local boy named Buzz, who happened to be playing with it at the time. Again, while drones function as deadly technology in warfare, in this case, we see its ambiguity as both toy and weapon; it reflects the position of these kids, at the border of playfulness and serious harm, childhood and adulthood. In the film, the drone serves as the "god's eye" that sees all; this role is enhanced when understood as an extension of its owner, Buzz. It plays on a traditional view of the child as unknowing seer of truth; another version of this is the child as vessel of unmediated truth who bears witness to the duplicities of adults (Malkki 2010). The drone provides a modern-day enactment of these ideas—it "sees" without understanding what it sees, but its recording can and will tell the truth to those who watch it.

The film shows the difficult, carceral context in which these kids grow up, shaping their frustration and anger; this is revealed in an early scene, where Chris, the white police officer, approaches a group of teenage girls waiting for the bus, and grabs one of them to smell her fingers, claiming she smells like marijuana. When the girls complain about his harassment and try to film him, he grabs their phone and smashes it. This police violence is part of everyday life. And while, like most *banlieue* films, we see the marginalization and urban decay in which they live, they are not turned into victims of their situation; they are constantly finding ways to act and challenge their circumstances. In this way, the film escapes carceral logics of innocence and guilt. Issa is a strong, captivating young kid, and yet either because of or despite that, he is not terribly likable; he is defiant, and refuses to listen.

NON-INNOCENT COLLECTIVE SUBJECTS: MOBS, CROWDS, MULTITUDES, COMMONERS

But it is not primarily through Issa that the innocence of children is re-worked: it is by shifting the focus from Issa as lone individual to the group or collective. I want to now turn to discuss forms of political appearance, and the formation of a popular (non-innocent) subject. *Les Misérables* ends with an encounter between the police and all the children of the neighbor-hood, where the police are trapped in a building, and the kids block their backup. They take charge, imbued with a different sense of power. This is il-lustrated by their treatment of the neighborhood character called "le maire" or "the mayor," a person from the community who generally keeps things in order. He hears the violence and comes into the building to ask what is going on. He repeatedly shouts at the kids, "Who gave *you* permission?" un-til they eventually surround him, beat him, and throw him down the stairs. There is clearly no one giving permission—no sovereign power. They have assumed authority themselves. Issa is poised to light a Molotov cocktail to kill Stéphane, the new cop, and incidentally the only one who tried to ap-proach their worlds with kindness; and Stéphane in turn draws his gun on Issa. While the film ends before this decisive moment is resolved, we locate the power in neither Issa nor Stéphane—child nor policeman—but in the collective, who have become something bigger and stronger than children. They are dressed similarly, all in black, with hoods and masks covering their faces; we only see them as a collective force. They are not a gang, since they have come together simply for this moment, in the movement against the police, in the occupation of this building and in this encounter with the state and its racist history. Individual liberal subjects are purposively flat-tened in order for a larger social or political entity to materialize.

As in the case here, activity is often central to the forming of a collec-tive subject. We can think of the power of collective movement by thinking about the word "mobility" and its etymology. In the seventeenth century, the word "mobility" was shortened to the word "mob." A mob referred to the disorderly part of the common people; it meant a riotous assem-blage, a crowd or gang. One part of the definition of mob is its fickleness, its movement. These children came together temporarily, not forever. In the eighteenth century, as Martina Tazzioli (2017) points out, the mob referred more specifically to vagabonds and vagrants; and as she states, here the mob refers to both the "people" and their troubling actions—in other words, it is not about the identity of a group per se, but precisely about how people come together as a group to unsettle or disrupt.

Alternatively, we might theorize this new collective political subject in relation to a crowd. Crowd theory discusses whether individuals are more than the sum of their parts, if they are smarter or dumber than the individuals that compose them (Hayden 2020). But the crowd also challenges liberal formations in pushing people to lose their individuality, rationality, and boundaries—crowds are susceptible to emotional contagion (Orr 2006). Crowd theory is a theory of de-individuation, where political will is not made of individuals (Hayden 2021; Dean 2016). Rather, as with these kids, it is about the coming together of unauthorized bodies in public space, in potentially radical forms of popular assembly.

The multitude is perhaps the most theorized collective subject of late, particularly around the idea of the common (Hardt and Negri 2009). This is a radically plural and open body politic, not defined by identity, but precisely, by activity or being together in moments of encounter. Like the history of the mob, the multitude has also been defined negatively: as lawless, headless, or ignorant (Hardt and Negri 2009, 41). It is counterposed to the Hobbesian idea of the political body, which must become a people—it must be reduced to one, to a singularity, governed by a sovereign. The multitude, on the other hand, is defined by encounters, such that it is impossible to grasp as a unified object of rule; therefore, it is threatening to particular ideas of property, and social order. In Rancière's terms, we might think of the multitude as precisely the part who have no part in politics—those who have no part in the management of the social order and who have been excluded from the common world. Indeed, the children in *Les Misérables* enact this very idea: they and their families, their communities, have been excluded, and yet they have come together without clear identity or affiliation in this moment to claim their part. They are simultaneously the ones who authorize action and those who are represented by it.

Through the eyes of children not as autonomous individuals, but as an emergent collective political force—mob, multitude, crowd, commoners—we see the resentment at futures stolen, the contempt for the state and larger society, and the anger at the lot they have been dealt. They embody the politics of the future. And we see it is far too late for liberal good intentions, embodied by Stéphane. No one is innocent; even as we may like none of them, we understand all of them.

The film acts to decolonize insofar as it opens new space in the French imagination to understand the impact of colonial history. It does this by reconfiguring our sense of time and space: the *banlieue* becomes the center rather than the margin, it becomes *France*. The classic Victor Hugo novel becomes a story of the *banlieue*; it swallows everything up, exploding the attempts to contain, confine, and quarantine the legacies of racial capitalism and colonialism. We see their current manifestations as joblessness, segregation, abandonment, and houselessness. France as a nation-state is condemned unless both state and society step up to face this history; the film gives us this verdict in a visceral register. But just as importantly, the film does not simply critique—it creates the stage for a rupture in common sense. It opens the way for change, while leaving the direction of that change ambiguous—the children could be a violent mob, bent on nihilistic destruction, or they could transform into a long-overdue force of reckoning and accountability.

Les Misérables blends reality and fiction, expanding the field of action and organizing. It builds on previous political events and anticipates or prefigures new ones. Indeed, I saw clear echoes and overlaps of the film in a protest or "manifestation" I attended in December 2019, called "Marche des Mamans: pour la justice et la dignité" ("Mothers' Protest: For Justice and Dignity"). The protest march took place on the one-year anniversary of police violence against kids from the banlieue of Mantes-la-Jolie, when the police handcuffed 151 kids—aged between twelve and twenty-one—in front of a high school and forced them onto the ground, on their knees, for hours, with their hands over their heads. In response to several days of protests in the area of Mantes-la-Jolie, this was a deliberate act of humiliation. It specifically targeted a group, a collective; the police did not have the proof to arrest each of the 151 kids. The goal, rather, was to make this community submit, obey, heel, by shaming and demeaning their children. In this sense, the police reveal that they too understand the political power of such collectives, and their role in shaping the future. In the march, the mothers took center stage, but they refused to enact the figure of oppressed Muslim women, they refused the position of victimhood (see figure 8). Instead, the women came together as powerful figures against the abuse of the police and the state, many veiled, leading the march and speaking strongly in the rally afterward. I was struck by the fact that during the protest march, none of the banners or posters played on images of innocence; refusing to objectify their children, they focused instead on challenging the humiliation and the injustice, calling the state to account for their violent and unlawful action. The women were angry and resolute, not tearful. As with Abounaddara, they insisted on reclaiming a form of dignity.

If these decolonial aesthetic projects—these "image-events" (Strassler 2020)—work to undo the innocence of the classic figures of the woman and child, they also work both visually and conceptually to create room for subjects who are neither victims nor heroes. We might say that the films enact their own grounding principle of anonymity: they render visible the lives of what Rancière calls the anonymous, those who, as the least likely to be seen

FIGURE 8. "Marche des Mamans," Paris, 2019. Photo by Miriam Ticktin.

as political actors, exemplify the political. The experiences of these people are tragically common, they are ordinary; yet they are rarely acknowledged, not only due to a lack of visual representation, but because the larger French public is unable to recognize them as political: once again, this is the distinction between visibility and appearance, where appearance requires political imagination. This is also the case for those featured in Abounaddara's films, who are ordinary in the extraordinary time of war; they are the unnamed casualties. The films work to rupture our frameworks, where everyday people finally appear as notable and significant.

RECLAIMING HUMANITY

I now return to the collective subjects that appear in these aesthetic projects, and that replace or reconfigure the innocent individual. While I mentioned the mob, the crowd, and the multitude in the case of Ladj Ly's film, Abounaddara insists on recuperating the category of *humanity* as their liberatory political collective. Unlike many who challenge the grammar of humanitarianism by finding fault with the category of humanity itself, Abounaddara's political ethos is still driven by the language of a shared or common humanity; it calls what's going on in Syria "a crime against humanity."

It uses this to call for equal standards for Syrians, Americans, and everyone else. This is a different subject of humanity than that of humanitarianism: not the suffering, pitiful humanity. But Abounaddara nevertheless appeals to universalist language, insofar as it says the dominant regimes of representation are grounded on universalist principles even as they function to discriminate and segregate (Fox 2018). Abounaddara suggests that everyday Syrians themselves speak in the language of higher principles; for this reason, following them, the collective focuses on the principle of dignity.

In thinking about how Abounaddara's work displaces a focus on innocence, this grounding in the category of humanity requires further exploration. Is it possible to disentangle the concept of humanity from its histories in colonial and neoliberal projects, and in humanitarian and human rights regimes? To be sure, humanity is a powerful way to name a broad, sweeping collective; but its Euro-American history has consistently required a constitutive outside, even as that outside shifts (Fanon 1963; Kim 2015; Feldman and Ticktin 2010). As we saw in the introduction, liberal ideas of humanity rely on innocence—it is difficult to disentangle the two concepts. Hannah Arendt's classic critique of this category is also worth revisiting: she cautioned against drawing on humanity as a political constituency (for instance, by way of human rights), arguing that the abstract nakedness of being human and nothing but human was the ultimate danger, as it left people without any form of political recognition or protection—it left them without "the right to have rights" (Arendt 1951).

Both human rights regimes and liberal traditions have shaped the category of humanity in ways that complicate easy understanding of it as liberatory. To be sure, Abounaddara's work undermines the idea and practice of humanitarianism, which itself is grounded on universalist principles such as humanity, and linked, but not identical, to human rights. But does continuing to work within a frame of human rights constrain their work? Although human rights regimes may not have started out this way—more recent histories show that the language of human rights was used very powerfully by those struggling against colonial regimes (Slaughter 2018)—today, the discourse of human rights has become a key tool of the neoliberal order (Moyn 2010). Legal scholar Vasuki Nesiah (2020) suggests that the problem with international law, and the category of "crime against humanity," is precisely that it promises the transcendence of race, while being saturated with racial significance—racial violence has been erased from the concept and the history of liberal rule of law, reproducing whiteness as the default content of humanity. Simply stated, certain forms of hierarchy are endemic to the legal category of humanity. To be sure, the language of "crime against humanity" was mobilized by South Africa in front of the International Criminal Court

(ICC) in March 2024 to hold Israel accountable for the genocide in Gaza, reversing the usual international racialized hierarchies of this charge. While a powerful claim, it has not yet stopped the violence. The danger is that human rights claims risk being activated in a way that predictably serves to reinforce the extant social order.

And yet, what if we did not cede humanity to its Euro-American histories? Abounaddara is not alone in recuperating or reclaiming a different version of humanity. There have been attempts to recover universalist pasts that were prematurely foreclosed (Mbembe 2024; Sarr 2019; Wilder 2015, 2022). Critical theorists such as Sylvia Wynter and Paul Gilroy have called for a different concept of humanity and opened space for it in their work. In particular, Sylvia Wynter (2003) calls the secular, liberal category of humanity a "monohumanist" ontology of man, suggesting that it has dominated all genres and ways of being human. Rather than an independently existing entity, humanity is the product of a particular epistemology (Mignolo 2012). This liberal notion is the same one that is co-constituted by innocence, and that forms the racialized basis of international law. But Wynter chooses not to close down the category; instead, she creates a different future for humanity, by giving it a different past. She does this by retelling its philosophical history, starting with the colonial encounters of 1492, and revealing humanity's (which she calls Man1 and Man2) specific ethnic-class origins. She argues that it originates in a fundamental colonial—and ultimately, racial—divide, mapped onto a distinction about who is rational, and who is irrational. What results is an idea of the human as naturally good and rational, one that nevertheless embodies the color line.

In Wynter's remaking of this mono-version, "humanity" becomes a verb, rather than a noun—to be human is a praxis, about the realization of living in interdependence and connectivity. The question, ultimately, is how to potentially retrieve coexisting ontologies of humanity—how to activate them. For this, Wynter turns to different forms of scientific knowledge; but could aesthetic experiments offer another possibility? That is, if aesthetics and politics are co-constituted, and if aesthetic experiments open the way to forms of being that aren't limited to the rational—the logic that Wynter says dominates the notion of humanity now—then perhaps it could open the way to new sensory forms and practices of humanity, too. Abounaddara has primarily used media technology to (re)make their political worlds, rather than appealing to liberal regimes of law. By producing and circulating their own images, with or without rights, Abounaddara is helping obviate the need for the *right* to the image. In Rancière's terms, they are enacting the rights they do not have. To be sure, this is not easy; Olympe de Gouges was beheaded for enacting the rights that she did not have (Rancière 2004).

Abounaddara does not control the media platforms, most of which are embedded in larger corporate structures, and they have been finding it hard to garner media space and funding.

For Abounaddara, humanity is grounded on the concept of dignity—to lose one's dignity is to be dehumanized. I briefly delve into this concept to understand what kind of humanity is being claimed as a liberatory collective subject, although I do not pretend to do justice to the concept's complexity here. The call for human dignity animated the uprisings that swept North Africa and the Middle East in 2010–2011, quickly dubbed the "Arab Spring." But as Behrooz Ghamari-Tabrizi states, naming it thus immediately circumscribed its possibility, "placing it in a conceptual and discursive universe with a written past and a known future direction" (2016, 2). That is, using the term "spring" imposes a Western frame of liberal democratic revolution, echoing the "Prague Spring" of 1968, and the "Spring of Nations" in 1848. Pulling it out of this conceptual universe might help us see the disruptive force of the collective that is being fought for.

As with any concept, dignity does not mean one thing, and can embody contradictory ideas, depending on the social and historical context. In France, for instance, Camille Robcis suggests that rather than enabling freedom, dignity—which has Catholic roots, in this case—has been used by the French state as a tool of biopolitical rule, to oppose individual rights and liberalism, and to enforce a form of public order that is difficult to disentangle from French nationalism. For instance, it was used to justify the legal ban on face coverings, that is, the burqa and niqab, suggesting that these were an "infringement on the dignity of the person" (Robcis 2016, 326), and it has been used to fight against same-sex domestic partnerships, to sterilize transsexuals, and much more. Carolyn Dean (2015) has criticized the way dignity signifies wholeness and bodily integrity, leaving little room for the weak and disabled. Yet in the context of the Arab uprisings, it has a different valence; to fight for dignity is to fight for material equality, including having a job. In Egypt, for instance, the politics of dignity focused on the poor. The Arabic word for dignity, *karama*, comes from the word *karam* or generosity; and in Egypt, in the major uprisings in 1956 and 2011, the call for dignity was about social equality, including the equality between West and non-West (El Bernoussi 2015).

Some scholars have understood the Egyptian call for dignity in the context of colonial history, and here, Fanon's writings are revealing. He argues that the colonized were entirely deprived of their dignity; this manifested in arbitrary arrests, beatings, and starvation. The only way to regain dignity is to decolonize; and for this, Fanon focused on the need for land (1963). The lack of dignity is tied to economic and political disempowerment and oppression; and in the case of North Africa and the Middle East, these cannot be thought of outside the frame of colonialism and its continued legacies. In this sense, the dignified humanity that is being reclaimed by Abounaddara seems more in line with Sylvia Wynter's idea of a decolonized humanity based on coexistence and interdependence; the category of humanity could be seen as a praxis of equality. It is also more in line with Marx's idea of "species being," where humanity is also about activity, and cannot be conceived of outside social or political-economic contexts. Abounaddara's work at this tense and tender threshold of political appearance, their beautiful and compelling work, disrupts our sensibilities, and holds out a hand into a world of new possibility.

No Borders: Political Experiments Beyond Innocence

I turn now to experiments in *being together* that undermine or challenge regimes of innocence and their associated forms of racial capitalism. I look to "no-borders" or border abolitionist movements because they are already pushing beyond many of our foundational liberal political terms and concepts; and insofar as this book has traced the way discourses and images of innocence get weaponized in secular liberal (and sometimes illiberal) contexts, I am left with the question of whether contemporary forms of secular liberalism can be compatible with non-innocent politics. These movements offer insight into this dilemma.

I came to my research on no-borders movements through fieldwork on the transnational politics of border walls and containment, which I conducted in part through collaborative research with the Multiple Mobilities Research Cluster. While investigating the politics and materiality of the walls themselves (for instance, at the US-Mexico and Ceuta-Morocco walls), I encountered everyday people working with people-on-the-move[5] with both old and new technologies. In the case of the US, I learned firsthand as I participated in the Sanctuary movement after Trump was elected the first time (and again, the second time!), and subsequently helped co-organize a series of workshops and events with colleagues, activists, and people-on-the-move from across the Americas, Europe, and North Africa, helping support and amplify transnational coalitions. And once I was aware of these movements and forms of collective living, I followed them in various locations: in Lesvos, Athens, Paris, Calais. I realized, in fact, that this is a set of political movements I have been thinking about and working with for a long time, as the *sans papiers* movement in France (the subject of my first book, *Casualties of Care*) was an early instantiation of this call for no borders.

In 2009, Bridget Anderson, Nandita Sharma, and Cynthia Wright wrote presciently and persuasively about no-borders movements as incarnating a struggle for the global commons. And since then, much of the literature on these movements—often from the perspective of the Marxist autonomist tradition of "autonomy of migration," which takes mobility as an ontological fact of the human condition, and sees migrants themselves as a transgressive political force[6]—describes a politics of the "mobile commons," which refers to the shared knowledge, affective cooperation, and mutual support between people-on-the-move when they are on the road or arrive somewhere (Papadopoulos and Tsianos 2013). This mobile commons is made up of the secret knowledges and survival tricks that help people cross borders, but perhaps more importantly, that also help build a larger politics of freedom of movement. It has also been spoken of as an "underground railroad."[7] At a Border Security Expo in Texas, I heard about this incarnation of the underground railroad—US Border Patrol officers spoke in bitter and resentful terms about an Indigenous man who had hooked up a generator deep in the forest in Panama to help those who were crossing to charge their phones, a crucial technology for people-on-the-move. Underground railroads or mobile commons also include the more organized activist organizations who stop people from drowning in the Mediterranean or dying in the desert.[8]

But in thinking about a non-innocent politics, my imagination was activated by a different, intimately related set of spaces, and a different set of praxes, which required thinking beyond the autonomy of migration approach, to ways of being together that touch all kinds of people and things, not just people-on-the-move, and imagine a very different world. *Occupations* are a key aspect of this embryonic politics: occupations of buildings and land. This requires a slight shift in focus, from mobility to immobility; people fighting not just for the freedom to move but the "freedom to inhabit" (Paik et al. 2019). In particular, I have been drawn to people-on-the-move attempting to create space to live, in ways not condoned by forms of liberal capitalist governance. If a focus on mobility draws attention to borders and border zones, a focus on immobility can draw our attention to the heart of the polis. Cities are a cauldron for experiments. In cities, the connective tissue of everyday life is on display—the unequal transportation systems, the opulent homes beside the houseless—the visibility and consciousness of inequality creates it as a space of possibility for both thinking and wanting an otherwise. And there have long been struggles over the right to the city (Harvey 2008).

I am aware of how troubling the term "occupation" is, particularly in relation to settler colonialism: as I write, the ongoing genocidal violence in

Palestine has put this issue front and center globally. The question is if such acts can be repurposed toward freedom; that is, if no-borders movements can practice decolonial politics, working with Indigenous communities against the nation-state to undo rather than further the settler colonial project (Fortier 2017; McNevin, forthcoming). The point is not to imagine or claim the land as empty or available or to encourage a liberal politics of inclusion, but precisely to refuse both the authority of the state and the logic of capital, challenging their right to decide who resides where. This can be a project of "unoccupying" the land—to use a term by Indigenous scholar Sandy Grande—in the name of redistribution or repair (Grande 2013). Indeed, Grande suggests that decolonizing involves autonomist formations, and this is in line with commoning. But even when evoked against the settler colonial project, the concept of occupation recalls violent histories, from Israel, Australia, and Canada to the US. Occupations are always sedimented (Orr 2013). In this sense, commoning is necessarily a non-innocent practice—we all inherit and live in the wake of these histories, we are all shaped by their violence, even if we are differently situated in relation to it. To claim innocence is a liberal aspiration; it is not a goal of commoning, where exclusion based on moral stratification is not an option.

Right from the start, then, the concept of occupation demonstrates that this is a form of non-innocent politics. Similarly, its form is not accidental; this is because people-on-the-move are reimagining space and how to be together, asserting their presence against experiences of dispossession and inequality. They are building autonomous, alternative forms of governance against the state and against what they see as unjust treatment, including the lack of basic care and shelter. They do this by occupying physically, legally and politically liminal spaces, challenging regimes of private property. While these may not be spaces of choice, they do serve as forms of "home" and not just shelter, insofar as people work together to create various forms of intimacy and belonging in the process (Van Isacker 2020). That is, sometimes necessity, or as disability scholar Arseli Dokumacı calls it, shrinkage of one's world—constraints, losses, failures—can lead to "activist affordances," or improvisatory performances that imagine the world and its materiality otherwise (Dokumacı 2023). But rather than see this as limited or as unchosen, we can see this shrunken world as the condition of possibility. Those who live there are not subject to judgments of deserving or undeserving, rescue and protection: the logics go beyond innocence or guilt. Togetherness and care are grounded on sharing resources, in ways that require reciprocity and mutuality, but not necessarily love or recognition—this is a form of care or concern that does not require liking those with whom one lives. These spaces require openness, and respect. Whoever needs a home—and for however long—can occupy any welcoming, unlived-in, or abandoned space, unsettling property regimes toward more egalitarian ends. In many ways, these occupations are forcing a more equitable distribution of resources: the necessity of producing a home elsewhere can serve as a way to produce other worlds.

In what follows, as I will describe, going beyond innocence includes the refusal of discourses, practices, and hierarchies of moral deservingness; it admits to violence, even as it tries to reduce it; and it refuses racial innocence, which pretends not to know about the history and intertwined roles of capitalism, imperialism, and racism, opening the way to think about forms of implicatedness. In the process, it also threatens to open the way to more egalitarian relations. Being together in different ways—incipient collective formations—are built in specific spaces and places and require various forms of affective attachment or detachment. In this sense, I explore various aspects of commoning and illustrate each with a particular example. First, building on the discussion of collective subjects in the films, I will discuss emergent collective *political subjects* of commoning; second, *the affective relations* that infuse commoning experiments, which admit to violence, and yet work to manage and not expel it; and third, the *scale* and spread of commoning. To be sure, occupations have taken different forms: and indeed, I want to admit to the tension between paying attention to the transnational or translocal connections, and the ways in which each experiment is shaped by specific, place-based histories. It is not easy to do justice to both.

FRENCH OCCUPATIONS AND MIGRANT MOBS

I begin with France, and the emergence of collective political subjects. Migrant occupations have a long history: the *sans papiers* movement of the 1990s began by occupying churches in Paris, as a demand for rights and papers, not as a quest for protection (Ticktin 2011a; McNevin 2011). "The Jungle"—the makeshift camp on the outskirts of Calais, France, that lasted from January 2015 to October 2016—was also a form of occupation. To be sure, the area around Calais has a long history with people-on-the-move, with its origins in the 1990s. Sangatte, which opened in 1999, was one of the many refugee camps in that area; it was administered by the Red Cross and became the center of controversy between France and the UK until it was closed in 2002. The first legal squat, established in 2013, was an explicitly feminist space on Rue Caillette (Van Isacker 2020). Informal encampments have cropped up over the years, served in part by charity or humanitarian organizations, and have been cyclically shut down by the government. But the Jungle was *not* a refugee camp. In 2015, it brought together the many autonomous occupations that existed in the city, in an effort—eventually enforced by police violence—by the French state to contain them and move them outside the city center. The goal was simply to dump people on the outskirts of the city, away from other people and services, so they would disperse. Perhaps precisely because of this abandonment, it grew into its own, new autonomous political formation, both socially and architecturally, organized and run by people-on-the-move themselves, as they stopped on their way to the UK or elsewhere (Van Isacker 2020; Agier et al. 2018; King 2019).

The Jungle was both a claim to and a launching pad toward freedom. The name itself reveals this history: it derives from the Pashto word "dzjangal," which means forest or woods, which was then bastardized into "la Jungle," with all its racist overtones. Indeed, the name paved the way for a form of racial innocence on the part of the humanitarians, who then came in to help and protect people living in "uncivilized" conditions. People-on-the-move claimed the area as a place they could live for however long it took them to cross over to the UK, by way of trains or ships or trucks; they made a home of it, created communities. The communities were not organized according to ideas of moral worth, protection, or innocence; it was not about who is a "real" refugee, and who is not. Anyone could set up a tent, participate in the local economy of makeshift shops, services, healthcare facilities, and places of worship, and stay for a day or a year (see figure 9). In this sense, it was a community of care by way of practice— "commoning" was entered into by labor and by action, in a very broad sense of action that does not require able-bodiedness. Labor and action replace communities based on blood, ethnicity, nationality, or any other such identity category—community here is simply a quality of relations, one that is ultimately non-exclusionary.

Without romanticizing it—there were certainly conflicts and attempts to organize along the lines of nationality and ethnicity—many agreed it was a burgeoning experiment in different forms of being together (Agier et al. 2018; King 2019). Ultimately, in the name of humanitarian care, the state razed the Jungle, replacing it with a limited number of shipping containers that they could manage in recognizable ways: they could be cleaned, controlled, counted, and surveilled (see figure 10). Again, this was *humanitarian* care, which promises to help and protect, and in the process, separates out the deserving from the undeserving. In contrast, the Jungle was a form of unruly but nonjudgmental, non-moralist, non-innocent care.

We see the incipient formation of a collective political subject in reaction to this move to humanitarianism: people-on-the-move ushered themselves

FIGURE 9. Haircut in the Jungle. Photo by Sipa via AP Images.

FIGURE 10. Containers in the Jungle, February 3, 2016. Photo by Léopold Lambert.

into a collective form of being in the Jungle, which they called the capital of Calais, effacing differences between city and camp. They called on this temporary collective formation when the state decided to bulldoze their space and deport or displace its inhabitants: they fought the government's desire to destroy their homes in the name of a "we": "we the united people of the Jungle" (Sanyal 2017). It was a provisional formation, but one that nevertheless named and called into being a permeable, changeable, yet emplaced, collective subject. In many ways, this "we" positively named the space of vital surplus; the space of exclusion and abandonment.

The Gilets Noirs or Black Vests—a play on the Gilets Jaunes or Yellow Vests movement in France—was one of the more recent incarnations of the *sans papiers* movement, although it subsequently split and morphed into the collective la Chapelle Debout! They offer us a slightly different model of collective subjectivity. They too are using a strategy of occupation, albeit a double-pronged one—on the one hand, they have claimed space to make a political appearance, rendering inequality and exclusion visible; on the other, in their incarnation as la Chapelle Debout!, they have occupied abandoned buildings, in order to live together collectively. On both fronts, they helped change the dynamics of the city, putting themselves at the heart of it, reclaiming space, but in the process, they were also prefiguring a new political subject: that of a *decolonized collective.*

The Gilets Noirs started by occupying Charles de Gaulle Airport in May 2019, as the country's largest airport, from which many migrants are deported. They then moved on to occupy the lobby of the multinational catering company, Elior, in June 2019, in La Défense business district of Paris. Elior represents the heart of French neo-imperialism: the Gilets Noirs pointed to their role in making profits from selling weapons to Africa, feeding conflicts that in turn have led many of these very same *sans papiers* to flee to Europe. The Gilets Noirs argued that their fight was against the twin forces of racism in France and imperialism in Africa; they refused to let Elior, or the French more broadly, claim racial innocence by ignoring the links between colonialism and contemporary racism and inequality, despite the French state's refusal to officially recognize the existence of race or racism. They also challenged private property regimes and the capital accumulation that has led to their disenfranchisement.

They then occupied the famous Pantheon, a mausoleum for distinguished French citizens—a potent symbol of the French republic from which they have been excluded. In their leaflets distributed on site, they stated, "We are the undocumented, voiceless, faceless for the French republic. We come to the graves of your great citizens to denounce your irreverence [and] . . . to demand the Prime Minister give papers to all undocumented migrants in France." Indeed, in this way, they were visually refiguring and decolonizing the collective political subject of France. They faced the cameras head-on, assuming their place at the heart of the

Pantheon, demanding an audience (see figure 11). Through their movement into and occupation of these various spaces, they disrupted order, they unsettled—they forced others to care about them, to think about French history differently. They made the explicit connection between their situation, the historic relationship between France and its former colonies, and the ongoing "pillaging" by French companies of the resources of the African continent. "France continues slavery through other means," their statement read (Butterly 2019).

Migrants and people of color are far too often described as unruly, but in fact, we might actually turn to this designation and its potential political power, returning to the earlier discussion of the concept "mob." While so many groups like the Gilets Noirs have been called "migrant mobs," perhaps the mob is precisely the political subject of commoning—the excess, those excluded from the current political and social order, those determined by their acts of unsettling care. As noted, one part of the definition of mob is its capriciousness, its movement. Could this constant changeability actually be at the root of its political potential?

In the spring of 2022, after they morphed into la Chapelle Debout! and after scoping out the many abandoned buildings in the city, they occupied a location in Paris's ninth arrondissement, and whoever needed a place to live moved in; they called it "L'Ambassade des Immigrés" (Embassy of

FIGURE 11. The Gilets Noirs occupy the Pantheon, July
12, 2019. Photo by Sipa via AP Images.

Immigrants) (see figure 12). Together with locals from the neighborhood, they transformed the space into a home: it was a place for collective living and learning. They worked to build a collective kitchen; they called on everyone with expertise. They stocked it with beds and began creating social infrastructures for people to access French and English language lessons, legal aid, medical care, and accompaniment to court. They were expelled by the state within months, but they continue to occupy different locales—in October 2022 they occupied Paris's Hôtel de Ville or City Hall, claiming space together, marking their presence, combining the two strategies of occupation, about both collective living and political appearance. And, as I later describe, there have been many occupations and squats since then in Paris. As a constantly coalescing, decolonized collective, mob, or a contingent "we," they are reshaping the nature of political subjectivity.

FIGURE 12. "Embassy of Immigrants," Paris, 2022.
Photo by Miriam Ticktin.

FROM SOLIDARITY TO COMMON CAUSE: ATHENS, AFFECT, AND FEMINIST ABOLITIONISM

The Gilets Noirs or Black Vests emerged in force in the past number of years in part because of new laws that double legal detention periods, limit asylum, and speed up deportations. But theirs is a much broader fight. They build on the Gilets Jaunes' movement against deepening forms of inequality, but they insist that they took their name because they are "black with anger." They never pretended to use the language of innocence and victimhood. The Gilets Noirs do not want to be saved. Two of the organizers explained to me that they shifted the affective regime of struggle away from a focus on suffering, toward an unrepentant and strident struggle for dignity and equality—dignity is once again significant in defining the liberated collective subject. They organized from the "foyers" or migrant hostels where they live, but along with la Chapelle Debout!, they organized with others in their neighborhoods. When they occupied Elior, for instance, they joined the striking cleaning workers. In this sense, they call for a politics that goes beyond identity, beyond deservingness. They insist that theirs is a movement for all—not just for people-on-the-move or *personnes exilés*—against a racist, capitalist, patriarchal system. It is a movement that recognizes histories of exploitation and extraction and pushes for freedom of circulation. They use a form of spatial politics, organizing in place, with common goals; but they do not argue for solidarity, admitting to forms of difference and conflict—just common cause.[9] In this sense, they are building new forms of being together that are not easy or innocent.

Solidarity, in their understanding, is about being in alliance with or in support of a certain group of people, while being outside it, rather than seeing oneself as part of that group's struggle. They point to the way that the Left has said they are in solidarity with *sans papiers* (or people-on-the-move), assuming that they can stand alongside, without understanding that they are implicated in the *sans papiers'* struggle. La Chapelle Debout! want to reframe the struggle to show that it is relevant to everyone—that liberation for *sans papiers* is a "concrete universal" (Wilder 2022)—it affects everyone, even if people come to it from different positions. They suggest that this is because we live in a common world, where the fate of each depends on all. To be sure, solidarity has contradictory histories and meanings: it can be both revolutionary and instrumentalized and co-opted. In France, solidarity was part of state ideology in the Third Republic; it was a normative principle and aided in consolidating capitalism. But it has also been the basis for struggle by and for workers, in the Pan-Africanist movement, as part of May 1968 and in relation to anticolonial internationalism, among many other revolutionary movements (Wilder 2022). There is also a tension between solidarity as sustaining or even requiring an a priori collective, community, or group, and it acting as a method of fighting in concert, whether or not one feels anything for the people one fights alongside. What la Chapelle Debout! are saying is that there is no a priori collective, but that the struggle requires people who do not agree or identify with one another to fight together in a contingent way against certain conditions of domination. It requires a contingent, transversal mutuality. With their critique of solidarity, we might better understand what la Chapelle Debout! are advocating for by returning to the concept of "association"; this preceded solidarity in the workers' movements. As Marx suggested, association indexes a form of sociality that cuts across the opposition between individual and society—freely *associated* people, who come together in activity with one another.

To be sure, France is not the only place where such occupations are occurring,[10] or where different ways of being together—the affective glues and repellants—are being worked out. In the summer of 2018, I went to the occupied Plaza Hotel in Athens, which, under the new right-wing government, has now been shut down. Reading across the French and the Greek political struggles, we learn more about the nature of affective relations in commoning spaces: they are not necessarily about solidarity, but anger, and common cause. What affective grammars do we need to understand these formations? How are conflict and violence managed?

City Plaza was initially another example of autonomous organization of people-on-the-move, without an NGO working top-down to manage them or provide services, although it later changed and the NGO logic seems to have largely won out. It was actually only one of about twelve occupied buildings in Athens. These occupations originated in the dissident history of the district of Exarcheia, where abandoned buildings have been the site of collective living and action since the 1970s—they have been shaped by a mix of autonomism and anarchism (Zaman 2019). As with the Gilets Noirs/la Chapelle Debout!, "refugees" and locals worked together, and occupied the hotel together, building on existing infrastructures and traditions, interweaving and complementing struggles (Tsavdaroglou and Kaika 2022). Rather than being contained on the margins of the Greek polity, as with so many refugee camps, these people-on-the-move live in Athens, indistinguishable from the many people who require shelter, particularly since Greece's debt crisis. They were all houseless, out-of-place, and as such, they reclaimed space together.[11]

Before it got taken over by the top-down logic associated with NGOs, Plaza challenged liberal models of care, recognition, and integration; for example, Plaza residents worked to enable children to go to school regardless of how long they would be in Athens, decoupling social services from nation-states—indeed, as one of the Plaza residents explained, the local teachers organized and went on strike to enable this. This was an experiment in how social services can be accessible to people beyond citizenship status, beyond identity, as part of a larger commoning experiment, driven by participation, presence, and mutuality. Indeed, Plaza was experimenting with what they themselves called "politicizing help" (see figure 13); they organized explicit discussions about what this could mean—how care could be reworked beyond hierarchical notions grounded on sympathy or pity. As part of this, in 2018, a contingent of people-on-the-move from Plaza went to help Greeks after devastating wildfires just outside Athens. Similarly, Tahir Zaman (2019) writes about refugee volunteers, who grew vegetables and made knafeh and shared this with people from the local villages, creating space for shared sociability and what they call "neighborliness."

FIGURE 13. "Politicizing Help," sign in the occupied Plaza Hotel, Athens, 2018. Photo by Miriam Ticktin.

In these circumstances, commoning is enacted by creating and sharing spaces to live, in a non-exclusionary manner; it manifests in other material concerns, such as creating access to healthcare and education for all. In Plaza, there were communal kitchens, so people could prepare food and eat as a collective. More broadly, these practices of collective living attempt to even out hierarchies and create a world where people all have access to resources to live. But this does not mean that such occupations work without violence or conflict. I learned that living in Plaza could be rough; there was violence, and it was not always safe. Even going to the bathroom was not without risks for women. In this experiment, violence is intertwined with care. These are decidedly not "safe spaces," in the liberal language of late. They reveal that violence is not something we can eradicate or quarantine; rather, it is something that people inevitably share from living under racial capitalism and imperialism. As abolitionist feminists have argued, interpersonal forms of violence are rooted in the structural violences of our world—racist, sexist, classist, supremacist, and so on—and cannot be separated from the primary institutions that perpetuate violence, including the carceral state itself (INCITE! 2016; West 2016; Kim 2020). If people are trying to reclaim their share in the common world, which includes deconstructing the state's monopoly on violence, we will all need to grapple with it. A non-innocent space cannot be pure; it comes with sedimented histories that cannot be ignored. This is not to say that we should condone violence, but that to aspire to purity or to expel or enclose those who commit violence is part of a carceral logic. It skips the necessary work of making another world where "humanity" is a praxis, not an identity, and where other sensibilities and ways of being together are cultivated.

More generally, as stated by the French activists, it is not clear that "solidarity" describes the way that people come together in these spaces, even as they come together to make common cause and participate in a form of sharing and mutuality. People-on-the-move come from different backgrounds, regions, languages, and perspectives, and most have already endured violence along their travels; they are mixing with anarchists, feminists, and other people who may be houseless. People come together in contingent ways, sometimes with trepidation and suspicion, sometimes with generosity and neighborliness, and sometimes with indifference. Sometimes it is simply about necessity. The question of what theories, strategies, and tactics to use to cultivate respect in these collective spaces is critical, and how to develop them together. How to create new affective forms and subjects? Must people be in solidarity and agree on a common goal or program, or even feel allied with a larger cause? Anarchist pedagogies have dominated in the Greek context. But abolitionist-inspired feminists in Athens and elsewhere are also teaching others how to manage conflict in ways that don't engage in carceral logics. Called "transformative justice," these rely on collective and community-based responses founded on connection rather than retribution. They require that everyone understands themselves as part of a system of structural violence, and as such, that everyone is a potential perpetrator of violence. In this way, they question adversarial binaries such as victim and perpetrator or abuser, preferring the language of "person who caused harm." They support accountability, but as democratic acts by everyday people such as friends, family, and community members, not state authorities or police (Kim 2021, 2020). And while committed to autonomy and horizontality, they do require experienced organizing and political (or better yet, popular) education, including teaching everyone that we are all entitled to be invested in a world liberated from violence. Horizontality can accommodate expertise, allowing certain people to temporarily lead; but how this plays out requires work and care. I witnessed this tension as activists tried to end the practice of gathering by nationality in Plaza Hotel. They urged migrants to share the kitchens and to cook with others they did not know, to break up predictable political formations based on national identity. Were they justified in suggesting that this was a better way of being together? It depends on the pedagogy—was it a form of popular education, where people are all taken seriously as both teachers and learners, and where everyone's experience matters, or was it imposed from above, a form of didactic paternalism?

Different social geometries—that is, going beyond hierarchy to other ways of coming together—must be enabled and produced, not assumed; there are multiple ways to do this, none of which are easy or innocent. Cultivating new affective grammars and ways of being are a critical part of this task.

TRANSLOCAL ARCHITECTURES OF FREEDOM: ABOLITIONIST SANCTUARY

I use my last example of experiments in politics beyond innocence to reflect on the scale of commoning, and the way space shapes incipient political formations. I look at the translocal manifestations of such experiments: across both types of struggle and nation-state borders. I turn to the new Sanctuary movement in the US, but I connect this to other (global) incarnations of sanctuary. The Sanctuary movement originally began in the 1980s, with interfaith communities along the American Southwest border providing protection to undocumented immigrants fleeing violence in Central America. They did so by accompanying them across the border and giving them safe haven in churches. It was reactivated in 2007 to protect immigrants under threat of deportation. Now it is increasingly affiliated with transnational no-borders movements.

Sanctuary is both a politico-legal technology and a form of architecture that challenges nation-state borders by creating spaces inside the nation-state not subject to its laws. Since the Middle Ages, the idea of sanctuary has been tied to a separation of church and state, with the church providing a space of refuge from the political sphere for those who are persecuted; this is rooted in an idea of a divine source of authority. While it may seem strange to look to the Sanctuary movement as a form of non-innocent politics when sanctuary is itself profoundly shaped by Judeo-Christian history, and there-fore by concepts such as innocence and guilt, the practice of sanctuary has moved away from a focus on the divine to a broader concern with alterna-tive sources of authority. This movement reclaims a much earlier tradition of sanctuary, which was not concerned with separating out the deserving from the undeserving, and included outlaws, petty criminals, subversives, and all those otherwise forced to flee the polis, and which later connected to the concept of refugee (Behrman 2015a; see also chapter 2). For many on the more radical end of the newly invigorated Sanctuary movement, the goal was to suspend and replace the current regime of nation-state sover-eignty with a new, more just, egalitarian juridical-political order: it was a broader project to challenge liberal tenets, to create a common world.

After Trump's election to president in 2016, the Sanctuary movement became a powerful, multifaceted political movement, increasingly joining with other transnational struggles. It was deployed across multiple domains: from sanctuary cities and states to sanctuary campuses, and increasingly, a range of different spaces in between, from the original churches and faith-based institutions that have long provided shelter for the undocumented, to restaurants, labor unions, private homes, and arts spaces. Sanctuary on campuses started by thinking of DACA (Deferred Action for Childhood Arrivals) and undocumented students and their families, but it quickly en-compassed people of many immigrant and citizenship statuses, those from the countries banned by Trump in 2017 under what was colloquially called "the Muslim ban," to Muslims more generally, to all those who were in vul-nerable positions in relation to the state. In this sense, sanctuary is a broad and evolving political concept: the fact that it has no particular legal status has allowed people to deploy it politically in new and powerful ways. They are doing so again, under the new Trump administration, as I will discuss.

I see it as a burgeoning experiment politics beyond innocence, insofar as it redefines the location, boundaries, and content of who and what matters. It creates space for those otherwise considered outsiders or "criminal"—it does away with guilt as a criterion. By literally harboring people and giving them safe haven, or by simply refusing to ask people for their citizenship status, it can transform the very nature of cities by subjecting them to a different juridical and spatial order. At the start of the COVID-19 pandemic, for example, sanctuary spaces were used to give vaccines to the undocumented. That is, in a moment when the state is increasingly using innocence as the distinguishing criterion for morally deserving and undeserving, it challenges ideas of liberal nation-state sovereignty, and the way the concept of innocence is used to create inclusions and exclusions.

To be sure, sanctuary is not easily or always a form of politics beyond innocence. Architectures of sanctuary are double-edged, insofar as these spaces of protection can also be sites of containment: walls to protect those on the inside can double as forms of imprisonment. Many churches report to ICE (Immigration and Customs Enforcement) about the migrants they keep in sanctuary, which can surely be seen as a form of complicity. Sanctuary creates safe spaces for those at risk of deportation, but with the premise that these spaces are enclosed and secure; while many churches are serving as sanctuaries, for those who are housed there, these spaces do not necessarily feel like freedom. Those in sanctuary cannot work, go home, or see friends, and their children often cannot go to school. We know the two-faced nature of spaces of protection from the case of refugee camps; while they are precisely created as zones of peace amid conflict, much scholarship has shown that these spaces are often less safe than conflict zones themselves, containing new forms of violence, policing, and suffering (Ticktin 2014b).

Furthermore, sanctuary risks playing into a logic of compassion, rather than of equality. In other words, one part of the Sanctuary movement remains very much governed by a liberal politics of protection and deservingness. Insofar as sanctuary serves a few exceptional individuals at a time, it risks reproducing a model based on humanitarian logics and the benevolence of the privileged, and their desire to help or save. Yet despite this, I believe that this invigorated Sanctuary movement has the potential to transform these risks into new political imaginations, to bring something new into being. In part, this is happening by way of scaling up and across: both thematically and geographically.

First, I turn to the way sanctuary is connecting different types of struggles domestically: thanks in large part to women and queer folks of color,[12] the Sanctuary movement has been expanding its mission, its own borders and spaces—for instance, in the US, the campaign for *expanded sanctuary* or *abolition sanctuary* has questioned why sanctuary is only for migrants, in a society where racist, sexist, and homophobic violence is rampant (Paik 2020). This was already happening under the first Trump administration, but under the second one, sanctuary struggles quickly expanded to include those fighting in solidarity with Palestine, along with the fight for justice for trans people, since these groups have been targeted for detention, deportation, or removal of citizenship and passports. This echoes what is happening in France with the expansion of what was once seen as the *sans papiers* movement to other struggles, establishing a set of common concerns and a general feeling of implicatedness for all. Abolitionist sanctuary asks how a movement to create spaces free from state violence for those who are undocumented can also take on the broader challenges of inequality in American cities, including police violence and mass incarceration. While I heard one pastor say they would refuse to give sanctuary to those with criminal records in order to protect their flock, I also witnessed pastors and many others committed to sanctuary as an abolitionist practice, who refuse no one. An abolitionist approach envisions a world that does not rely on policing and incarceration as tools for social control, for migrants or anyone else (Gilmore 2022; Loyd 2019; Paik 2017). It is engaged in creating new autonomous spaces of support and care that counter the conjoined pipelines that lead into detention and prison, and that refuse the language of innocence in relation to a larger set of carceral geographies, whether these distinguish good and bad migrants, or good or bad people. Abolitionism in this sense is not about getting rid of borders in the present conditions, but it is precisely about transforming the conditions to which borders are a response (Bradley and De Noronha 2022). It is about challenging the nation-state form, insofar as it enables exclusion, violence, and abandonment. Abolitionist Sanctuary movements link struggles for Black, brown, and migrant communities with questions of Indigenous sovereignty, and antifascist groups.

Second, let's consider the way sanctuary works transnationally, across borders and geographies. Sanctuary activists have joined with other global no-borders activists, to share and elaborate on strategies. These include the political coalitions that work to rescue people crossing the Mediterranean—these have been called "sanctuary ships." One activist group, Alarm Phone, which directs emergency calls from people in distress at sea to those who can rescue them, thinks of what they do as "sanctuary in motion" (see Maira 2019, 154). While not everyone calls their work "sanctuary," they all contest liberal, democratic approaches that seek to provide safe haven to migrants without challenging border regimes. They share strategies, and each learns from the specific contexts of the others: for instance, the US coalitions have brought questions of white supremacy to bear to help explain the right-wing populist backlash against people-on-the-move in Europe, while the European struggles have brought their knowledge of antifascism and anticapitalism to help illuminate what is going on with migrants in the Biden-Trump era (Maira 2019). Together, they work translocally, across borders. That said, they do not necessarily aspire to scale to the level of global capital, as they do not want to standardize or flatten their struggles. As activists said in the context of City Plaza: they work on a "humane scale" (Scott-Smith 2024, 77). McNevin (forthcoming) suggests that abolitionism is partly about playing with and reinventing scale, balancing between scalable and non-scalable projects, insofar as abolitionism is prefigurative and provisional; it leaves space to imagine beyond linear notions of space and time, and to be responsive to the specific conditions of oppression and domination. The idea of transversality—with its capaciousness and flexibility—is more appropriate in imagining how it works.

In 2017, I helped co-organize a series of workshops with activists and scholars, and those engaged in expanding sanctuary had a lively debate about whether the term "sanctuary" should be replaced, to signal the expansive nature of this set of political practices, and to create the possibility of a radically different future. In the second workshop, which included people-on-the-move and sanctuary activists from across the Americas, Europe, and North Africa, we debated the idea of sanctuary as civil disobedience or civil initiative; as radical hospitality; as community defense; as a web of resistance; as the eye of the storm; as a praxis of abolition; a space of imagination; a shared fate; as a legal replacement; as a space where all the so-called undeserving finally activate as a collective; and as the common.[13]

Radical practices of sanctuary are morphing into movements that are reimagining the nature of the political. They work outside of nation-state territoriality. The question is, ultimately, can the architectural features of sanctuary spaces or any occupation not serve as borders, but as Hector Amaya has written (2017), as "markers intended to convey the threshold of ethical behavior"? Even if we are not yet there, the movement has pushed many of us to imagine a world where "sanctuary" or occupation is deployed not to create an inside or an outside, but to get rid of the outsides and border structures altogether, by creating a world where resources are shared and risks redistributed. The goal is to create a non-innocent, interconnected political formation which, while not pure or without conflict, nevertheless offers the potential for more of us to flourish (Ticktin 2017b; Paik 2020).

Exploring the Liveliness of the World

In this chapter, I have argued that political experiments in both the visual and social realms are helping forge or prefigure what I think of as non-innocent commoning practices, grounded on structural forms of care (Woodly 2020b), collective struggle, and political imagination.

These connections do not rely on sentiments such as compassion, sympathy, or pity, or the more moralized judgments, such as deserving or undeserving. These latter are liberal sentiments, which work to connect the autonomous individuals of liberal politics. The affective ties cultivated by these emerging political forms are less about individuality than the collective, more about equality (or other social geometries) than hierarchy. The experiments in film and representation discussed in the first half, and the occupying migrant mobs discussed in the second half, both magnify a certain generic set of relationships involved in this collective subject formation—they do not rely on whether one likes each other or not; people may not want any sentimental affiliation at all. Rather, they are often grounded on a basic respect and reciprocity, or what Jodi Dean (2019) calls "comradeship"—this is a political relation, not a personal one, one that we can learn to practice with even the most disagreeable of characters. We might even call these relations of indifference, following Naisargi Davé (2023), insofar as this means respect for opaqueness and unknowability of the Other. If we think of association as a guiding principle, these formations are about freely associated people, who become implicated in each other's histories, in a messy, uneven way, where power differences are acknowledged.

While some of these experiments have already come to a halt, such as the Jungle in Calais, and City Plaza and other occupied buildings in Athens, I want to point again to the spaces of alterpolitics that they have opened: the breaks in common sense, the alter-frequencies, the thresholds they have crossed into other worlds. Commoning is necessarily an iterative praxis—perhaps more to the point, it is a constant struggle. What if we understood that there are different logics that inform commoning, and its contingent political imagination? What if we took seriously that these political experiments spread not just by way of reason, but by political contagion? How might we work with them, harness them? To be sure, they change material conditions and subjectivities, but they do not immediately produce equality or redistribute risk; the goal is not to escape history, but to live in and with it, to create forms of accountability even as those involved work toward better forms of life for all. As Tom Scott-Smith writes, quoting Nasim, one of the activists at Plaza Hotel, who himself came to Greece from Afghanistan: City Plaza "is not the solution to the refugee crisis . . . but it is a good example of how to do it better" (Scott-Smith 2024, 79).

Just as with abolitionism, which I see as part of the same larger political project, commoning is a horizon, not an event (Rodríguez 2012, 2019; Dilts 2017; Chua 2020). While the squats in Athens were closed, the commoning/communing relationships formed in City Plaza and Exarcheia were reassembled during the pandemic, in a mutual aid response, called Kropotkin-19, as feminist scholar-activist Penny Travlou writes; they created a network of spaces across Athens—an informal supply chain—with one building as the distribution center. She talks about the mutations of the refugee solidarity network, and its redirected energy, which in this version incorporated rent strike activists, initiatives for housing action, and so on.

In Paris, occupations and squats continue to gather steam and power: we could point to the March 2024 occupation by undocumented minors and others of 104, a cultural institution in the nineteenth arrondissement, organized by the youth collective of Belleville parc, along with the twentieth arrondissement's Collective Solidaire (Le collectif des jeunes du parc de Belleville et le collectif Paris 20eme solidaire); they occupied this location after they were expelled from their squat by the Seine, where they were living in tents. Or, there is the occupation of an abandoned bus company headquarters in Vitry-sur-Seine, in the south of Paris—and the subsequent eviction of hundreds of people, including refugees with papers, asylum seekers, homeless people—to make space for the 2024 Summer Olympics.[14]

Even if none of these experiments have all the answers, neither does a politics based on innocence. These alternative forms of togetherness are about coexisting in ways that ensure everyone's survival. They are about creating new subjects, and new desires, including the desire to live in ways that are more equitable for all, to make this idea contagious, and to make it spread as such; the goal is for people to realize that everyone is implicated in maintaining a world based on hierarchy and violence, and that we need to take responsibility for creating a different, common world.

Both the new political formations enacted in the films, and the experimental forms of occupation, proliferate horizontally, in partially commensurable spaces. They are scaling out and across in multiple ways across both time and space, not necessarily scaling up; there is no reason that these different spaces would match the scale of capital, or even work with forms of scale that are recognizable, insofar as abolitionism tries to build new worlds, not reproduce old ones. Black feminist scholar Barbara Ransby has an excellent term for this horizontal spread—"political quilting" (Nadasen 2023). The way I interpret it, a political quilt can mean a series of mismatched collectives that nevertheless meet at their edges and get stitched together into a larger common world, through different forms of political, affective, and sensory engagement; it does not mean that each collective is of the same size, shape, texture, or color. The edges line up well for some, and not for others; some may be sewn onto and on top of each other, overlapping in ways that create lumpiness, unevenness. Maybe others remain fragmented, partially joined; still others may be obscure, their edges detectable only by touch. Yet we recognize something in common—a quilt—however imperfect.

These experiments abandon any hope of purity—they are saturated in ambiguity and uncertainty. A politics beyond innocence plays with the constant provisionality of its visions, engaging in practical experiments and pivoting if these do not produce greater flourishing. In this sense, there must be room for partial vision, for imagination, and the prefiguration of reality without determining it a priori. These emerging political formations do not propose or protect a territory of belonging, but a constant state of becoming, and commitment to exploring and embracing the liveliness of the world. This is simply a space to begin—not to end.

Notes

INTRODUCTION

1. "Advocating for the Sanctity of Life," Office of Senator Rand Paul, accessed April 2, 2025, https://www.paul.senate.gov/issues/advocating-for-sanctity-of-life/.

2. Tovah Lazaroff, "'There Are No Innocents in Gaza,' Says Israeli Defense Minister," *The Jerusalem Post*, April 8, 2018, https://www.jpost.com/arab-israeli-conflict/there -are-no-innocents-in-gaza-says-israeli-defense-minister-549173. He accused all Gazans of having a connection to Hamas, voiding their claims to innocence.

3. On October 7, 2023, Hamas-supported militants, responding to over seventy-five years of occupation and oppression of the Palestinian people, carried out attacks on residential communities, social events, and military bases in southern Israel, killing close to 1,200 Israelis and taking others hostage. The Israeli state retaliated with a genocidal military offensive on Gaza's residents and civilian infrastructure, and has since killed more than 56,000 people.

4. Jonathan Ofir, "As an Israeli, I Believe There Is Just One Way Forward: Freedom, Justice, and Equality for Palestinians," *Mondoweiss*, October 15, 2023, https://mondoweiss.net/2023/10/as-an-israeli-i-believe-there-is-just-one-way -forward-freedom-justice-and-equality-for-palestinians/.

5. I am grateful to both Ann Stoler and Léopold Lambert for the encouragement!

6. To be sure, there are many books written on innocence in other, more discrete domains: the aesthetics of innocence (Higonnet 1998), innocence and childhood (Bernstein 2011; Kincaid 1998; Faulkner 2011), the politics of innocence and refugees (Turner 2010), and racial innocence (Wekker 2016; Gray 2013), among others.

7. See Mawuna Remarque Koutonin, "14 African Countries Forced by France to Pay Colonial Tax for the Benefits of Slavery and Colonization," *Pan African Visions*, January 14, 2014. See also Mehmet Demiryay, "Black Vests: France's Undocumented Movement," *Gaia Dergi*, October 5, 2019, https://gaiadergi.com/kara-yelekliler -fransanin-belgelenmemis-hareketi-video/.

8. For example, see Frederic Jameson, *An American Utopia* (2016); Erik Olin Wright, *Envisioning Real Utopias* (2010); Gary Wilder, *Concrete Utopianism: The Politics of Temporality and Solidarity* (2022); José Muñoz, *Cruising Utopia: The Then and There of Queer Futurity* (2009); Avery Gordon, *The Hawthorn Archive: Letters from the Utopian Margins* (2017).

9. Here, Arendt argues that the exception to this rule of compassion is Jesus Christ, as portrayed by Fyodor Dostoevsky; the sign of Jesus's divinity was his ability to have compassion for all men in their singularity, without lumping them together into one suffering mankind.

10. *Oxford English Dictionary*, s.v. "innocence, n.," accessed December 22, 2024, https://www.oed.com/dictionary/innocence_n?tab=meaning_and_use.

11. For Joanna Faulkner (2011, 333), carnal knowledge assumes a kind of ignorance that in turn makes way for pleasure.

12. MSF, however, grew out of a revolutionary context in which populations in danger, not simply individuals, were also part of its mandate (Redfield 2013).

13. In July 1995, the Armed Islamic Group of Algeria (GIA) attacked the transport systems in Paris and Lyon, trying to expand their civil war from Algeria to France, killing eight people and injuring 190.

14. "'Roof Knocking': Israel Warning System Under Scrutiny in Gaza Conflict," *France 24*, May 20, 2021, https://www.france24.com/en/live-news/20210520-roof-knocking-israel-warning-system-under-scrutiny-in-gaza-conflict.

CHAPTER ONE

1. Noah Robertson, "After Blackface Scandal, Va. Governor Has Hung On—And Is Making Amends," *Christian Science Monitor*, October 3, 2019, https://www.csmonitor.com/USA/Politics/2019/1003/After-blackface-scandal-Va.-governor-has-hung-on-and-is-making-amends.

2. Leyland Cecco, "Trudeau Says He Can't Recall How Many Times He Wore Blackface Makeup," *The Guardian*, September 20, 2019, https://www.theguardian.com/world/2019/sep/19/justin-trudeau-wearing-blackface-details-emerge-third-incident.

3. See also Rothberg 2019.

4. For more on these concepts, see Rothberg (2019); Robbins (2017); Meister (2011).

5. Charlotte McDonald-Gibson, "How Dutch Anti-Racism Campaigners Took on 'Black Pete,'" *Time*, November 14, 2020, https://time.com/5910949/black-pete-netherlands-zwarte-piet/.

6. Lauren Collins, "The Campaign to Remove a Shocking Painting from the French National Assembly," *The New Yorker*, April 12, 2019, https://www.newyorker.com/culture/cultural-comment/the-campaign-to-remove-a-shocking-painting-from-the-french-national-assembly.

7. Others, like Jodi Byrd (2011), have used the concept of "colonial agnosia," to mark this colonial aporia, which is similarly likened to a neurological condition, in this case, one that entails trouble assembling elements of an image into a whole. Colonial agnosia is somewhere between a refusal and the inability to put the pieces of colonial history together, to see who benefits most from it. While finding use in both the concepts of colonial agnosia and aphasia, Vimalassery et al. (2016) are also wary of associating impairment or disability with a white supremacist or colonial condition; rather, they urge us to see that none of these forms of being can be collapsed into one another, even

as they shape each other. The question is how to explain such occlusions in ways that do not rely on pathologized or medicalized terms, but instead, allow for culpability.

8. Lici Beveridge, "Mississippi Mayor Refuses to Resign After Facing Backlash for George Floyd Comments: 'I Didn't See Anything Unreasonable,'" *USA Today*, May 28, 2020, https://www.usatoday.com/story/news/nation/2020/05/28/petal-mississippi -mayor-hal-marx-slammed-george-floyd-comments/5276933002/.

9. "Woman Fired by Franklin Templeton After Backlash from Racist Park Confrontation," *CNBC*, May 26, 2020, https://www.cnbc.com/2020/05/26/woman -fired-by-franklin-templeton-after-backlash-from-racist-park-confrontation.html.

10. Abandoned Angels Cocker Spaniel Rescue, Inc., "Abandoned Angels would like to express its gratitude for the outpouring of support regarding the dog that was recently placed in our custody, following release of a troubling video that was brought to our attention," Facebook, June 3, 2020, https://www.facebook.com/ AbandonedAngels/posts/10157529978973723.

11. Amir Vera and Laura Ly, "White Woman Who Called Police on a Black Man Bird-Watching in Central Park Has Been Fired," *CNN*, May 26, 2020, https://www .cnn.com/2020/05/26/us/central-park-video-dog-video-african-american-trnd/index .html. For a discussion of Cooper as liberal, see also Al-Gharbi 2020.

12. This refers to Trump's nativist, white supremacist slogan "Make America Great Again."

13. Nylah Burton, "It Looks Like Amy Cooper, the White Woman in the Viral Central Park Video, Is a Liberal: That's Important," *The Independent*, May 27, 2020, https://www.independent.co.uk/voices/amy-cooper-central-park-racist-dog-walker -trump-a9533581.html.

14. Christian Cooper, "Christian Cooper: Why I Have Chosen Not to Aid the Investigation of Amy Cooper," *Washington Post*, July 14, 2020, https://www .washingtonpost.com/opinions/christian-cooper-why-i-am-declining-to-be-involved -in-amy-coopers-prosecution/2020/07/14/1ba3a920-c5d4-11ea-b037-f9711f89ee46 _story.html.

15. The rapes have been a point of deep contestation. First, the UN was accused of not covering the issue with sufficient attention—for instance, Sheryl Sandberg co-organized a presentation at the UN on December 4, 2023. This was refuted, for instance, by Judith Levine, "There Was No Cover-Up of Hamas's Sexual Violence on October 7" (*The Intercept*, December 24, 2023). Then the *New York Times* published an exposé in December 2023 that purportedly detailed this violence (Jeffrey Gettleman, Anat Schwartz, and Adam Sella, "Screams Without Words," *New York Times*, December 31, 2023), but the article was then exposed for bias and complete lack of evidence (Jeremy Scahill, Ryan Grim, and Daniel Boguslaw, "'Between the Hammer and the Anvil': The Story Behind the *New York Times* October 7 Exposé," *The Intercept*, February 28, 2024). The Christian right denounced Hamas, as did liberal feminists; but many others condemned the weaponization of rape. Feminists for a Free Palestine wrote an open letter condemning this and the way it was used to render Hamas (and Palestinians) monstrous, and deserving of ever more depraved militarized violence.

16. Office of Senator Kirsten Gillibrand, "At United Nations, Gillibrand Delivers Remarks Condemning Rape and Sexual Violence Committed by Hamas Against

Israelis," press release, December 4, 2023, https://www.gillibrand.senate.gov/news/press/release/at-united-nations-gillibrand-delivers-remarks-condemning-rape-and-sexual-violence-committed-by-hamas-against-israelis/#.

17. Sarah Fortinsky, "CNN's Bash Has Tense Exchange over Hamas Rapes with Jayapal," *The Hill*, December 4, 2023, https://thehill.com/policy/international/4340811-cnn-bash-jayapal-hamas-violence-rape-women-israel/.

18. Christie Renick, "The Nation's First Family Separation Policy," *The Imprint*, October 9, 2018, https://imprintnews.org/child-welfare-2/nations-first-family-separation-policy-indian-child-welfare-act/32431.

19. Center for Gender and Refugee Studies, "Title 42 Challenges," https://cgrs.uchastings.edu/our-work/title-42-challenges.

20. Jillian Kestler-D'Amours, "The Trump-Era Order Biden Is Using to Turn away Most Migrants," *Al Jazeera*, April 7, 2021, https://www.aljazeera.com/news/2021/4/7/the-trump-era-rule-biden-is-using-to-turn-asylum-seekers-away.

21. Department of Health and Human Services, "Public Health Reassessment and Immediate Termination of Order Suspending the Right to Introduce Certain Persons from Countries Where a Quarantinable Communicable Disease Exists with Respect to Unaccompanied Noncitizen Children," *Federal Register* 87, no. 7 (March 17, 2022): 15243, https://www.govinfo.gov/content/pkg/FR-2022-03-17/pdf/2022-05687.pdf.

22. Camilo Montoya-Galvez, "White House Open to New Border Expulsion Law, Mandatory Detention and Increased Deportations in Talks with Congress," *CBS News*, December 12, 2023, https://www.cbsnews.com/news/immigration-white-house-congress-border-security-detention-deportation/.

23. Karl Jaspers discusses four types of guilt in relation to collective violence, specifically that of the National Socialist regime: criminal guilt, political guilt, moral guilt, and metaphysical guilt. Political guilt comes closest to a form of collective responsibility (Jaspers [1946] 2000; Rothberg 2019, 43–44).

24. Jewish American-Russian writer Masha Gessen is one case in point: the Hannah Arendt award for political thinking was withdrawn after she compared Gaza to a Jewish ghetto in Nazi-occupied Germany. But there are many others: Jewish philosopher Nancy Fraser and anthropologist Ghassan Hage are among them.

25. For a discussion of the censoring of descriptions of Israel as a settler state, see Corey Robin, "Non-Jews Banning Jewish Texts to Protect Jews," *Jacobin*, February 28, 2025, https://jacobin.com/2025/02/hunter-cuny-palestine-hochul-censorship.

CHAPTER TWO

1. The furor over migrant children separated from their parents at the US-Mexico border in 2018 by Trump's draconian policies is also about the distinction between deserving and undeserving, innocent and guilty: the majority of Americans were outraged at the treatment of the children, but many fewer have suggested that their parents do not deserve to be held in detention centers. See chapter 1.

2. Aamna Mohdin, "These Are the Routes Being Closed off to Refugees Fleeing into Europe," *Quartz*, March 10, 2016, https://qz.com/635110/these-are-the-routes-being-closed-off-to-refugees-fleeing-into-europe/.

3. Helena Smith and Mark Tran, "Germany Says It Could Take 500,000 Refugees a Year," *The Guardian*, September 8, 2015, https://www.theguardian.com/world/2015/sep/08/germany-500000-refugees-a-year-clashes-lesbos.

4. Jillian Jorgenson, "'Is This What He Wants to See Happen?': De Blasio Rips Christie on Syrian Refugees," *Observer*, November 18, 2015, https://observer.com/2015/11/is-this-what-he-wants-to-see-happen-de-blasio-rips-christie-on-syrian-refugees/.

5. Charles Homans, "The Boy on the Beach," *New York Times*, September 3, 2015, https://www.nytimes.com/2015/09/03/magazine/the-boy-on-the-beach.html.

6. Moustafa Bayoumi, "They Are 'Civilised' and 'Look Like Us': The Racist Coverage of Ukraine," *The Guardian*, March 2, 2022, https://www.theguardian.com/commentisfree/2022/mar/02/civilised-european-look-like-us-racist-coverage-ukraine.

7. Jonathan Ofir, "Israeli Politician Says 'Children of Gaza Have Brought This upon Themselves,'" *Truthout*, October 18, 2023, https://truthout.org/articles/israeli-politician-says-children-of-gaza-have-brought-this-upon-themselves/.

8. "Israel's War on Gaza Has Killed 50,000 Palestinians Since October 2023," *Al Jazeera*, March 23, 2025, https://www.aljazeera.com/news/2025/3/23/israeli-offensive-in-gaza-has-killed-50000-palestinians-since-october-2023.

9. Collier Meyerson, "Adults Think Black Girls Are Older Than They Are—and It Matters," *The Nation*, July 6, 2017, https://www.thenation.com/article/archive/adults-thinks-black-girls-are-older-than-they-are-and-it-matters/.

10. Maya King, "Someone Called the Police on a Girl Catching Lanternflies: Then Yale Honored Her," *New York Times*, February 2, 2023, https://www.nytimes.com/2023/02/02/nyregion/bobbi-wilson-lanternfly-yale.html.

11. "Turkey Tries Father of Refugee Alan Kurdi for His Drowning," *Middle East Eye*, February 11, 2016, https://www.middleeasteye.net/news/turkey-tries-father-refugee-alan-kurdi-his-drowning.

12. While trafficking is often defined as coercive, exploiting people for the purposes of sex or labor, smuggling is understood as a consensual act, paying for a service, such as help with border crossing. European political discourses often conflate the two, assuming that smuggling is coerced.

13. Michael Powell and Zia Weise, "Aylan and His Father's Real Story: Abdullah Kurdi Forced to Deny Being a Smuggler After New Questions Emerge from Picture That Shook the World," *Daily Mail*, September 12, 2015, https://www.dailymail.co.uk/news/article-3232251/Aylan-father-s-REAL-story-Abdullah-Kurdi-forced-deny-smuggler-new-questions-emerge-picture-shook-world.html; "Human Smugglers on Trial over Syrian Toddler Aylan Kurdi's Death," *France 24*, November 2, 2016, https://www.france24.com/en/20160211-turkey-syria-aylan-kurdi-toddler-human-traffickers-trial-refugees-death.

14. Lizzy Davies, "Lampedusa Boat Tragedy Is 'Slaughter of Innocents' Says Italian President," *The Guardian*, October 3, 2013, https://www.theguardian.com/world/2013/oct/03/lampedusa-boat-tragedy-italy-migrants.

15. Lorenzo Tondo, "Italy Using Anti-Mafia Laws to Scapegoat Migrant Boat Drivers, Report Finds," *The Guardian*, October 15, 2021, https://www.theguardian.com/global-development/2021/oct/15/italy-using-anti-mafia-laws-to-scapegoat-migrant-boat-drivers-report-finds; see also Dutch Council for Refugees, "Aliou:

Driving a Migrant Boat Makes Me a Hero or a Criminal?," October 2, 2023, https://www.vluchtelingenwerk.nl/en/stories/aliou-driving-migrant-boat-makes-me-hero-or-criminal.

16. Eva Ruth Moravec, Arelis R. Hernández, Nick Miroff, and Maria Sacchetti, "Deaths of 53 Migrants in Texas Stoke Grief, Fears of a Deadly Summer," *Washington Post*, June 28, 2022, https://www.washingtonpost.com/nation/2022/06/28/san-antonio-migrants-trailer/.

17. The photograph can be seen here, taken by famous Indian photographer Rohit Chawla: https://www.indiatoday.in/india/photo/syrian-refugee-crisis-artist-ai-weiwei-poses-as-aylan-kurdi-for-india-today-magazine-377881-2016-02-05.

18. Henri Neuendorf, "Ai Weiwei Hits a New Low by Crassly Recreating Photo of Drowned Syrian Toddler," *artnet*, February 1, 2016, https://news.artnet.com/market/ai-weiwei-reenactment-drowned-syrian-toddler-417275.

19. Kevin Carter struggled with the conditions under which he was a photojournalist and ultimately took his own life not long after taking this famous photograph, at age thirty-three. In his suicide note, he said that he was haunted by the killings and corpses and by starving and wounded children. After he took this photograph, many called him unethical for having taken the photograph rather than immediately helping the child. In fact, he was not able to help as he was surrounded by soldiers; the story is told in the short documentary film *The Death of Kevin Carter: The Story of the Bang-Bang Club*. See also Kleinman and Kleinman (1996).

CHAPTER THREE

1. "Born-this-way" theorizations first appeared in psychoanalytic discourse, in Robert Stoller's accounts of gender identity (1964, 1966), where he considered core gender identity a biological force. See also Saketopoulou and Pellegrini (2023).

2. See Rebecca Jordan-Young, *Brain Storm: The Flaws in the Science of Sex Differences* (2010), which soundly debunks the science around sexual orientation, showing both its internal contradictions and how sexual orientation is multidimensional.

3. To be sure, Daston and Galison suggest that subjectivity is never fully erased, but that certain aspects of subjectivity are understood as irrelevant, or simply non-contaminating, depending on the context. There are different scientific selves cultivated to produce objective knowledge; these include trained subjects who know how to evaluate and submit to the weight of evidence. Interestingly, as Nadia Abu El-Haj (2012) argues, in genetic research, to declare personal or social attachments to the research at hand is not understood to have epistemological consequences: scientists nevertheless present their findings as reliable, impartial, and experimentally determined. For instance, it was not understood as biased that LeVay and Hammer are gay and personally invested in their research. This is in part because the research into the human genome is itself framed as an egalitarian undertaking, displacing ideas of population or racial inequality by focusing on molecular data. Rather, their ethical attachment to the question gives them legitimacy to do that particular research—they care to get it right (Abu El-Haj 2012). The idea is still that their research is grounded on objectivity, and their findings can be replicated by anyone else.

4. Since its early days, AIDS has been increasingly criminalized, rather than the other way around, albeit in different terms (Tomso 2017).

5. Similarly, a common explanation by doctors about the trans people they work with is that trans people were born in the wrong body; as Sadjadi points out, scientists have suggested that trans people have the brain or soul (they often use these interchangeably) of one gender, and the body of another (Sadjadi 2019). Najmabadi notes a similar conflation between soul and psyche in discourses about trans people in Iran (2011). Once again, this is a biological explanation, rooted in theologically inflected dualist ideas of mind/body. While fully in support of trans rights and justice, Sadjadi asks whether this is necessarily the best way to further rights and to allow trans people to live freely and flourish. For more, see my section on "queering innocence," which discusses queer theory.

6. To be clear, as Janet Halley states, there are four positions in the pro- and anti-gay struggle: pro-gay essentialism, and pro-gay constructivism; and anti-gay essentialism, and anti-gay constructivism (Halley 1994, 516). I focus on pro-gay essentialism and anti-gay constructivism here.

7. Makana Eyre and Martin Goillandeau, "Europe Is Telling Gay Asylum Seekers They Are Not Gay Enough," *The Nation*, January 3, 2020, https://www.thenation.com/article/archive/gay-asylum-netherlands-ind/.

8. Larry Kramer, "Sex and Sensibility," *The Advocate*, May 27, 1997.

9. According to the *OED*, Thomas Hobbes invoked this meaning in *Leviathan* (1651) in speaking of a sovereign prince who put to death an innocent subject.

10. There are many, many incredible scholar/activists engaged in this struggle: Naomi Murakawa, Beth Richie, Mariame Kaba, Andrea Ritchie, Nadine Naber, and Ujju Aggarwal are among many others in the large pool of activists and scholars.

11. As Gilmore (2017) suggests, half of the prison population are descendants of chattel slavery, and while this is enormous, it is not a direct correlation.

12. "David Vasquez," Innocence Project, accessed July 26, 2022, https://innocenceproject.org/cases/david-vasquez/. See also Findley and Golden (2014).

13. "The National Registry of Exonerations," University of California Irvine Newkirk Center for Science and Society, University of Michigan Law School, and Michigan State University College of Law, accessed April 2, 2024, https://www.law.umich.edu/special/exoneration/Pages/browse.aspx.

14. Marvin Zalman (2011) refers to "innocence consciousness" as the awareness of systemic justice problems, leading to the need for structural reform.

15. Taken from an interview I conducted with Meryl Schwartz at the Innocence Project in New York, August 8, 2016.

16. See "Transforming the Criminal Justice System Through Science," Innocence Project 2015 Annual Report.

17. Innocence Project, "Texas Court of Criminal Appeals Officially Exonerates Steven Mark Chaney," news release, January 17, 2019, https://innocenceproject.org/texas-court-officially-exonerates-steven-chaney/.

18. Innocence Project, "'Actually Innocent': Texas Court of Appeals Vacates Wrongful Conviction Based on False Bite Mark Testimony," news release, December

19, 2018, https://innocenceproject.org/court-vacates-wrongful-conviction-steven
-chaney/.

19. Innocence Project, "Remembering Exoneree Steven Mark Chaney," news
release, June 1, 2021, https://innocenceproject.org/remembering-exoneree-steven
-mark-chaney/.

20. Linda Greenhouse, "Requiem for the Supreme Court," *New York Times*, June 24,
2022, https://www.nytimes.com/2022/06/24/opinion/roe-v-wade-dobbs-decision.html.

21. Noah Feldman, "Supreme Court Erodes Wall Between Church and State," *Seattle
Times*, June 29, 2022, https://www.seattletimes.com/opinion/supreme-court-erodes
-wall-between-church-and-state/.

22. Noah Bernstein, Sarah Huddleston, Shea Vance, and Esha Karam, "'Columbia
in Crisis': Shafik Testifies Before Congress about Antisemitism at Columbia," *Columbia
Spectator*, April 21, 2024, https://www.columbiaspectator.com/news/2024/04/21/
columbia-in-crisis-shafik-testifies-before-congress-about-antisemitism-at-columbia/.

23. People have called this notion of racism "color-blind racism" (Bonilla-Silva
2001) or "laissez-faire racism" (Bobo et al. 1997).

24. "Race and Wrongful Conviction," Innocence Project, accessed April 2,
2024, https://innocenceproject.org/race-and-wrongful-conviction/#:~:text=
This%20demographic%20rate%20is%20consistent,13.6%25%20of%20the%20U.S.
%20population.

25. See "Transforming the Criminal Justice System Through Science," Innocence
Project 2015 Annual Report.

CHAPTER FOUR

1. See the Wildlife Society, "Western and Southwest Sections Weigh-In on Border
Wall," press release, May 31, 2018, https://wildlife.org/western-and-southwest-sections
-weigh-in-on-border-wall/.

2. See https://www.multiplemobilities.org/. Our collaboration began in 2014: we
were all at the New School, but from different disciplinary backgrounds (Victoria
Hattam, politics; Laura Liu, global studies and geography; Radhika Subramaniam, art
and design, and curator; Rafi Youatt, politics; and myself, in anthropology).

3. Vanessa O'Brien, "Animal Migration," *DW*, February 11, 2012, https://www.dw
.com/en/israeli-army-opens-west-bank-barrier-for-animals/a-16351700.

4. This is the size of bureaucracy, as Shannon Mattern so insightfully commented in
a discussion of a different version of this chapter.

5. I did the interview with my Spanish colleague Liliana Suárez Navaz, and I thank
her for her help translating.

6. "Fort Vert: Nature Conservation as Border Regime in Calais," *Statewatch*,
February 24, 2020, https://www.statewatch.org/analyses/2020/fort-vert-nature
-conservation-as-border-regime-in-calais/.

7. See the work of Forensic Oceanography, and the work of Charles Heller and
Lorenzo Pezzani.

8. Simon Rosc, "Žica je smrtonosna prepreka" [Wire is a deadly obstacle], *Svet*,
November 21, 2015, http://svet24.si/clanek/novice/slovenija/564fb68807a50/kopot
-preseka-bodeca-zica.

9. "What's That Owl Doing Strapped to the Chest of an Israeli Border Police Officer?," *Jerusalem Post*, June 27, 2011, https://www.jpost.com/israel-news/what-is-an-owl-doing-strapped-to-the-chest-of-an-israeli-border-police-officer-407304.

10. Lynn Paltrow, "PersonhoodUSA's Radical, Fetal-Separatist Agenda," *Truthout*, October 7, 2010, https://truthout.org/articles/personhoodusas-radical-fetalseparatist-agenda/.

11. Lynn Paltrow, "Life After Roe," *New York Times*, September 1, 2018, https://www.nytimes.com/2018/09/01/opinion/sunday/brett-kavanaugh-roe-abortion.html.

12. "State Bans on Abortion Throughout Pregnancy," Guttmacher Institute, accessed April 2, 2025, https://www.guttmacher.org/state-policy/explore/state-policies-abortion-bans.

13. Office of Representative Paul Gosar, "Gosar Lauds Supreme Court Decision to Hear Pro-Life Case," press release, December 1, 2021, https://gosar.house.gov/news/documentsingle.aspx?DocumentID=4719.

14. Planned Parenthood, "Rand Paul and the Race to the Bottom on Women's Health," news release, April 20, 2015, https://www.plannedparenthoodaction.org/pressroom/rand-paul-and-race-bottom-womens-health.

15. Stefan Becket, "Read the Full VP Debate Transcript from the Walz-Vance Showdown," *CBS News*, October 2, 2024, https://www.cbsnews.com/news/full-vp-debate-transcript-walz-vance-2024/.

16. In the US, in September 2020, nurse practitioner Dawn Wooten served as whistleblower for the sterilizations being performed at Irwin County Detention Center (ICDC) in Georgia. In addition to witnessing the lack of testing and medical care for those who had been exposed to COVID-19, and the general unsanitary and neglectful living conditions, Wooten said that nearly all the detained women who went to see the assigned gynecologist returned without ovaries and/or uteruses. These operations were performed without proper consent, in a coercive manner—often the women did not even know they had had hysterectomies. This echoes the long history of Black Americans being forcibly sterilized, named already in the 1974 case *Relf v. Reinberger* when two Black sisters, aged twelve and fourteen, were forcibly sterilized because their mother, who was illiterate, was made to sign a form she did not understand.

17. See, among many others, the work of scholars such as M. Murphy (2017); Max Liboiron (2021); Nick Estes (2019); and Nick Estes and Jaskiran Dhillon (2019).

18. "Greta Thunberg: TIME's Person of the Year 2019," *Time*, December 23, 2019.

19. See for instance the work of Vanessa Agard Jones (2014); Katherine McKittrick (2006, 2013); J. T. Roane (2017, 2018); Christina Sharpe (2018); and Marisa Solomon (2022).

CHAPTER FIVE

1. Jeanne Van Heeswijk spoke at "Toward Sanctuary Summits," Vera List Center for Art and Politics, February 15, 2018. Van Heeswijk is a Dutch artist.

2. For recent examples, in addition to the powerful work of abolitionist feminists (Ruth Wilson Gilmore, Mariame Kaba, Naomi Murakawa, Nadine Naber, Naomi Paik, etc.), see Saidiya Hartman (2007, 2019), Sara Ahmed (2017), M. Murphy (2017), María Puig de la Bellacasa (2017), and Lata Mani (2022), who all engage creativity and political imagination to open new worlds. See also bell hooks (1994) for a formative

take on this. Decolonial feminism also goes beyond critique, focusing on building new futures where multiple worlds can coexist (Avtar Brah 2022).

3. This has its own geographically distributed racialized regime, where white children are the focus in the Global North as pure, and Black children are the focus in the Global South—seen as the most victimized by their families or societies.

4. Melena Ryzik, "Life Behind the Scenes of a Conflict," *New York Times*, October 19, 2015.

5. "People-on-the-move" can be translated in many different ways; for instance, in France it is sometimes "personnes exilées" (people in exile) and sometimes "personnes bloquées à la frontière" (people stuck at the border).

6. See Ticktin and Youatt (2022) for more on this approach, in relation to no-borders approaches.

7. I refer here to the network of secret routes and safe houses for those who were enslaved in the US during the early to mid-nineteenth century, to escape into free states and Canada. See also Stierl (2019) and Haro and Coles (2019).

8. For instance, see the Alarm Phone, an activist hotline for refugees in distress in the Mediterranean and Aegean Sea: https://alarmphone.org/en/.

9. See Plateforme d'Enquêtes Militantes, "Les Gilets Noirs, c'est pas un collectif c'est un mouvement! Archéologie d'une lutte antiraciste," *ACTA*, September 1, 2019, https://acta.zone/les-gilets-noirs-cest-pas-un-collectif-cest-un-mouvement-archeologie-dunstiere-lutte-antiraciste/.

10. For instance, there are also occupations in Italy, in Piazza Indipendenza: see Carla Hung (2019). They also exist in the Netherlands, Germany, Spain, etc.

11. I think of houseless encampments as a similar form of occupation. While on the one hand, they can be seen as marginal spaces where the unwanted are warehoused, on the other hand, they reclaim both public and privatized space, enacting a slow and steady occupation, an assertion of presence against experiences of dispossession and inequality. Both of these claim a right to the city (Harvey 2008).

12. This includes organizations such as the Black Youth Project (BYP100), the Black Alliance for Just Immigration (Baji), and Mijente, among others.

13. See "Sanctuary Says," in *Migration and Society* (2021). As part of the New School's Expanded Sanctuary Working Group, a few of my colleagues/co-organizers and I (Alexandra Delano; Abou Farman and Anne McNevin) helped compile this set of poetic and imaginative expressions that all those who attended contributed to. We see it as a contingent collaboration that engages sanctuary as an ongoing question.

14. Angelique Chrisafis, "Hundreds Evicted from France's Biggest Squat Months Before Paris Olympics," April 17, 2024, https://www.theguardian.com/world/2024/apr/17/hundreds-evicted-france-squat-paris-olympics.

Bibliography

Abounaddara. 2017. "Dignity Has Never Been Photographed." *Documenta*, March 24. http://www.documenta14.de/en/notes-and-works/15348/dignity-has-never-been -photographed.

Abreu, Jessica de. 2018. "Reclaiming Our Voices: The Anti–Black Pete Movement from a Black Woman's Perspective." In *Smash the Pillars: Decoloniality and the Imaginary of Color in the Dutch Kingdom*, edited by Melissa F. Weiner and Antonio Carmona Báez. Lexington Books.

Abu El-Haj, Nadia. 2012. *The Genealogical Science: The Search for Jewish Origins and the Politics of Epistemology*. University of Chicago Press.

Abu El-Haj, Nadia. 2022. *Combat Trauma: Imaginaries of War and Citizenship in Post-9/11 America*. Verso.

Abu-Lughod, Lila. 2013. *Do Muslim Women Need Saving?* Harvard University Press.

Achiume, E. Tendayi. 2019. "Migration as Decolonization." *Stanford Law Review* 71 (6): 1509–74.

Adler-Nissen, Rebecca, Katrine Emilie Andersen, and Lene Hansen. 2020. "Images, Emotions, and International Politics: The Death of Alan Kurdi." *Review of International Studies* 46 (1): 75–95. https://doi.org/10.1017/S0260210519000317.

Agamben, Giorgio. 1998. *Homo Sacer: Sovereign Power and Bare Life*. Stanford University Press.

Agard-Jones, Vanessa. 2014. "Spray." *Somatosphere*, May. https://somatosphere.com/ 2014/spray.html/.

Agier, Michel, Yasmine Bouagga, Maël Galisson, Cyrille Hanappe, Mathilde Pette, Philippe Wannesson, Madeleine Trépanier, et al. 2018. *La jungle de Calais: les migrants, la frontière et le camp*. PUF.

Ahmed, Sara. 2017. *Living a Feminist Life*. Duke University Press.

Aizeki, Mizue, Geoffrey Boyce, Todd Miller, Joseph Nevins, and Miriam Ticktin. 2021. "Smart Borders or a Humane World?" Immigrant Defense Project's Surveillance, Tech & Immigration Policing Project, and the Transnational Institute. https:// issuelab.org/resources/39039/39039.pdf.

Aleinikoff, T. Alexander. 2019a. *The Arc of Protection: Reforming the International Refugee Regime*. Stanford University Press.

Aleinikoff, T Alexander. 2019b. "The Unfinished Work of the Global Compact on Refugees." *International Journal of Refugee Law* 30 (4): 611–17. https://doi.org/10 .1093/ijrl/eey057.

Alexander, Michelle. 2010. *The New Jim Crow*. The New Press.

Al-Gharbi, Musa. 2020. "Amy Cooper: The Paradox of the Shameless White Liberal." *Public Seminar*, May 29. https://publicseminar.org/essays/amy-cooper-the -paradox-of-the-shameless-white-liberal/.

Al-Ghazzi, Omar. 2019. "An Archetypal Digital Witness: The Child Figure and the Media Conflict over Syria." *International Journal of Communication* 13: 3225–43.

Allen, Lori. 2021. *A History of False Hope: Investigative Commissions in Palestine*. Stanford University Press.

Alonso, Alexandra Délano, Abou Farman, Anne McNevin, and Miriam Ticktin. 2021. "Sanctuary Says." *Migration and Society* 4 (1): 16–18. https://doi.org/10.3167/arms .2021.040103.

Amaya, Hector. 2017. "The Big Picture: The Promise of Sanctuary." *Public Books*, November 20. https://www.publicbooks.org/big-picture-promise-sanctuary/.

Anderson, Bridget. 2017. "The Politics of Pests Immigration and the Invasive Other." *Social Research* 84 (1): 7–28.

Anderson, Bridget, Nandita Sharma, and Cynthia Wright. 2009. "Editorial: Why No Borders?" *Refuge* 26 (2): 5.

Anzaldúa, Gloria. 1987. *Borderlands/La Frontera: The New Mestiza*. Spinsters/Aunt Lute.

Arendt, Hannah. [1943] 1996. "We Refugees." In *Altogether Elsewhere, Writers in Exile*, edited by Marc Robinson. Harvest Books.

Arendt, Hannah. 1951. *The Origins of Totalitarianism*. Harcourt, Brace and Co.

Arendt, Hannah. 1968. "Collective Responsibility." In *Responsibility and Judgment*, edited by Jerome Kohn. Schocken Books.

Arendt, Hannah. 1990. *On Revolution*. Penguin Books.

Ariès, Philippe. 1965. *Centuries of Childhood: A Social History of Family Life*. Translated by Robert Baldick. Vintage Books.

Asad, Talal. 2003. *Formations of the Secular: Christianity, Islam, Modernity*. Stanford University Press.

Asad, Talal. 2007. *On Suicide Bombing*. New York: Columbia University Press.

Asad, Talal. 2015. "Reflections on Violence, Law, and Humanitarianism." *Critical Inquiry* 41 (2): 390–427. https://doi.org/10.1086/679081.

Baldwin, James. 1998. *Collected Essays*. Edited by Gene Berry and Jeffrey Campbell. Library of America.

Balfour, Lawrie. 1999. "The Appeal of Innocence: Baldwin, Walzer, and the Bounds of Social Criticism." *The Review of Politics* 61 (3): 373–402. https://doi.org/10.1017/ S0034670500028898.

Barnett, Michael N. 2011. *Empire of Humanity: A History of Humanitarianism*. Cornell University Press.

Barthes, Roland. 1977. *Image, Music, Text*. Translated by Stephen Heath. Hill and Wang.

Behrman, Simon. 2014. "Accidents, Agency and Asylum: Constructing the Refugee Subject." *Law and Critique* 25 (3): 249–70. https://doi.org/10.1007/s10978-014 -9140-x.

Behrman, Simon. 2015a. "Grassroots Asylum and Legal Strategies: A Case Study of the US Sanctuary Movement." *Birkbeck Law Review* 3 (2): 200–221.

Behrman, Simon. 2015b. "Reconfiguring the Concept of Asylum." *Policies and Practices*, no. 70. https://pure.royalholloway.ac.uk/en/publications/reconfiguring-the -concept-of-asylum.

Bereni, Laure, Renaud Epstein, and Manon Torres. 2020. "Colour-Blind Diversity: How the 'Diversity Label' Reshaped Anti-Discrimination Policies in Three French Local Governments." *Ethnic and Racial Studies* 43 (11): 1942–60. https://doi.org/10.1080/01419870.2020.1738523.

Bernstein, Elizabeth. 2018. *Brokered Subjects: Sex, Trafficking, and the Politics of Freedom.* University of Chicago Press.

Bernstein, Robin. 2011. *Racial Innocence: Performing American Childhood from Slavery to Civil Rights.* New York University Press.

Bersani, Leo. 1995. *Homos.* Harvard University Press.

Berthold, Dana. 2010. "Tidy Whiteness: A Genealogy of Race, Purity, and Hygiene." *Ethics & the Environment* 15 (1): 1–26.

Biri, Despina. 2016. "Ai Weiwei and the Aestheticization of Refugees." *Greek Left Review*, February. https://greekleftreview.wordpress.com/2016/02/06/ai-weiwei-the-aestheticization-of-refugees/.

Blay, Zeba. 2020. "Amy Cooper Knew Exactly What She Was Doing." *Huffpost*, May 26. https://www.huffpost.com/entry/amy-cooper-knew-exactly-what-she-was-doing_n_5ecd1d89c5b6c1f281e0fbc5.

Blumenau, Bernhard. 2014. "The Other Battleground of the Cold War: The UN and the Struggle Against International Terrorism in the 1970s." *Journal of Cold War Studies* 16 (1): 61–84. https://doi.org/10.1162/JCWS_a_00431.

Bobo, Lawrence, James R. Kluegel, and Ryan A. Smith. 1997. "Laissez-Faire Racism: The Crystallization of a Kinder, Gentler, Antiblack Ideology." In *Racial Attitudes in the 1990s: Continuity and Change*, edited by Steven A. Tuch and Jack K. Martin. Praeger.

Boisseron, Bénédicte. 2018. *Afro-Dog: Blackness and the Animal Question.* Columbia University Press.

Boltanski, Luc. 1999. *Distant Suffering: Morality, Media, and Politics.* Cambridge University Press.

Bonilla-Silva, Eduardo. 2001. *White Supremacy and Racism in the Post–Civil Rights Era.* Lynne Rienner Publishers.

Bourke, Joanna. 2011. *What It Means to Be Human: Reflections from 1791 to the Present.* Counterpoint.

Bradley, Gracie Mae, and Luke de Noronha. 2022. *Against Borders: The Case for Abolition.* Verso.

Bradol, Jean-Hervé. 2003. "How Images of Adversity Affect the Quality of Aid." In *Civilians Under Fire: Humanitarian Practices in the Congo Republic, 1998–2000*, edited by Marc Le Pape and Pierre Salignon, translated by Andrew Long. Médecins sans frontières/Doctors Without Borders.

Brah, Avtar. 2022. *Decolonial Imaginings: Intersectional Conversations and Contestations.* Goldsmith Press.

Bratton, Benjamin H. 2015. *The Stack: On Software and Sovereignty.* MIT Press.

Brauman, Rony. 1993. "When Suffering Makes a Good Story." In *Life, Death, and Aid: The Médecins sans Frontières Report on World Crisis Intervention*, edited by François Jean. Routledge.

Brodkin, Karen. 1998. *How Jews Became White Folks and What That Says About Race in America.* Rutgers University Press.

Brown, Jayna. 2021. *Black Utopias: Speculative Life and the Music of Other Worlds.* Duke University Press.

Brown, Wendy. 1995. *States of Injury: Power and Freedom in Late Modernity*. Princeton University Press.

Brown, Wendy. 2018. "Neoliberalism's Frankenstein: Authoritarian Freedom in Twenty-First Century 'Democracies.'" *Critical Times* 1 (1): 60–79. https://doi.org/10.1215/26410478-1.1.60.

Bruyneel, Kevin. 2021. *Settler Memory: The Disavowal of Indigeneity and the Politics of Race in the United States*. University of North Carolina Press.

Butler, Judith. 2006. *Gender Trouble: Feminism and the Subversion of Identity*. Routledge.

Butler, Judith. 2009. *Frames of War: When Is Life Grievable?* Verso.

Butler, Judith. 2016. *Notes Toward a Performative Theory of Assembly*. Harvard University Press.

Butler, Judith, Zeynep Gambetti, and Leticia Sabsay, eds. 2016. *Vulnerability in Resistance*. Duke University Press.

Butterly, Luke. 2020. "'There Is No Future Without Equal Rights for All!': Migrant Struggles in France." *Verso* (blog), January 23. https://www.versobooks.com/blogs/news/4554-there-is-no-future-without-equal-rights-for-all-migrant-struggles-in-france.

Byrd, Jodi A. 2011. *The Transit of Empire: Indigenous Critiques of Colonialism*. University of Minnesota Press.

Caldwell, Christopher. 2009. "Communiste et Rastignac." *The London Review of Books* 31 (13): 7–10.

Chakrabarty, Dipesh. 2021. *The Climate of History in a Planetary Age*. University of Chicago Press.

Chen, Mel Y. 2021. "Feminisms in the Air." *Signs: Journal of Women in Culture and Society* 47 (1): 22–29. https://doi.org/10.1086/715733.

Chu, Andrea Long. 2018. "On Liking Women." *N+1* 30, https://www.nplusonemag.com/issue-30/essays/on-liking-women/.

Chua, Charmaine. 2020. "Abolition Is a Constant Struggle: Five Lessons from Minneapolis." *Theory & Event* 23 (5): S-127–S-147.

Clarke, Jessica A. 2015. "Against Immutability." *The Yale Law Journal* 125 (1): 2–102.

Coates, Ta-Nehisi. 2014. "The Case for Reparations." *The Atlantic* 313 (5): 54–71.

Collins, Patricia Hill. 1997. "Defining Black Feminist Thought." In *The Second Wave: A Reader in Feminist Theory*, edited by Linda J. Nicholson. Routledge.

Crimp, Douglas. 2003. "Melancholia and Moralism." In *Loss: The Politics of Mourning*, edited by David L. Eng and David Kazanjian. University of California Press.

Dardot, Pierre, Haud Guéguen, Christian Laval, and Pierre Sauvêtre. 2021. *Le Choix de La Guerre Civile Une Autre Histoire Du Neoliberalisme*. Lux Editeur.

Dardot, Pierre, and Christian Laval. 2019. *Common: On Revolution in the 21st Century*. Translated by Matthew MacLellan. Bloomsbury Academic.

Daston, Lorraine, and Peter Galison. 2007. *Objectivity*. Zone Books.

Davé, Naisargi N. 2023. *Indifference: On the Praxis of Interspecies Being*. Duke University Press.

Davis, Angela Y. 2003. *Are Prisons Obsolete?* Seven Stories Press.

Davis, Dána-Ain. 2019. *Reproductive Injustice: Racism, Pregnancy, and Premature Birth*. Anthropologies of American Medicine: Culture, Power, and Practice. New York University Press.

Dawson, Ashley. 2024. *Environmentalism from Below: How Global People's Movements Are Leading the Fight for Our Planet*. Haymarket Books.

De Leon, Jason. 2015. *The Land of Open Graves*. University of California Press.

Dean, Carolyn. 2010. *A Culture of Stone: Inka Perspectives on Rock*. Duke University Press.

Dean, Carolyn J. 2015. "Atrocity Photographs, Dignity, and Human Vulnerability." *Humanity* 6 (2): 239–64. https://doi.org/10.1353/hum.2015.0020.

Dean, Jodi. 2016. *Crowds and Party*. Verso.

Dean, Jodi. 2019. *Comrade: An Essay on Political Belonging*. Verso.

Dhesi, Surindar, Arshad Isakjee, and Thom Davies. 2018. "Public Health in the Calais Refugee Camp: Environment, Health and Exclusion." *Critical Public Health* 28 (2): 140–52. https://doi.org/10.1080/09581596.2017.1335860.

Dilts, Andrew. 2017. "Toward Abolitionist Genealogy." *The Southern Journal of Philosophy* 55 (S1): 51–77. https://doi.org/10.1111/sjp.12237.

Dilts, Andrew. 2019. "Crisis, Critique, and Abolition." In *A Time for Critique*, edited by Bernard E. Harcourt and Didier Fassin. Columbia University Press.

Dokumacı, Arseli. 2023. *Activist Affordances: How Disabled People Improvise More Habitable Worlds*. Duke University Press.

Du Bois, W. E. B. 1920. *The Souls of Black Folk*. A. C. McClurg & Co.

Dubois, Laurent. 2000. "La République Métissée: Citizenship, Colonialism, and the Borders of French History." *Cultural Studies* 14 (1): 15–34.

Duden, Barbara. 1999. "The Fetus on the 'Farther Shore': Toward a History of the Unborn." In *Fetal Subjects, Feminist Positions*, edited by Lynn M. Morgan and Meredith Wilson Michaels. University of Pennsylvania Press.

Dunne, Anthony, and Fiona Raby. 2018. "Design for the Unreal World." In *Studio Time: Future Thinking in Art and Design*, edited by Jan Boelen, Ils Huygens, and Heini Lehtinin. Black Dog Press.

Dwyer, Jim, Peter Neufeld, and Barry Scheck. 2001. *Actual Innocence: When Justice Goes Wrong and How to Make It Right*. New American Library.

Edelman, Lee. 2004. *No Future: Queer Theory and the Death Drive*. Duke University Press.

El Bernoussi, Zaynab. 2015. "The Postcolonial Politics of Dignity: From the 1956 Suez Nationalization to the 2011 Revolution in Egypt." *International Sociology* 30 (4): 367–82. https://doi.org/10.1177/0268580914537848.

Epstein, Steven. 1992. "Gay Politics, Ethnic Identity: The Limits of Social Constructionism." In *Forms of Desire: Sexual Orientation and the Social Constructionist Controversy*, edited by Edward Stein. Routledge.

Esmeir, Samera. 2012. *Juridical Humanity: A Colonial History*. Stanford University Press.

Esposito, Addie. 2022. "The Limitations of Humanity: Differential Refugee Treatment in the EU." *Harvard International Review*, September 14. https://hir.harvard.edu/the-limitations-of-humanity-differential-refugee-treatment-in-the-eu/.

Estes, Nick. 2019. *Our History Is the Future: Standing Rock Versus the Dakota Access Pipeline, and the Long Tradition of Indigenous Resistance*. Verso.

Estes, Nick, and Jaskiran Dhillon, eds. 2019. *Standing with Standing Rock: Voices from the #nodapl Movement*. University of Minnesota Press.

Fanon, Frantz. 1963. *The Wretched of the Earth*. Grove Press.

Fanon, Frantz. 2008. *Black Skin, White Masks*. Grove Press.

Farris, Sara R. 2017. *In the Name of Women's Rights: The Rise of Femonationalism*. Duke University Press.

Fassin, Didier. 2010. "Inequality of Lives, Hierarchies of Humanity: Moral Commitments and Ethical Dilemmas of Humanitarianism." In *In the Name of Humanity: The Government of Threat and Care*, edited by Miriam Ticktin and Ilana Feldman. Duke University Press.

Fassin, Didier. 2011. *Humanitarian Reason: A Moral History of the Present Times*. University of California Press.

Fassin, Didier. 2013. "On Resentment and Ressentiment: The Politics and Ethics of Moral Emotions." *Current Anthropology* 54 (3): 249–67. https://doi.org/10.1086/670390.

Fassin, Didier, and Richard Rechtman. 2009. *The Empire of Trauma: An Inquiry into the Condition of Victimhood*. Princeton University Press.

Faulkner, Joanne. 2008. "The Innocence of Victimhood Versus the 'Innocence of Becoming': Nietzsche, 9/11, and the 'Falling Man.'" *Journal of Nietzsche Studies* 35–36 (1): 67–85. https://doi.org/10.2307/jnietstud.35.2008.0067.

Faulkner, Joanne. 2011. "Innocents and Oracles: The Child as a Figure of Knowledge and Critique in the Middle-Class Philosophical Imagination." *Critical Horizons: Journal of Social & Critical Theory* 12 (3): 323–46. https://doi.org/10.1558/crit.v12i3.323.

Federici, Silvia. 2019. *Re-Enchanting the World: Feminism and the Politics of the Commons*. PM Press.

Feldman, Allen. 1994. "On Cultural Anesthesia: From Desert Storm to Rodney King." *American Ethnologist* 21 (2): 404–18. https://doi.org/10.1525/ae.1994.21.2.02a00100.

Feldman, Ilana, and Miriam Ticktin. 2010. "Introduction: Government and Humanity." In *In the Name of Humanity: The Government of Threat and Care*, edited by Miriam Ticktin and Ilana Feldman. Duke University Press.

Feldman, Noah. 2005. *Divided by God: America's Church-State Problem—and What We Should Do About It*. Farrar, Straus & Giroux.

Fellows, Mary Louise, and Sherene Razack. 1998. "The Race to Innocence: Confronting Hierarchical Relations Among Women." *The Journal of Gender, Race & Justice* 1: 335–52.

Ferguson, James, and Akhil Gupta. 2002. "Spatializing States: Toward an Ethnography of Neoliberal Governmentality." *American Ethnologist* 29 (4): 981–1002.

Festa, Lynn M. (Lynn Mary). 2010. "Humanity without Feathers." *Humanity: An International Journal of Human Rights, Humanitarianism, and Development* 1 (1): 3–27.

Findley, Keith A., and Larry Golden. 2014. "The Innocence Movement, the Innocence Network, and Policy Reform." In *Wrongful Conviction and Criminal Justice Reform: Making Justice*, edited by Marvin Zalman and Julia Carrano. Routledge.

Fischel, Joseph J. 2016. *Sex and Harm in the Age of Consent*. University of Minnesota Press.

Forti, Simona. 2014. *New Demons: Rethinking Power and Evil Today*. Translated by Zakiya Hanafi. Stanford University Press.

Fortier, Craig. 2017. *Unsettling the Commons: Social Movements Within, Against, and Beyond Settler Colonialism*. ARP Books.

Foucault, Michel. 1978. *The History of Sexuality*. Translated by Robert Hurley. Pantheon Books.

Fox, Jason. 2018. "Representational Regimes: A Conversation with Abounaddara." https://worldrecordsjournal.org/representational-regimes-a-conversation-with -abounaddara/.

Frank, Jason A. 2021. *The Democratic Sublime: On Aesthetics and Popular Assembly.* Oxford University Press.

Ghamari-Tabrizi, Behrooz. 2016. *Foucault in Iran: Islamic Revolution after the Enlightenment.* University of Minnesota Press.

Gilich, Yulia. 2020. "'This Is Not a Pig': Settler Innocence and Visuality of Zoos." *Image & Text* 34: 1–15. https://doi.org/10.17159/2617-3255/2020/n34a25.

Gilmore, Ruth Wilson. 1998. "Globalisation and US Prison Growth: From Military Keynesianism to Post-Keynesian Militarism." *Race & Class* 40 (2–3): 171–88.

Gilmore, Ruth Wilson. 2007. *Golden Gulag: Prisons, Surplus, Crisis, and Opposition in Globalizing California.* Berkeley: University of California Press.

Gilmore, Ruth Wilson. 2009. "In the Shadow of the Shadow State." In *The Revolution Will Not Be Funded: Beyond the Non-Profit Industrial Complex.* South End Press.

Gilmore, Ruth Wilson. 2017. "Abolition Geography and the Problem of Innocence." In *Futures of Black Radicalism*, edited by Gaye Theresa Johnson and Alex Lubin. Verso.

Gilmore, Ruth Wilson. 2020. "The Case for Prison Abolition: Ruth Wilson Gilmore on COVID-19, Racial Capitalism & Decarceration." Democracy Now! https://www .democracynow.org/2020/5/5/ruth_wilson_gilmore_abolition_coronavirus.

Gilmore, Ruth Wilson. 2022. *Abolition Geography: Essays Towards Liberation.* Edited by Brenna Bhandar and Alberto Toscano. Verso.

Gordon, Avery F. 2017. *The Hawthorn Archive: Letters from the Utopian Margins.* Fordham University Press.

Gramsci, Antonio. 1971. *Selections from the Prison Notebooks of Antonio Gramsci.* Edited by Quintin Hoare and Geoffrey Nowell-Smith. International Publishers.

Grande, Sandy. 2013. "Accumulation of the Primitive: The Limits of Liberalism and the Politics of Occupy Wall Street." *Settler Colonial Studies* 3 (3–4): 369–80. https://doi .org/10.1080/2201473X.2013.810704.

Gray, Jonathan W. 2013. *Civil Rights in the White Literary Imagination: Innocence by Association.* University Press of Mississippi.

Grewal, Inderpal. 2017. *Saving the Security State: Exceptional Citizens in Twenty-First-Century America.* Duke University Press.

Gruber, Aya. 2007. "The Feminist War on Crime." *Iowa Law Review* 92 (3): 741–833.

Hage, Ghassan. 2015. *Alter-Politics: Critical Anthropology and the Radical Imagination.* Melbourne University Press.

Hage, Ghassan. 2017. *Is Racism an Environmental Threat?* Polity.

Hall, Stuart. 1988. *The Hard Road to Renewal: Thatcherism and the Crisis of the Left.* Verso.

Hall, Stuart, Chas Critcher, Tony Jefferson, John Clarke, and Brian Roberts. 1978. *Policing the Crisis: Mugging, the State, and Law and Order.* Macmillan.

Hall, Stuart, and Alan O'Shea. 2013. "Common-Sense Neoliberalism." *Soundings* (55): 9–25. https://doi.org/10.3898/136266213809450194.

Halley, Janet E. 1993. "Reasoning about Sodomy: Act and Identity in and After *Bowers v. Hardwick.*" *Virginia Law Review* 79 (7): 1721–80. https://doi.org/10.2307/1073385.

Halley, Janet E. 1994. "Sexual Orientation and the Politics of Biology: A Critique of the Argument from Immutability." *Stanford Law Review* 46 (3): 503–68. https://doi .org/10.2307/1229101.

Halley, Janet E., Prabha Kotiswaran, Rachel Rebouché, and Hila Shamir, eds. 2019. *Governance Feminism: Notes from the Field*. University of Minnesota Press.

Hamburger, Philip. 2002. *Separation of Church and State*. Harvard University Press.

Haraway, Donna J. 1991. "Situated Knowledges: The Science Question in Feminism and the Privilege of Partial Perspective." In *Simians, Cyborgs, and Women: The Reinvention of Nature*. Routledge.

Haraway, Donna J. 2008. *When Species Meet*. University of Minnesota Press.

Haraway, Donna J. 2016. *Staying with the Trouble: Making Kin in the Chthulucene*. Duke University Press.

Hardin, Garrett. 1968. "The Tragedy of the Commons." *Science* 162 (3859): 1243–48. https://doi.org/10.1126/science.162.3859.1243.

Harding, Sandra G. 1986. *The Science Question in Feminism*. Cornell University Press.

Hardt, Michael, and Antonio Negri. 2009. *Commonwealth*. Harvard University Press.

Haro, Lia, and Romand Coles. 2019. "Reimagining Fugitive Democracy and Transformative Sanctuary with Black Frontline Communities in the Underground Railroad." *Political Theory* 47 (5): 1–28. https://doi.org/10.1177/0090591719828725.

Harris, Christopher Paul, Deva Woodly, Rachel H. Brown, Mara Marin, Shatema Threadcraft, Jasmine Syedullah, and Miriam Ticktin. 2021. "(Caring for) the World That Must Be Undone." *Contemporary Political Theory* 20 (4): 890–925. https://doi .org/10.1057/s41296-021-00515-8.

Hartman, Saidiya V. 2007. *Lose Your Mother: A Journey along the Atlantic Slave Route*. Farrar, Straus & Giroux.

Hartman, Saidiya V. 2019. *Wayward Lives, Beautiful Experiments: Intimate Histories of Social Upheaval*. W. W. Norton & Company.

Hartsock, Nancy. 1983. "The Feminist Standpoint: Developing the Ground for a Specifically Feminist Historical Materialism." In *Discovering Reality*, edited by Merrill B. P. Hintikka and Sandra Harding. Springer Netherlands.

Harvey, David. 2008. "The Right to the City." *New Left Review* 53 (53): 23–40.

Hathaway, James C. 2008. "The Human Rights Quagmire of 'Human Trafficking.'" *Virginia Journal of International Law* 49 (1): 1–59.

Hayden, Cori. 2021. "Crowding the Elements." In *Reactivating Elements: Chemistry, Ecology, Practice*, edited by Dimitris Papadopoulos, María Puig de la Bellacasa, and Natasha Myers. Duke University Press.

Heller, Charles, and Lorenzo Pezzani. n.d. "Forensic Oceanography." https://forensic -architecture.org/subdomain/forensic-oceanography.

Herman, Judith Lewis. 1992. *Trauma and Recovery: The Aftermath of Violence—From Domestic Abuse to Political Terror*. Basic Books.

Higonnet, Anne. 1998. *Pictures of Innocence: The History and Crisis of Ideal Childhood*. Thames and Hudson.

Hinton, Elizabeth. 2017. *From the War on Poverty to the War on Crime*. Harvard University Press.

Hlavka, Heather R., and Sameena Mulla. 2021. *Bodies in Evidence: Race, Gender, and Science in Sexual Assault Adjudication*. New York University Press.

Hooker, Juliet. 2017. "Black Protest / White Grievance: On the Problem of White Political Imaginations Not Shaped by Loss." *The South Atlantic Quarterly* 116 (3): 483–504. https://doi.org/10.1215/00382876-3961450.

hooks, bell. 1994. *Teaching to Transgress: Education as the Practice of Freedom.* Routledge.

hooks, bell. 2013. "Beyond the Body?" Lecture, New School for Social Research, November 5.

Hultgren, John. 2015. *Border Walls Gone Green: Nature and Anti-Immigrant Politics in America.* University of Minnesota Press.

Hung, Carla. 2019. "Sanctuary Squats: The Political Contestations of Piazza Indipendenza Refugee Occupiers." *Radical History Review* (135): 119–37. https://doi.org/10.1215/01636545-7607872.

INCITE! Women of Color Against Violence, eds. 2016. *Color of Violence: The INCITE! Anthology.* Duke University Press.

Inwood, Joshua F. J. 2018. "'It Is the Innocence Which Constitutes the Crime': Political Geographies of White Supremacy, the Construction of White Innocence, and the Flint Water Crisis." *Geography Compass* 12 (3): e12361. https://doi.org/10.1111/gec3.12361.

Jakobsen, Janet R., and Ann Pellegrini. 2003. *Love the Sin: Sexual Regulation and the Limits of Religious Tolerance.* New York University Press.

Jameson, Fredric. 2016. *An American Utopia: Dual Power and the Universal Army.* Edited by Slavoj Žižek. Verso.

Jaspers, Karl. (1946) 2000. *The Question of German Guilt.* Fordham University Press.

Jordan-Young, Rebecca M. 2010. *Brain Storm: The Flaws in the Science of Sex Differences.* Harvard University Press.

Kafadar, Karen. 2019. "The Need for Objective Measures in Forensic Evidence." *Significance* 16 (2): 16–20. https://doi.org/10.1111/j.1740-9713.2019.01249.x.

Kapur, Ratna. 2002. "The Tragedy of Victimization Rhetoric: Resurrecting the 'Native' Subject in International/Post-Colonial Feminist Legal Politics." *Harvard Human Rights Journal* 15 (April): 1–37.

Kaushal, Asha, and Catherine Dauvergne. 2011. "The Growing Culture of Exclusion: Trends in Canadian Refugee Exclusions." *International Journal of Refugee Law* 23 (1): 54–92. https://doi.org/10.1093/ijrl/eeq046.

Kelley, Robin D. G. 2024. "American Thanatocracy." Podcast with Christina Heatherton and Peter Linebaugh. *Conjuncture*, January 24. https://trinitysocialjustice.com/american-thanatocracy/.

Kelly, Lisa M. 2014. "Reckoning with Narratives of Innocent Suffering in Transnational Abortion Litigation." In *Abortion Law in Transnational Perspective: Cases and Controversies.* De Gruyter.

Keshavarz, Mahmoud, and Shahram Khosravi, eds. 2022. *Seeing Like a Smuggler: Borders from Below.* Pluto Press.

Kim, Claire Jean. 2015. *Dangerous Crossings: Race, Species, and Nature in a Multicultural Age.* Cambridge University Press.

Kim, Mimi E. 2020. "Anti-Carceral Feminism: The Contradictions of Progress and the Possibilities of Counter-Hegemonic Struggle." *Affilia* 35 (3): 309–26. https://doi.org/10.1177/0886109919878276.

Kim, Mimi E. 2021. "Transformative Justice and Restorative Justice: Gender-Based Violence and Alternative Visions of Justice in the United States." *International Review of Victimology* 27 (2): 162–72. https://doi.org/10.1177/0269758020970414.

Kincaid, James R. 1998. *Erotic Innocence: The Culture of Child Molesting.* Duke University Press.

King, Natasha. 2019. "Radical Migrant Solidarity in Calais." In *Open Borders: In Defense of Free Movement*, edited by Reece Jones. University of Georgia Press.

Kleinman, Arthur, and Joan Kleinman. 1996. "The Appeal of Experience; the Dismay of Images: Cultural Appropriations of Suffering in Our Times." *Daedalus* 125 (1): 1–23.

Krug, Nora. 2018. *Belonging: A German Reckons with History and Home*. Scribner.

Laqueur, Thomas W. 2009. "Mourning, Pity, and the Work of Narrative in the Making of 'Humanity.'" In *Humanitarianism and Suffering: The Mobilization of Empathy*, edited by Richard Wilson and Richard D. Brown. Cambridge University Press.

Le Pape, Marc, and Pierre Salignon, eds. 2003. *Civilians Under Fire: Humanitarian Practices in the Congo Republic, 1998–2000*. Translated by Andrew Long. Médecins sans frontières/Doctors Without Borders.

LeVay, Simon. 1991. "A Difference in Hypothalamic Structure Between Heterosexual and Homosexual Men." *Science* 253 (5023): 1034–37. https://doi.org/10.1126/science.1887219.

Lepore, Jill. 2018. "The Rise of the Victims'-Rights Movement." *New Yorker*, May 14. https://www.newyorker.com/magazine/2018/05/21/the-rise-of-the-victims-rights-movement.

Levi, Primo. 2015. "The Gray Zone." In *The Complete Works of Primo Levi*, vol. 3, edited by Ann Goldstein. Translated by Michael F. Moore. Liveright.

Liboiron, Max. 2021. *Pollution Is Colonialism*. Duke University Press.

Linfield, Susie. 2012. *The Cruel Radiance: Photography and Political Violence*. University of Chicago Press.

Livingston, Julie. 2020. "To Heal the Body, Heal the Body Politic." *Public Books*, November 19. https://www.publicbooks.org/to-heal-the-body-heal-the-body-politic/.

Locke, John. 1975. *An Essay Concerning Human Understanding*. Edited by P. H. Nidditch. Clarendon Press.

Loescher, Gil. 1993. *Beyond Charity: International Cooperation and the Global Refugee Crisis*. Oxford University Press.

Lorenz, Konrad. 1971. *Studies in Animal and Human Behaviour*. Translated by Robert Martin. Harvard University Press.

Lorimer, Jamie. 2007. "Nonhuman Charisma." *Environment and Planning D: Society and Space* 25 (5): 911–32. https://doi.org/10.1068/d71j.

Loyd, Jenna M. 2019. "Prison Abolitionist Perspectives on No Borders." In *Open Borders: In Defense of Free Movement*, edited by Reece Jones. University of Georgia Press.

Macas, Luis. 2010. "El Sumak Kawsay." *Revista Yachaykuna* 13: 13–39.

Maira, Sunaina. 2019. "Freedom to Move, Freedom to Stay, Freedom to Return: A Transnational Roundtable on Sanctuary Activism." *Radical History Review* 135: 138–59. https://doi.org/10.1215/01636545-7607884.

Malkki, Liisa. 1996. "Speechless Emissaries: Refugees, Humanitarianism, and Dehistoricization." *Cultural Anthropology* 11 (3): 377–404. https://doi.org/10.1525/can.1996.11.3.02a00050.

Malkki, Liisa. 2010. "Children, Humanity, and the Infantilization of Peace." In *In the Name of Humanity: The Government of Threat and Care*, edited by Miriam Ticktin and Ilana Feldman. Duke University Press.

Mani, Lata. 2022. *Myriad Intimacies*. Duke University Press Books.

Manzo, Kate. 2008. "Imaging Humanitarianism: NGO Identity and the Iconography of Childhood." *Antipode* 40 (4): 632–57. https://doi.org/10.1111/j.1467-8330.2008 .00627.x.

Margulies, Joseph. 2018. "Managing Innocence." *Boston Review*, October. https://www .bostonreview.net/articles/joseph-margulies-slouching-toward-innocence/.

Marshall, Lawrence C. 2004. "The Innocence Revolution and the Death Penalty." *Ohio State Journal of Criminal Law* 1: 573–84.

Maskovsky, Jeff, and Sophie Bjork-James. 2020. "Introduction." In *Beyond Populism: Angry Politics and the Twilight of Neoliberalism*, edited by Jeff Maskovsky and Sophie Bjork-James. West Virginia University Press.

Mason, Carol. 2000. "Cracked Babies and the Partial Birth of a Nation: Millennialism and Fetal Citizenship." *Cultural Studies* 14 (1): 35–60. https://doi.org/10.1080/ 095023800334977.

Mbembe, Achille. 2011. "Provincializing France?" *Public Culture* 23 (1): 85–119. https:// doi.org/10.1215/08992363-2010-017.

Mbembe, Achille. 2019. "Bodies as Borders." *From the European South* 4: 5–18.

Mbembe, Achille. 2024. *Brutalism*. Duke University Press.

McKittrick, Katherine. 2006. *Demonic Grounds: Black Women and the Cartographies of Struggle*. University of Minnesota Press.

McKittrick, Katherine. 2013. "Plantation Futures." *Small Axe: A Journal of Criticism* 17 (3): 1–15. https://doi.org/10.1215/07990537-2378892.

McLaughlin, Carly. 2018. "'They Don't Look like Children': Child Asylum-Seekers, the Dubs Amendment and the Politics of Childhood." *Journal of Ethnic and Migration Studies* 44 (11): 1757–73.

McNevin, Anne. 2011. *Contesting Citizenship: Irregular Migrants and New Frontiers of the Political*. Columbia University Press.

McNevin, Anne. Forthcoming. *Worldmaking and Border Politics*. Stanford University Press.

Meister, Robert. 2011. *After Evil: A Politics of Human Rights*. Columbia University Press.

Meyers, Diana T. 2011. "Two Victim Paradigms and the Problem of 'Impure' Victims." *Humanity: An International Journal of Human Rights, Humanitarianism, and Development* 2 (2): 255–75.

Meyerson, Collier. 2017. "Adults Think Black Girls Are Older Than They Are—and It Matters." *The Nation*, July 6. https://www.thenation.com/article/archive/adults -thinks-black-girls-are-older-than-they-are-and-it-matters/.

Mignolo, Walter. 2012. *Local Histories/Global Designs: Coloniality, Subaltern Knowledges, and Border Thinking*. Princeton University Press.

Miller, Alice M. 2004. "Sexuality, Violence against Women, and Human Rights: Women Make Demands and Ladies Get Protection." *Health and Human Rights* 7 (2): 16–47. https://doi.org/10.2307/4065347.

Miller, Todd. 2019. *Empire of Borders: The Expansion of the US Border Around the World*. Verso.

Mills, Charles. 2007. "White Ignorance." In *Race and Epistemologies of Ignorance*, edited by Shannon Sullivan and Nancy Tuana. State University of New York Press.

Mohanty, Chandra. 1988. "Under Western Eyes: Feminist Scholarship and Colonial Discourses." *Feminist Review* 30 (1): 61–88. https://doi.org/10.1057/fr.1988.42.

Mortensen, Mette. 2017. "Constructing, Confirming, and Contesting Icons: The Alan Kurdi Imagery Appropriated by #humanitywashedashore, Ai Weiwei, and

Charlie Hebdo." *Media, Culture & Society* 39 (8): 1142–61. https://doi.org/10.1177/
0163443717725572.

Moyn, Samuel. 2010. *The Last Utopia: Human Rights in History*. Harvard University
Press.

MTL Collective. 2020. "Principles for Decolonial Film." *World Records Journal* 4:
81–82.

Muehlebach, Andrea. 2016. "Camp in the City." Society for Cultural Anthropology,
June 28. https://culanth.org/fieldsights/camp-in-the-city.

Muñoz, José Esteban. 2009. *Cruising Utopia: The Then and There of Queer Futurity*.
New York University Press.

Muñoz, José Esteban. 2020. *The Sense of Brown*. Edited by Tavia Amolo Ochieng'
Nyongó and Joshua Takano Chambers-Letson. Duke University Press.

Murakawa, Naomi. 2014. *The First Civil Right: How Liberals Built Prison America*.
Oxford University Press.

Murakawa, Naomi, and Katherine Beckett. 2010. "The Penology of Racial Innocence:
The Erasure of Racism in the Study and Practice of Punishment." *Law & Society
Review* 44 (3–4): 695–730. https://doi.org/10.1111/j.1540-5893.2010.00420.x.

Murphy, M. 2017. "Afterlife and Decolonial Chemical Relations." *Cultural Anthropology*
32 (4): 494–503. https://doi.org/10.14506/ca32.4.02.

Murphy, M. 2018. "Against Population, Towards Alterlife." In *Making Kin Not
Population: Reconceiving Generations*, edited by Adele E. Clarke and Donna
Harraway. Prickly Paradigm Press.

Naber, Nadine, Souzan Nasser, and Johnaé Strong. 2020. "Radical Mothering for
Abolitionist Futures Post-COVID-19." *Abolition: A Journal of Insurgent Politics*,
June. https://abolitionjournal.org/radical-mothering/.

Naber, Nadine Suleiman. 2014. "Imperial Whiteness and the Diasporas of Empire."
American Quarterly 66 (4): 1107–15. https://doi.org/10.1353/aq.2014.0068.

Nadasen, Premilla. 2023. *Care: The Highest Stage of Capitalism*. Haymarket Books.

Najmabadi, Afsaneh. 2011. "Verdicts of Science, Rulings of Faith: Transgender/
Sexuality in Contemporary Iran." *Social Research* 78 (2): 533–56.

Nesiah, Vasuki. 2020. "The Law of Humanity Has a Canon: Translating Racialized
World Order into 'Colorblind' Law." *PoLAR: Political and Legal Anthropology
Review*, November 15. https://polarjournal.org/2020/11/15/the-law-of-humanity
-has-a-canon-translating-racialized-world-order-into-colorblind-law/.

Nevins, Joseph. 2019. "Migration as Reparations." In *Open Borders: In Defense of Free
Movement*, edited by Reece Jones. University of Georgia Press.

Newman, Karen. 1996. *Fetal Positions: Individualism, Science, Visuality*. Stanford
University Press.

Ngai, Sianne. 2005. "The Cuteness of the Avant-Garde." *Critical Inquiry* 31 (4): 811–47.
https://doi.org/10.1086/444516.

Niang, Mame-Fatou, and Julien Suaudeau. 2022. *Universalisme*. ANAMOSA.

Nietzsche, Friedrich Wilhelm. [1887] 1998. *On the Genealogy of Morality*. Translated by
Maudemarie Clark and Alan J. Swensen. Hackett.

Obadia, Julienne. 2020. "Responsibility, Respectability, Recognition, and Polyamory:
Lessons in Subject Formation in the Age of Sexual Identity." *Feminist Studies* 46 (2):
287–315. https://doi.org/10.1353/fem.2020.0040.

Ordover, Nancy. 2003. *American Eugenics: Race, Queer Anatomy, and the Science of
Nationalism*. University of Minnesota Press.

Orr, Jackie. 2006. *Panic Diaries: A Genealogy of Panic Disorder*. Duke University Press.

Orr, Jackie. 2013. "A Possible History of Oblivion." *Social Text*, June. https://socialtextjournal.org/periscope_article/a-possible-history-of-oblivion/.

Ostrom, Elinor. 1990. *Governing the Commons: The Evolution of Institutions for Collective Action*. Cambridge University Press.

Ostrom, Elinor. 2000. "Reformulating the Commons." *Schweizerische Zeitschrift für Politikwissenschaft* 6 (1): 29–52. https://doi.org/10.1002/j.1662-6370.2000.tb00285.x.

Pacari, Nina. 2009. "Naturaleza y Territorio de La Mirada de Los Pueblos Indígena." In *Derechos de La Naturaleza: El Futuro Es Ahora*, edited by Alberto Acosta and Esperanza Martínez, 31–37. Abya Yala.

Paik, A. Naomi. 2017. "Abolitionist Futures and the US Sanctuary Movement." *Race & Class* 59 (2): 3–25. https://doi.org/10.1177/0306396817717858.

Paik, A. Naomi. 2020. *Bans, Walls, Raids, Sanctuary: Understanding U.S. Immigration for the Twenty-First Century*. American Studies Now; Critical Histories of the Present; 12. University of California Press.

Paik, A. Naomi, Jason Ruiz, and Rebecca M. Schreiber. 2019. "Sanctuary's Radical Networks." *Radical History Review* 2019 (135): 1–13. https://doi.org/10.1215/01636545-7607797.

Papadopoulos, Dimitris, and Vassilis S. Tsianos. 2013. "After Citizenship: Autonomy of Migration, Organisational Ontology and Mobile Commons." *Citizenship Studies* 17 (2): 178–96. https://doi.org/10.1080/13621025.2013.780736.

Park, Lisa Sun-Hee, and David N. Pellow. 2013. *The Slums of Aspen: Immigrants vs. the Environment in America's Eden*. New York University Press.

Paumgarten, Nick. 2021. "What Will Become of the Pandemic Pets?" *New Yorker*, June 21. https://www.newyorker.com/magazine/2021/06/28/what-will-become-of-the-pandemic-pets.

Petchesky, Rosalind Pollack. 1987. "Fetal Images: The Power of Visual Culture in the Politics of Reproduction." *Feminist Studies* 13 (2): 263–92.

Pierce, Jennifer L. 2012. *Racing for Innocence: Whiteness, Gender, and the Backlash Against Affirmative Action*. Stanford University Press.

Pillard, R. C., and J. M. Bailey. 1995. "A Biologic Perspective on Sexual Orientation: Clinical Sexuality." *The Psychiatric Clinics of North America* 18 (1): 71–84.

Povinelli, Elizabeth A. 2011. *Economies of Abandonment: Social Belonging and Endurance in Late Liberalism*. Duke University Press.

Proctor, Robert, and Londa L. Schiebinger. 2008. *Agnotology: The Making and Unmaking of Ignorance*. Stanford University Press.

Puig de la Bellacasa, María. 2017. *Matters of Care: Speculative Ethics in More Than Human Worlds*. University of Minnesota Press.

Rancière, Jacques. 2004. *The Politics of Aesthetics: The Distribution of the Sensible*. Continuum.

Rancière, Jacques. 2010. *Dissensus: On Politics and Aesthetics*. Translated by Steve Corcoran. Continuum.

Razack, Sherene H. 2007. "Stealing the Pain of Others: Reflections on Canadian Humanitarian Responses." *The Review of Education/Pedagogy/Cultural Studies* 29 (4): 375–94. https://doi.org/10.1080/10714410701454198.

Razsa, Maple, and Milton Guillén, dirs. 2017. *The Maribor Uprisings*. EnMasse Films.

Reaven, Daria. 2023. "Afflicted by Innocence: An Examination of the Innocence Revolution and Its Failures." *Law, Culture and the Humanities* 19 (2): 406–28. https://doi.org/10.1177/1743872119893085.

Redfield, Peter. 2013. *Life in Crisis: The Ethical Journey of Doctors Without Borders*. University of California Press.

Rifkin, Mark. 2014. *Settler Common Sense: Queerness and Everyday Colonialism in the American Renaissance*. University of Minnesota Press.

Roane, J. T. 2017. "Towards Usable Histories of the Black Commons." *Black Perspectives*, February. https://www.aaihs.org/towards-usable-histories-of-the -black-commons/.

Roane, J. T. 2018. "Plotting the Black Commons." *Souls* 20 (3): 239–66. https://doi .org/10.1080/10999949.2018.1532757.

Robbins, Bruce. 2017. *The Beneficiary*. Duke University Press.

Robcis, Camille. 2015. "Catholics, the 'Theory of Gender,' and the Turn to the Human in France: A New Dreyfus Affair?" *The Journal of Modern History* 87 (4): 892–923. https://doi.org/10.1086/683599.

Robcis, Camille. 2016. "The Biopolitics of Dignity." *The South Atlantic Quarterly* 115 (2): 313–30. https://doi.org/10.1215/00382876-3488431.

Robinson, Cedric J. 1983. "Racial Capitalism: The Nonobjective Character of Capitalist Development." In *Black Marxism*. University of North Carolina Press.

Rodríguez, Dylan. 2012. "Beyond 'Police Brutality': Racist State Violence and the University of California." *American Quarterly* 64 (2): 301–13. https://doi.org/10 .1353/aq.2012.0012.

Rodríguez, Dylan. 2019. "Abolition as Praxis of Human Being: A Foreword." *Harvard Law Review* 132 (6): 1575–612.

Rosen, Rachel, and Sarah Crafter. 2018. "Media Representations of Separated Child Migrants: From Dubs to Doubt." *Migration and Society: Advances in Research* 1 (1): 66–81. https://doi.org/10.3167/arms.2018.010107.

Ross, Andrew A. G. 2014. *Mixed Emotions: Beyond Fear and Hatred in International Conflict*. University of Chicago Press.

Ross, Kristin. 2002. *May '68 and Its Afterlives*. University of Chicago Press.

Ross, Kristin. 2024. *The Commune Form: The Transformation of Everyday Life*. Verso.

Rothberg, Michael. 2019. *The Implicated Subject: Beyond Victims and Perpetrators*. Stanford University Press.

Rousseau, Jean-Jacques. 1987a. "Discourse on the Origin and Foundations of Inequality Among Men." In *The Basic Political Writings*, translated by Donald Cress. Hackett.

Rousseau, Jean-Jacques. 1987b. "On the Social Contract." In *The Basic Political Writings*, translated by Donald Cress. Hackett.

Rubin, Gayle S. 1993. "Thinking Sex: Notes for a Radical Theory of the Politics of Sexuality." In *The Lesbian and Gay Studies Reader*, edited by Henry Abelove, Michèle Aina Barale, and David M. Halperin. Routledge.

Rullmann, Hanna. 2020. "Fort Vert: Nature Conservation as Border Regime in Calais." Statewatch. https://www.statewatch.org/analyses/2020/fort-vert-nature -conservation-as-border-regime-in-calais/.

Sackett, Robert. 2006. "Pictures of Atrocity: Public Discussion of Der Gelbe Stern in Early 1960s West Germany." *German History* 24 (4): 526–61. https://doi.org/10 .1177/0266355406070329.

Sadjadi, Sahar. 2019. "Deep in the Brain: Identity and Authenticity in Pediatric Gender Transition." *Cultural Anthropology* 34 (1): 103–29. https://doi.org/10.14506/ca34.1.10.

Saketopoulou, Avgi, and Ann Pellegrini. 2023. *Gender Without Identity*. The Unconscious in Translation.

Sanyal, Debarati. 2017. "Calais 'Jungle': Refugees, Biopolitics and the Arts of Resistance." *Representations* 139: 1–33.

Sarr, Felwine. 2019. *Afrotopia*. Translated by Drew Burk and Sarah Jones-Boardman. University of Minnesota Press.

Schoenberner, Gerhard. 1960. *Der gelbe Stern: Die Judenverfolgung in Europa 1933 bis 1945*. Rütten & Loening.

Schumacher, Günter, Andreas Schmeling, and Ernst Rudolf. 2018. "Medical Age Assessment of Juvenile Migrants." EUR, Scientific and Technical Research Series, 29358.

Scott, Joan. 2018. *Sex and Secularism*. Princeton University Press.

Scott, Joan Wallach. 1996. *Only Paradoxes to Offer: French Feminists and the Rights of Man*. Harvard University Press.

Scott-Smith, Tom. 2024. *Fragments of Home: Refugee Housing and the Politics of Shelter*. Stanford University Press.

Sedgwick, Eve Kosofsky. 1990. *Epistemology of the Closet*. University of California Press.

Shalhoub-Kevorkian, Nadera. 2020. "Gun to Body: Mental Health against Unchilding." *International Journal of Applied Psychoanalytic Studies* 17 (2): 126–45. https://doi.org/10.1002/aps.1652.

Sharpe, Christina. 2018. "And to Survive." *Small Axe: A Journal of Criticism* 22 (3): 171–80. https://doi.org/10.1215/07990537-7249304.

Singh, Bhrigupati. 2010. "Asceticism and Eroticism in Gandhi, Thoreau and Nietzsche: An Essay in Geo-Philosophy." *Borderlands* 9 (3): 1–34.

Slaughter, Joseph R. 2007. *Human Rights, Inc.: The World Novel, Narrative Form, and International Law*. Fordham University Press.

Slaughter, Joseph R. 2018. "Hijacking Human Rights: Neoliberalism, the New Historiography, and the End of the Third World." *Human Rights Quarterly* 40 (4): 735–75. https://doi.org/10.1353/hrq.2018.0044.

Smith, Abbe. 2010. "In Praise of the Guilty Project: A Criminal Defense Lawyer's Growing Anxiety About Innocence Projects." *University of Pennsylvania Journal of Law and Social Change*, no. 13, 315–29.

Solomon, Marisa. 2022. "Ecologies Elsewhere: Flyness, Fill, and Black Women's Fugitive Matter(s)." *GLQ* 28 (4): 567–87. https://doi.org/10.1215/10642684-9991341.

Sontag, Susan. 2003. *Regarding the Pain of Others*. Farrar, Straus & Giroux.

Spivak, Gayatri Chakravorty. 1988. "Can the Subaltern Speak?" *Die Philosophin* 14 (27): 42–58.

Stierl, Maurice. 2019. "Of Migrant Slaves and Underground Railroads: Movement, Containment, Freedom." *American Behavioral Scientist* 64 (4): 456–79. https://doi.org/10.1177/0002764219883006.

Stoler, Ann Laura. 2016. *Duress: Imperial Durabilities in Our Times*. Duke University Press.

Stoller, Robert. 1964. "A Contribution to the Study of Gender Identity." *International Journal of Psychoanalysis* 45:220–26.

Stoller, Robert. 1966. "The Mother's Contribution to Infantile Transvestic Behaviour." *International Journal of Psychoanalysis* 47 (2): 384–95.

Strassler, Karen. 2020. *Demanding Images: Democracy, Mediation, and the Image-Event in Indonesia*. Duke University Press.

Strauss, David Levi, Yasmine El Rashidi, Allan Sekula, Abigail Solomon-Godeau, Mark Sealy, Thomas Keenan, Atom Egoyan, et al. 2011. "The Anxiety of Images." *Aperture* 204: 50–73.

Sundberg, Juanita. 2011. "Diabolic Caminos in the Desert and Cat Fights on the Río: A Posthumanist Political Ecology of Boundary Enforcement in the United States–Mexico Borderlands." *Annals of the Association of American Geographers* 101 (2): 318–36.

Syedullah, Jasmine. 2014. "'Is This Freedom?' A Political Theory of Harriet Jacobs's Loopholes of Emancipation." PhD diss., UC Santa Cruz.

Sznaider, Natan. 2001. *The Compassionate Temperament: Care and Cruelty in Modern Society*. Rowman & Littlefield Publishers.

Tadiar, Neferti X. M. 2022. *Remaindered Life*. Duke University Press.

Taylor, Kirstine. 2015. "Untimely Subjects: White Trash and the Making of Racial Innocence in the Postwar South." *American Quarterly* 67 (1): 55–79. https://doi .org/10.1353/aq.2015.0014.

Tazzioli, Martina. 2017. "The Government of Migrant Mobs: Temporary Divisible Multiplicities in Border Zones." *European Journal of Social Theory* 20 (4): 473–90. https://doi.org/10.1177/1368431016658894.

Ticktin, Miriam. 2011a. *Casualties of Care Immigration and the Politics of Humanitarianism in France*. University of California Press.

Ticktin, Miriam. 2011b. "The Gendered Human of Humanitarianism: Medicalising and Politicising Sexual Violence." *Gender & History* 23 (2): 250–65. https://doi.org/10 .1111/j.1468-0424.2011.01637.x.

Ticktin, Miriam. 2014a. "Humanitarianism as Planetary Politics." In *At the Limits of Justice*, edited by Sherene Razack and Suvendrini Perera, 406–20. University of Toronto Press. https://doi.org/10.3138/9781442616455-025.

Ticktin, Miriam. 2014b. "Transnational Humanitarianism." *Annual Review of Anthropology* 43: 273–89. https://doi.org/10.1146/annurev-anthro-102313-030403.

Ticktin, Miriam. 2016. "Thinking Beyond Humanitarian Borders." Edited by Alexandra Delano and Benjamin Nienass. *Social Research: An International Quarterly, Special Issue on Borders and the Politics of Mourning* 83 (2): 255–71.

Ticktin, Miriam. 2017a. "A World Without Innocence." *American Ethnologist* 44 (4): 577–90. https://doi.org/10.1111/amet.12558.

Ticktin, Miriam. 2017b. "Invasive Others: Toward a Contaminated World." *Social Research* 84 (1): xxi–xxxiv. https://doi.org/10.1353/sor.2017.0001.

Ticktin, Miriam. 2017c. "The Sanctuary Movement and Women's Rights: Sister Struggles." *Truthout*, April 29. https://truthout.org/articles/the-sanctuary -movement-and-women-s-rights-sister-struggles/.

Ticktin, Miriam. 2020. "On Refugees and Innocence." Public Seminar, January 16. https://publicseminar.org/2020/01/on-refugees-and-innocence/.

Ticktin, Miriam. 2022. "Borders: A Story of Political Imagination." *Borderlands Journal* 21 (1): 138–70. https://doi.org/10.21307/borderlands-2022-007.

Ticktin, Miriam, and Rafi Youatt. 2022. "Intersecting Mobilities: Beyond the Autonomy of Movement and Power of Place." *Borderlands Journal* 21 (1): 1–17. https://doi.org/ 10.21307/borderlands-2022-001.

Tola, Miriam. 2018. "Between Pachamama and Mother Earth: Gender, Political Ontology and the Rights of Nature in Contemporary Bolivia." *Feminist Review* 118 (1): 25–40. https://doi.org/10.1057/s41305-018-0100-4.

Tomso, Gregory. 2017. "HIV Monsters: Gay Men, Criminal Law, and the New Political Economy of HIV." In *The War on Sex*, edited by David M. Halperin and Trevor Hoppe. Duke University Press.

Torrenté, Nicolas de. 2004. "Humanitarian Action Under Attack: Reflections on the Iraq War." *Harvard Human Rights Journal* 17 (5): 1–29.

Toscano, Alberto. 2021. "Fascists, Freedom, and the Anti-State State." *Historical Materialism: Research in Critical Marxist Theory* 29 (4): 3–21. https://doi.org/10.1163/1569206X-12342233.

Touray, Maimuna. 2021. "Plotting Liberation: A Scheme for the Commons as Reparations." *ATM Magazine*, March 28. https://www.atm-magazine.com/online/plotting-liberation.

Tsavdaroglou, Charalampos, and Maria Kaika. 2022. "The Refugees' Right to the Centre of the City: City Branding Versus City Commoning in Athens." *Urban Studies (Edinburgh, Scotland)* 59 (6): 1130–47. https://doi.org/10.1177/0042098021997009.

Turner, Simon. 2010. *Politics of Innocence: Hutu Identity, Conflict, and Camp Life*. Berghahn Books.

Vallaeys, Anne. 2004. *Médecins Sans Frontières: la biographie*. Fayard.

Van Isacker, Travis. 2020. "Counter-Mapping Citizenship: Bordering Through Domicide in Calais, France." PhD diss., University of Brighton.

Vance, Carole S. 2012. "Innocence and Experience: Melodramatic Narratives of Sex Trafficking and Their Consequences for Law and Policy." *History of the Present* 2 (2): 200–218. https://doi.org/10.5406/historypresent.2.2.0200.

Vimalassery, Manu, Juliana Hu Pegues, and Alyosha Goldstein. 2016. "Introduction: On Colonial Unknowing." *Theory & Event* 19 (4). https://muse.jhu.edu/article/633283.

Volpp, Leti. 2015. "Saving Muslim Women." *Public Books*, August 1. https://www.publicbooks.org/saving-muslim-women/.

Wacquant, Loïc. 2007. "Social Identity and the Ethics of Punishment." Center for Ethics in Society, Stanford University.

Walters, Suzanna Danuta. 2014. *The Tolerance Trap: How God, Genes, and Good Intentions Are Sabotaging Gay Equality*. NYU Press.

Wang, Jackie. 2018. *Carceral Capitalism*. Semiotext(e).

Weizman, Eyal. 2011. *The Least of All Possible Evils: Humanitarian Violence from Arendt to Gaza*. Verso.

Wekker, Gloria. 2016. *White Innocence: Paradoxes of Colonialism and Race*. Duke University Press.

West, Traci C. 2016. "An Antiracist Christian Ethical Approach to Violence Resistance." In *Color of Violence: The INCITE! Anthology*, edited by INCITE! Women of Color Against Violence. Duke University Press.

Wilder, Gary. 2015. *Freedom Time: Negritude, Decolonization, and the Future of the World*. Duke University Press.

Wilder, Gary. 2022. *Concrete Utopianism: The Politics of Temporality and Solidarity*. Fordham University Press.

Williams, Raymond. 1977. *Marxism and Literature*. Oxford University Press.

Wittgenstein, Ludwig. 1958. *Philosophical Investigations: The English Text of the Third Edition*. Prentice Hall.

Woodly, Deva. 2020a. "Black Feminist Visions and the Politics of Healing in the Movement for Black Lives." In *Women Mobilizing Memory*. Columbia University Press. https://doi.org/10.7312/alti19184-014.

Woodly, Deva. 2020b. "The Politics of Care." Lecture, New School for Social Research, June 18. https://youtu.be/ih6F6N9pg-A?si=kCmsuMMGCiMCoF1k.

Woodly, Deva, Rachel H. Brown, Mara Marin, Shatema Threadcraft, Christopher Paul Harris, Jasmine Syedullah, and Miriam Ticktin. 2021. "The Politics of Care." *Contemporary Political Theory* 20 (4): 890–925. https://doi.org/10.1057/s41296-021 -00515-8.

Wright, Erik Olin. 2010. *Envisioning Real Utopias*. Verso.

Wynter, Sylvia. 2003. "Unsettling the Coloniality of Being/Power/Truth/Freedom: Towards the Human, After Man, Its Overrepresentation—An Argument." *CR* 3 (3): 257–337. https://doi.org/10.1353/ncr.2004.0015.

Zalman, Marvin. 2011. "An Integrated Justice Model of Wrongful Convictions." *Albany Law Review* 74 (3): 1465.

Zaman, Tahir, 2019. "What's So Radical About Refugee Squats? An Exploration of Urban Community Based Responses to Mass Displacement in Athens." In *Challenging the Political Across Borders: Migrants' and Solidarity Struggles*, edited by Tegiye Birey, Celine Cantat, Ewa Maczynska, and Eda Sevinin. Central European University.

Zigon, Jarrett. 2019. *A War on People: Drug User Politics and a New Ethics of Community*. University of California Press.

Index

WHAT IF I KNEW YOU

ANAHEIM STARS
BOOK THREE

SUSAN RENEE

WHAT IF I KNEW YOU

SUSAN RENEE

Editing by Brandi Zelenka, Notes in the Margin

Reader Team: Kristan Anderson, Stephani Brown,

Jenn Hager, Jennifer Wilson

Cover Design by Quirky Bird Covers

 Created with Vellum

To all the men of the world who are still virgins.
If you're not reading romance books to learn what women want,
you're doing it wrong.